FLIGHT FROM DHAHRAN

FLIGHT FROM DHAHRAN

The True Experiences of an
American Businessman
Held Hostage in Saudi Arabia

John McDonald
with Clyde Burleson

Prentice-Hall, Inc., Englewood Cliffs, New Jersey 07632

Book Designer: Donna Kurdock
Art Director: Hal Siegel

Flight from Dhahran by
John McDonald with Clyde Burleson
Copyright © 1981 by John McDonald and Suzy Burleson

Printed in the United States of America

10 9 8 7 6 5 4 3 2 1

Library of Congress Cataloging in Publication Data

McDonald, John, date
    Flight from Dhahran.

    1. Saudi Arabia—Description and travel.
2. McDonald, John, date.   3. Escapes—
Saudi Arabia.   I. Burleson, Clyde W.,
date.   II. Title.
DS208.M32   953'.8053   81-10574
                                      AACR2
ISBN 0-13-322453-8

Contents

Preface

This book is more than an adventure story. The adventure is there, all right, but it comes naturally packaged in a closeup look at another way of life: a culture as foreign to those of us in the West as an Eskimo's life-style would be to a New York City banker.

When Westerners are suddenly exposed to the Arabic world by stepping off a jet airliner and into the streets of Dhahran, Dubai, or some other port of entry, there is an immediate recognition shock brought on by the foreignness of it all. As days pass, and they hold meetings, stay in hotels, go out into the countryside, eat in restaurants, and do the hundred normal things all humans do, the feeling of shock, in most, doesn't go away. It increases because added exposure to the culture gives greater opportunity for alien experiences.

One of the purposes of this book is to give a Westerner the same kind of shock he or she would receive stepping into the Moslem world of Saudi Arabia. It's not a "sun sinking slowly in the West" type of travelogue. Obviously, a person steeped in anthropology or one who has lived in other Arabic or Moslem countries for a length of time might see this culture in a different light.

Many Arabs who have visited in the West, and especially in the United States, have gone back to their homes carrying tales of unheard-of waste, decadence, and debauched behavior.

That a stranger in a strange land should view what the inhabitants of the area consider normal from a framework or cultural orientation which makes it appear abnormal is nothing new. Historians and travelers have done this since the time of the early Greeks.

It's also necessary to remember that there is no "Arab." There is no typical "Saudi" any more than there is a typical "American," "German," or "Englishman." Yet to each of us, the designation of nationality conjures up some image of distinct national traits. The Germans are precise, well organized, and emotionless; the English are very proper and have an odd sense of humor, and so on. In the West, the term "Saudi," to most people, brings a visual image of a sheikh in flowing white robes, but no sense of his character. The people who live behind that shifting, white-hot wall of sand are an enigma to us.

This book shows what the Saudi is like at home. Not all the scenes are pretty, but they are real, and are presented as they were perceived through the eyes of a Middle American businessman who went there, on his own, without the backing of one of the major oil companies, Aramco, or a giant multinational conglomerate corporation.

There is no desire to be contemptuous, but, rather, to give you the thoughts and feelings of one person exposed to cultural electrocution. In so doing, it probably says something about that person, too, who is, after all, both Western and human, thus subject to all the frailties and prejudices of other Western humans.

Foreword

Notes, Pronunciations, and Comments

First, there are no correct English language spellings for Arabic words. At best, our version of a written Arabic word is an approximation, a phonetic spelling, and in our language where *c* can sound with an "sss," as in "certificate" or more like a *k*, as in "cave," a lot depends on where the speller is from and how English is used there. For this book, we've tried to stick close to the phonetics as they might be heard in Middle America.

Next, while still Arabic, the Persian Gulf has a slang or shortened form of the language all its own, different from village dialects, classical Arabic, or Modern Standard Arabic. "Welcome," for example, is properly *Ahlan Wa Sahlan*. Along the Gulf, you hear *Aleikum Alsallem*, or "Greetings, God be with you," because Saudi Arabia is the birthplace of Mohammed and a center of the Moslem faith.

I guess, because of interest in the subject, there are a number of different words for the veil worn by all women away from their intimates outside their homes. There are also different kinds of veils. In the book, we've tried to stay with one word, or at most two, so as not to confuse.

An important point. Here, we say "sheikh" as in "The Sheikh of Araby," but in the Kingdom, it's pronounced more like "shake." Any man strong enough, important enough, or rich enough to demand to be called sheikh and gets called sheikh, is one—a simple criterion, simple test, for the use of the title, which signifies a man of importance, but does not have an official, governmental meaning. If you ever meet one, be sure and call him "shake." It makes dealing easier and shows you know his importance. Finally, we have, after considerable thought, changed the names of some of the people who are characters in this book because they might be inconvenienced or face serious problems.

FLIGHT FROM DHAHRAN

1 In the Majlis of the Sheikh

Saudi Arabia: November 1977

Dinner wasn't very pleasant. Neither from the standpoint of the food nor the company.

A Pakistani had come in from the kitchen, which was attached to the back part of the house across the open center courtyard, carrying a cheap, shiny, thin aluminum tray about four feet in diameter covered with rice and broiled goat. The fire-blackened remains of the unfortunate animal had been hacked into five or six slabs and arranged tastefully on top of some brownish rice. He unrolled a red plastic cloth on the floor and placed the tray carefully. Eight barefoot men adjusted their robes as they hunkered down around it.

Without a word, the servant left, then returned with a wicker basket of flat bread, which he put between two of the diners. None of the already eating men paid the slightest attention to him. They just concentrated on tearing off hunks of the cooked, greasy flesh and stuffing it into their noisily chewing mouths. On friendly nights, one or two would always rip off a choice morsel and toss it onto the rice in front of me to show hospitality. But not tonight.

I sat there with them, parked so my butt rested on my right ankle. Like the pack, I ate with my right hand only, keeping my left behind my back. Practical custom: one hand, the right, for eating, the other, the left, for performing the daily ablution of washing your asshole after answering Mother Nature's morning call.

Using fingers and thumb, I made an irregular ball of the cooked rice and popped it into my mouth. It, and the goat, were almost cold. But not half as cold as the conversation had become.

1

Even Abdallah Fazza, my usually cordial host, seemed tense and subdued. Almost totally blind since childhood, the fat rascal was King Khaled's brother-in-law and had the reputation of being a tough cagey character. When I'd come over to Saudi Arabia the first time, months before, I'd liked him immediately. He seemed to like me as well, because he'd taken the almost unheard-of step, in that small, strict Moslem village, of asking me to be a guest in his home. Then we could work out the details of our business deal and oversee assembly of the precast-concrete forms into components for a new housing project.

I'd accepted instantly. Both because I wanted to live with an Arabic family and because the construction site was a dangerous seventy kilometers from the nearest hotel. Six hundred people a year, give or take a few, are killed in traffic accidents on that one stretch of blacktop—worse than any freeway! Besides, the word hotel was a complete misnomer when applied to the hovel on a side street of downtown Jubail. As a Westerner, I'd have been fair game for every con man or homosexual lecher in the area, and the rats would have been larger than those that prowled around my room in Abdallah's house all night.

I smiled as I sipped my large glass of unsweetened instant tea. Cut off from beer, scotch, bourbon, and all other alcoholic beverages because of the Saudi Arabian's strict recognition of Shari'a, the revealed law of Islam, I'd taken to Lipton's with a vengeance. It had always been a favorite of mine but now I consumed it morning till dark.

I hoped I didn't feel as bad as I must have looked under the bluish shine of the fluorescent lights. I wasn't hung over. I hadn't had a drink in weeks. I wasn't tired. If anything, I'd been getting too much sleep. There wasn't much to do at night.

I was just beat down. Depressed. The constant haggling and lack of good faith was finally getting to me. I was homesick, and I'd had it.

Speaking carefully, in my inimitable mixture of English and Arabic, I swallowed a mouthful of stringy goat, moved back away from the now almost bare tray, to remove myself from the polite protocol of dining, and got down to my final point.

"Since the work has not been done, and the site not prepared for the installation of the forms, we don't have any choice.

Christmas is on us and the men from my country will be going home. It's our Ramadan. Our holy time. That means we won't be able to start until well after the first of the year."

This statement was met with the same hard silence which had filled the room since I'd started talking. I regretted ruining their dinners, but considering what we'd been served, nothing could do it much damage. The only sound was the soft swish of the overhead fan.

I sat there with the uneasy disadvantage of a visitor, not quite certain of what was being said around me. Looking and speaking pleasantly during a meal was an obligation and I'd trod near the edge of discourtesy.

The Pakistani servant was wiping up the few stray grains of rice which had missed the plastic drop cloth. He wanted out of there. I did too. Nervously, I stuck my greasy hands into the pockets of my khakis so no one would see my fingers tremble. The sheikh across from me worried his beads a little harder.

The Pakistani left and came in again with openmouthed brass pots of coffee. Reacting to a motion from Abdallah, he removed the huge tray and the vinyl "tablecloth." The men, obviously contented, settled back, arranging themselves on small cushions, and started sipping tiny, fragile cups of boiled green coffee. They were watching me patiently.

"So," I concluded, taking a long pull at my tea, "I'll be leaving in a few days, too, since there is nothing more I can do here at this time."

There was a pause while they continued to drink. I began to work a string of goat out of a crevice between two teeth with my tongue. Then one of them smiled. "Ah, Mr. John. You mustn't try to use your mixture of Arabic and English. You only confuse them. I will translate."

"Suliman," I said in a low voice, "my partner George and I both know how you translate. You select what you want everyone to hear and skip the rest. Even Abdallah is complaining about it. We need straight talk now."

The small, mustached man looked at me for a long moment. Anger was written across his forehead. His English, when he finally contained himself enough to speak, had a British overtone.

"Mr. John, you speak of leaving. But you will not leave until you have paid me the final installment of six thousand American dollars on the commission you owe me. I'll have you placed in jail first."

The other men, seeing his intensity, moved away from the two of us, scooting their foam-rubber cushions back so they could sit and lean against the wall, listening.

I knew Suliman had to be careful, because none of the other partners knew of his commission scheme. If they found out, they'd all want a share.

Not everyone present had an interest in our little drama. In a Saudi house, men come and go like in a bus station, especially around meal times. Cousins, brothers, uncles, wives' relations, friends, acquaintances, enemies, you name it—anyone with business or curiosity drops by whenever he likes, to stay for however long something is up. Guests, at least male guests, are received in a single large room, the majlis, where they are free to sit. Getting involved is another matter, because speaking out in a family fight or inadvertently taking sides in a minor quarrel can result in blood feuds which last through generations. Only men, naturally, are included in this open-house invitation to visit and do nothing. Women, who come in two classifications, are not so welcomed. Single women stay home. Or, on the rare occasion they are allowed to visit, are escorted by a male family member to their destination. There they are received at the back of the house into the female area. Married women have little more freedom, but do seem to move about easier, in pairs or small groups. In some of the bigger cities, things are changing. A little, but changing. There is strong opposition to reform from the strict Wahhabi sect, though, and King Khaled, recognizing the potential for trouble, moves with wise slowness.

I looked at the group who had stayed close after Suliman threatened me. Abdallah, our host, of course, remained intensely interested. The blind fat man just sat quietly, listening. I knew he didn't understand three words of English but I respected his ability to judge the meaning of emotions by tone of voice.

His Honor the Emir, Bidoon Ismek, mayor of the little town of Jubail, leaned forward, too. *Emir,* literally, translates as "army commander" or "military ruler." It's a title used on the Persian Gulf to denote an official of some city or state. I'd only learned earlier that same afternoon of his entry into the partnership. He was, as we say in the States, a "silent" participant, and he kept his silence now. Bidoon worried me. First, because *Bidoon* is "without" and *Ismek* reads "my name" in English, which meant to me he was remaining anonymous. Then, because he had political stroke, which told of a strong family tie somewhere up high. No one is elected anything in Saudi. A man is appointed, and the appointment shows power. It also worried me that I had seen his eyebrow raise slightly when I said my going-home line. How much English he knew, I didn't know. But some, to be sure. He was light-complexioned, which allowed the pits on his acne-scarred cheeks to show up under his black beard. Skin damage from severe acne is common among men in the Kingdom. Maybe in women, too, but with the *ghishura*, or veil, it was impossible to tell.

I was certain of Sheikh Saba, the man next to Bidoon. He knew nothing of the English language. His son, however, seated on his right, spoke a few words. They were in the act, but I didn't know how much they were involved. Neither was too dangerous, because we were in Abdallah's majlis. The rules were the same there as they were for a tent in the desert. As long as you were inside, Allah's law gave you safety. They seemed calm enough, half squatting, flowing robes and bare feet, running short chains of ivory and amber worry beads through their fingers again and again.

Bidoon was nervous. He was wearing, of all things, a golden-handled sword. Not some namby-pamby decorative item, but a real, honest-to-god sword, which had probably chopped off a few hands and possibly a head or two. He kept caressing the raised portion of the white ivory grip with his long brown fingers, twisting the pommel one way, then the other.

Except for the soft murmur of voices from the other men, who had now stopped watching and gathered into a small circle across the twenty-foot expanse of gray tile floor, there was no noise. The two suspended fans turned slowly, moving the hot air about. Two installations of fluorescent tubes, running across the high ceiling, cast a soft but not too flattering light on us, making our lips and the small areas under our eyes darkly sinister.

Abdallah, my host, always carried a chrome-plated, pearl-handled .32-caliber automatic of some odd make stuck down in a fold of his gold-threaded white robe. He said it was for use against rats. The fat man could see nothing, but was accustomed to shooting at sounds. I was concerned about him because he was the only one present I had ever seen get mad enough to kill. Besides, a reputation like his wasn't come by easily in the desert. Or peacefully.

Suliman Nasir Rasi, who had originally put this charming group together and was the only one fluent in English, liked to throw his weight around. I'd been able to see him at it firsthand during the months and months of parlaying we'd done. His threat to have me thrown in jail was more bluster than fact, to show his associates he had political influence. They didn't seem to notice. Suliman was small potatoes compared to the money sitting across from me. He was somehow in or connected with the Saudi Royal Navy. Short, dark, wiry, but with the beginnings of a paunch, his looks didn't match the command presence he could muster in his voice when he wanted to.

When the deal had started, Suliman had visited me in Houston on three occasions. He was the hanger-on, the fixer-upper, the putter-together. He had contacts with the money. For his efforts, he would receive a commission when the deal was done, as well as partial payment, a fee, and expenses while we were conducting business. I could tell by his new sureness he'd managed to somehow include himself into the partnership for a cut of the big action. Plus his secret commission.

"Hell, Suliman, you know the deal better than that. You get expenses, and when we collect for the work, then you get the rest of the twenty grand."

He stared at me. For an Arab, he was a real hard case. He had a laugh which was a long way from the enjoyment of anything funny. His coarse black mustache grew down to his chin and partially obscured his pink-lipped mouth. Right now, it was shiny with grease from dinner. When he talked, his tongue showed like some small red living creature.

There was a pause as the five of them began to work over a piece of equipment that looked like a cross between a nineteen-thirties-modern floor lamp and a goldfish bowl. A servant packed the burner with a mixture of dried fruit and other vegetable matter, checked the level of rose water used to cool-filter the smoke, then lit it. The smell of the burning mess was strong, somewhere between perfume and garbage on a hot day. The bubbling sucking was the loudest sound in the room.

An ornately carved wooden mouthpiece, mounted on a four-foot length of silk-wrapped rubber hose, was passed from man to man. Each took a toke, blew the smoke into the air, and seemed inordinately pleased with himself.

Suliman used the break to compose himself.

"Mr. John, Mr. John. We speak as enemies, not as friends and partners. The situation is not so bad as you make it to be. I'll tell you what. We'll start site preparation bukra. Tomorrow. You can't leave now. We are just commencing to need your skills and services."

This time I was the one who let a long silence linger. The man was bullshitting me. The same way I'd been BSed for months now. *Bukra* was like "mañana." It might never come. My position made it imperative to be careful.

Suliman broke into my thoughts. One of the group across the room farted and his friends laughed.

"I promise, Mr. John. Site work starts tomorrow. You'll stay, right? We can't let you leave until we're through."

That was it; finally said. I'd thought to myself several times during the past few days my Saudi partners were going to pass off not having performed on their end of the bargain and there it was, just a calm, casual statement. Nothing had been done, even though they'd told me a hundred stories about the progress.

I had to be cautious. But firm.

"Suliman, translate what I said. I'm going home tomorrow whether you start work or not. If you do start before I leave, I'll be back in January. By then, the damn site should be ready for the first forms. Though God only knows if they'll work after sitting out there on the dock in the salt air."

The man instantly became livid. His face, red under the swarthy tan, his narrowed black eyes, and the sound of his voice as he shouted showed his anger.

"You'll not leave until the job is done."

The others, watching, smoking stoically, looked at him, waiting for the Arabic version.

I was on uncertain ground. I'd never seen Suliman really pissed off before, and for my first time I had to do it as a lone ranger in a small room of a house on the edge of a desert village miles from a city or any sample of Western civilization. Neat move.

Then the humor of the situation struck me. Here I was, tucked away in a desolate corner of the world, on a legitimate business deal, and one of the partners, who was shortchanging the rest, was getting set to throw off his group's failure onto me.

I went back to my Saudi-English and addressed Abdallah, who was still fingering the smooth, cold, pearl-handled pistol. We'd managed to communicate on a limited basis for weeks through a mixture of gestures, pointing, Arabic and pidgin English, so I felt I might be able to get through to him now.

"Abdallah, do you believe my company is at fault because your partners did not prepare the site as you said you would? Your group even sent me telexes on its completion before I came over this time."

The man smiled back at me, sweetly. But without warmth.

Here it comes, I thought. When an Arab gets that flat smile on his face he's getting set to tell a well-thought-out lie, not one he uses every day. Lying is a fine Arabic art, much respected and revered, to be used without dishonor. I was about to get a terrific sample for my collection. The shit was getting deep.

Suliman spoke again. "As you know, Mr. John, I am very well aware of the terms of Abdallah's agreement with you and your company. But how could you truly have expected him, being without heavy equipment, to have the site ready? Besides, he was not able to complete the transaction to purchase the land until this afternoon."

Now I was getting hot. Six months ago, I'd been told something entirely different and had spent a thousand bucks on a soil-analysis coring job, to be sure the site would be suitable for the erection of a small plant.

"You told me yourself, Suliman, that your group had purchased the land months ago. You also said you'd leveled it and were through with compacting the soil, so we could start installing the forms."

He went on, blandly, but with his voice raised, so as to cover mine. Outshouting another person is one more Arab custom. It's an act of machismo and not supposed to be offensive.

"So obviously, if your firm were responsible for the erection of the housing shells within a specified period of time, your responsibility included the manufacturing site for the forms themselves. One goes with the other. It is obvious."

"Obvious, hell." I was mad now, and I had little trouble making my voice carry over his. "Not where I come from. You all said you'd have the site ready, and I said I'd be here to supervise the erection of the forms. You guys aren't ready, so I'm telling you now, like I've told you before, there is nothing I can damn well do. So I'm going home. Tomorrow, or the day after. As soon as I can get the damn reservations."

I flinched as the four men, acting as one, came to their feet. I hadn't seen Sheikh Saba look at his watch, but he must have, because he signaled the others. In a group, they moved to a corner where they got down on their knees on prayer mats. Qibla, the direction to face with prayers to direct the voice to Mecca, was understood. The praying routine was well known to each of them and they went through it automatically. I always wondered how much they faked it. Like we did as kids, with the nuns, back in St. Stephen's grammar school. In Saudi, if a man doesn't go through the motions, someone will mention it to the religious police, who will arrest the offender. But no one can see what's inside a praying man's head· After ten minutes they were back facing me, sitting on their pillows, silent.

The pipe bubbled. Somewhere off in the back, across the walled courtyard which kept guests from seeing the women of the house, the noise of children's clatter carried in with the faint smell of hot sesame seed oil.

I took the opportunity to light a small Havana cigar. I'd always liked cigars, especially Havana. There was no Cuban embargo in Saudi Arabia, so their smokes were available in the expatriate stores in the city. They tended to be dry, though, because no one bothered to keep them in a humidor.

Emir Bidoon went back to playing with his sword hilt, the sheikh and his son continued to worry their beads. It gave me a chance to think.

I'd said what I'd wanted to say. I was leaving. Suliman would translate that okay. Not wanting the situation to get out of hand, I rose to my feet, knees popping. I was stiff, as usual, from sitting on the floor. "Tell them this, Suliman. Thank Abdallah for me for the very excellent dinner."

I waited as he did so.

"Then say for them not to be anxious. My company wants to do this job more than your group wants it done. There are millions in profit for us. Altogether, three and a half million bucks. Tell them not to be anxious. I'll be back in January. And if you've completed your part, we'll quickly do ours."

Smiling pleasantly, shaking hands, I bowed to each gentleman as a means of avoiding their kisses, then walked soundlessly across the gray tile floor to where I'd left my shoes when I'd entered the majlis.

I stopped before reaching the door, and turned. "Also, tell 'em if they don't hurry, my partner will change his plans and not move here on a permanent basis. There's a lot of good work we can get, and all they have to do is stop stalling." Still smiling, I left the room.

Outside, in the narrow courtyard, as I slipped into my shoes, I could hear the congregation begin to argue. Suliman's high voice, almost squeaky with excitement as he told them what had transpired, was already bringing grunts and admonitions. The grimace which I hoped had passed for a smile turned sour as I listened to the Marx Brothers plan their next move.

It was another typical Saudi night. As I walked across the black-and-white-tiled court toward my room, I could see stars high overhead. There was a hint of wind and the temperature was near 90. But it would fall during the dark hours to a relatively comfortable 80. The stars, and their hazy brightness, made me conscious of the contribution the Arabian peoples had made to astronomy. Most of the brighter bodies in the heavens had Arabic names, even in the West.

The side of the house where I was quartered seemed strangely silent after the row of the majlis. I could still hear kids messing around, an occasional rat scurrying somewhere, and the light noise of the evening wind, a moist body-temperature breeze which sprang up every night after sundown.

At the door of my room my watch showed 8 P.M. There was nothing to do but bed. Saudi Arabia offers little in the way of night life even in the largest cities. Out here, in the boondocks next to the start of what is known as "the Empty Quarter," there is nothing. Just miles and miles of rock, sand, and hard-clay soil rolling away forever into an endless landscape of drought. Through the narrow window I could clearly see the orange flare from the burning of gas at the oil operation eight kilometers away. Parts of the flame went over two hundred feet into the dark Arabian sky. They burned more gas in a day than was flared in the United States in a week. The entire village was cast by an orange glow from the reflected light.

Bed wasn't too inviting, but I had to be up early to go out to the port of Dammam before I left for a final look at the forms which had been sitting on the docks gathering demurrage and rust for over a month. I had a stupid love affair with those forms. They'd been designed by George and me to meet the specific requirements of the Saudi climate, and it bugged me to think of them owned by some bunch of wastrels who would shorten their normal life by better than half. That was provided I ever got to install them in the first place. In the Middle East there was always someone sitting around waiting to make a few bucks by selling unclaimed freight out from under the owner.

I did a little work at my drawing board, on the plans for what I called the Moon Plaza Hotel, a project being developed for downtown Jubail, once we had the factory to build the proper precast shapes.

Then, about nine o'clock, I decided to go to bed. It wasn't late, I wasn't tired, but that was all there was to do. I'd read the two books I'd brought from home cover to cover, twice, including the copyright information. I had also almost erased the single Arabic-English language tape my family had given me by playing it so many times. Of the two pastimes left, killing flies, which swarmed everywhere, was better than watching the TV a servant had placed on the floor in one corner of the room. It was a beat-up old set, but it got a good black and white picture on two channels from Southern Iran and Oman. Highly rated evening entertainment consisted of four Arabs sitting in a small circle doing a Saudi talk show or a string music group which played three notes forward, then backward, changing tempo as they went along. I enjoyed Arabic music, although it is simpler than a symphony, but it wasn't much to see being performed.

A low wood table in the corner was equipped with a bowl and a pitcher of water. No mirror. Mirrors were considered a device of Western vanity. I kept a small one in my suitcase for shaving. I set it up and stripped off my shirt. The reflection showed how much darker my neck and face had become than my chest. The sun had also etched crow's-feet at the edges of my green eyes. Green eyes, brown hair, six feet, and a hundred eighty pounds. I'd slimmed down some since arriving, and if I got much more tan, I might pass for an Arab myself, except for my clothes. I'd refused a traditional thauba and kafiya headdress offered by Abdallah shortly after my arrival, feeling the need to be myself. It was a good idea, as my difference in dress helped maintain my independence.

I brushed my teeth, smiling like a mad dog with frothing foam at the edges of my lips. Me looking like an Arab was funny, because I was clean-shaven, and none of them would be caught dead without at least a mustache.

I looked older to myself tonight, older than my forty-seven years. That was usually a sign I was under stress. The happy scene at dinnertime hadn't helped.

Bed was a foam-rubber pallet laid in one corner, and, after killing as many flies as I could, it didn't take me long to slip out of my khaki work pants and roll in. Not too comfy, but I'd gotten used to it, more or less. The fan above moved the air, so down where I was, inches off the floor, it was relatively cool.

We'd been to the village shopping yesterday, and I'd purchased an English edition of *Better Homes & Gardens*. Not my ideal selection, but all I could find. As usual, the censors had been there before me. Parts of articles were clipped out and all photos of females showing any décolletage were doctored with black felt-tip. The magazine looked like a kindergarten had used it for a school project.

As I turned over in my narrow bunk, covered by a sheet to keep off the insects, I could hear, far away, the sound of impassioned voices. I recognized Abdallah's and realized the four men were still at it in the majlis. I must have dozed for a couple of hours, tossing uneasily as hard spots pressed through. It was no wonder I woke quickly at a noise in the courtyard outside my door.

"Who's there?"

I reached for the light switch to flick on the twin fluorescent lamps twelve feet up on the pink stucco-covered ceiling. Fishing for it, I hit a lump on the floor, which was warm and moved rapidly out the door, causing my caller to swear loudly as the rat ran over his bare foot. Before I could find the switch, the brilliant beam of a flashlight blinded me.

"Mr. John, you must come with us, on a small matter." Suliman's British accent identified him.

I was instantly nervous. When an Arab says, "It's a small

matter," he means it's a large one. They have mastered the art of saying the opposite of what's on their minds.

Confused by my broken sleep and the bright intensity of the light, I got to my feet. Suddenly, he placed my pants and shirt over my arm.

There was no way of telling what was about to happen. I might be in real danger. I could make a stand in the narrow room, inside the house, where I might have a hell of a time getting away, or I could put on my pants and go along with them. Some choice! I decided to go. There was a chance I would find myself in a more opportune situation. Besides, as nervous as I was, I didn't think they were hauling me away on a one-way camel ride, a common practice among the Bedouin desert tribes. Except for Fazza, my partners were city folk, more like drug-store Bedouins.

I could see Suliman, Abdallah, Saba, and the sheikh's son. Bidoon was missing, which was typical, because he was always worrying about his job. The four seemed embarrassed, but hurried me as much as they could.

"Come along, Mr. John," Suliman said, motioning me with the flashlight. "We need to go."

"Go? Where? Why?" I was fully dressed.

"We need to meet again. With the mayor."

There were no telephones in the village, or, for that matter, anywhere else for miles. I glanced at my watch. Eleven o'clock. It was late to be summoned to the emir's home. I slipped my feet into my shoes as Suliman quivered.

"Come along, come along."

I moved with Suliman and Saba into the rough-walled courtyard. The dim fluorescence at the far end exaggerated shadows. Abdallah, the rascal, stood at the open door of my room, his keen ears and blind eyes looking after us. No one touched me, because by Islamic law violent or unfriendly physical contact between two people is considered a grave insult. At least they were still treating me civilly.

At the ornate iron door of the house, on the side exposed to the narrow, rough street, Suliman again urged me on. "Please hurry, Mr. John," he said, speaking in a hushed voice. His commanding tone began to irritate me. Hurry, hell, after all the waiting I'd been doing.

It was a short walk to the dark-green Chevrolet Suburban and the activity brought me back to full consciousness.

"Where in the hell are we going?" I balked at the door. Now, outside so I could get some distance between us, Abdallah's gun didn't bother me so much. He had followed us.

"Into Jubail to see Bidoon. To talk again." All this in Arabic.

"Just the four of us?" If it were only me and the three Arabs, I knew it wasn't going to be a one-way drive. I believed I could handle them, but I knew I'd have to keep an eye on the fat man and his .32.

"Just us. Bidoon is waiting to see you."

"Why?"

"You will find out. He is an important man."

"He'd better be. You got me up from a sound sleep for this little joyride." .

Suliman stepped close. I could make him out clearly in the light from the house and the faraway orange glow of the Aramco gas flare. Behind him, the rocky countryside, covered with dark, ominous shadows, undulated off into the distance. I'd spent hours marveling at the khaki-tan color of the wasteland which makes up most of eastern Saudi Arabia and how different it was from a Hollywood desert. In the moonlight, the terrain seemed distorted and unworldly. Only the sight and smell of several large rats digging through the many weeks' supply of garbage piled outside against one wall of the courtyard brought me back to the Saudi I had grown to know and love.

Suliman, facing me, wore the traditional thauba, a long, flowing white robe, as well as the elaborate rope-and-cloth headpiece. The rope part, called "aqal," was, in earlier times, used to hobble the family camel. In the dark, his outfit made him look like a creature from a second-rate science-fiction film.

"Do come along, Mr. John."

I'd heard that line and had his urging until I was getting tired of it. Since I felt I could take all of them on at the same time if it came to action, I slowed.

"Suliman, I'm going to ask you once more, nicely. Why in the hell are we going to Bidoon's?"

"To talk. We, as well as you, wish to settle this matter."

Saba, sensing that Suliman's tone was making me angry, stepped forward. He was dressed traditionally, too. In the entire time I'd known him, he had worn what seemed to be the same thauba, like Abdallah's, with gold embroidery to denote wealth and position.

Saba motioned placatingly, and the next few steps brought us to the Suburban. It belonged to Abdallah Fazza, who had purchased it shortly after his ten-year-old boy, who usually acted as his chauffeur, had smashed his Mercedes into a mud-brick wall. I'd been along that evening and it had taught me a lesson about Saudi drivers.

Abdallah dearly wanted to drive. Enough so he had asked me on an earlier visit to look into the possibility of his coming to the United States for an operation to restore his vision. Like many Saudis, he believed anything was possible in the great United States. I'd conferred with a specialist, who, understanding the conditions, had given me a short course in what to look for. It had been very hard for me to tell Fazza his eyes had completely atrophied.

You might think Abdallah's lack of vision would temper his motor mania, but that wasn't the case. He drove with gusto across desert where there was nothing to hit.

Oddly enough, Fahad, his ten-year-old son, was very responsible as a chauffeur. And he loved his father. It was a treat for him to take his dad roaring off though the sand and scrub.

I wasn't hot to ride with the kid, though, due to the earlier Mercedes and mud-wall incident, so I breathed an honest sigh of relief when Sheikh Saba got behind the wheel. Misplaced faith.

Suliman paused at the door of the back seat, looked skyward for an instant, and in a barely perceptible voice said quickly, "In the name of Allah, the Compassionate, the Merciful." Then he got in. What he'd just recited was a phrase which begins each of the chapters of the Koran, except one, and is a kind of quickie prayer used to start a venture, a trip, or anything else, when the starter has some doubt as to the final outcome. I couldn't tell if I was the point of doubt or it was simply a quick protection against Saba's driving.

I joined him in the back, but not too eagerly. With the windows down, the flies had come into the cab after sunset to feast on the morsels of food strewn about inside. Getting in disturbed them from under the seats, so we were all sitting in a cloud of the buzzing bastards. They wouldn't clear out until we took off down the road.

One of the most useless things on a car as far as most Saudi drivers are concerned is air conditioning. Not because it's too hot to work well, but because for some reason they just don't use it. They all prefer to blaze along the highway with the windows down, allowing hundred-plus-degree air, desert grit, and an occasional insect to flow through.

From my seat in the rear, two of my friends would have their backs to me. If I didn't like where we were going, I was in a good position to do something about it.

If you've never ridden with a Saudi driver then you have a treat coming. A normal crosstown trip on paved streets is like every wild ride in a carnival thrown in together. It's a guaranteed thrill a second. In addition to not being overly adept at steering, the use of the accelerator, or understanding the distance it takes to stop without smoking the tires, they have a mandatory period of inattention. The driver will turn and talk to those in the back, eyes off the road, head screwed around, for a minute at a time. He will join into any argument and, at the proper point, compound his lack of vision by taking both hands from the wheel to wave his arms, accenting a point. Between chain-smoking and fumbling new stereo tapes into the player, which is usually installed by connecting a wire to the cigar lighter, he doesn't have much time for steering anyway. But every little bit helps.

Saba turned the key and didn't release it until long after the engine roared into life. The horrible grinding sound, as the starter raced faster and faster trying to match the accelerating flywheel, was unnerving. Then, with a sudden jerk, he let loose the ignition key, jammed his foot flat to the floor, and as the belabored engine screamed, knocked the gear-selection lever into drive. The big green Suburban sat perfectly still for a moment, there was a loud metallic thunk from the rear end, and with a shower of rocks and sand it lurched forward, fishtailing. The noise of the sprayed gravel rattled under the body. Saba swung the wheel with verve, bringing the nose of the moving Suburban in line with the narrow track between the courtyard walls of the houses, and we hit a mound of carelessly dumped rock fill which threw us all around in our seats. In a minute, accompanied by screaming tires, we were on the two-lane asphalt road, rocketing toward what passed for downtown. That's when I learned the reason for Suliman's short prayer.

Saba's driving frightened me more than the mystery of our destination. In addition to one completely bad eye, he had a continual spastic jerking of his head caused by an unending effort to get the folds of his silk kafiya headdress away from the edges of his greasy, extra thick glasses. Some distance from the house, he finally turned on the headlights. We could see well enough without them for most things, thanks to the Aramco fire storm, but wandering Arabs have a habit of going to sleep on the roads, where the blacktop holds the sun's heat during the night. A body, outline obliterated by the puddling effect of the robe and drifting sand, can be hard to see even in bright beams, much less by flarelight.

Saba settled down at what he thought was a reasonable, honorable speed, with the needle indicating something over ninety kilometers, all the suspension could handle over the rough, potholed pavement. In places, it was more than the chassis could manage so we bounced and squealed alarmingly. Old hands in the Middle East say Arabs drive as they handle camels: whipping the animal to go faster, never looking right or left, and allowing the beast to do the thinking for both of them. There is more than a modicum of truth in this viewpoint.

"Saba," I spoke in a low voice, using my limited Arabic and deliberately keeping what I was saying from Suliman. I knew it would bother him. He tried to lean forward to hear my conversation, but we hit a corrugated section of road and the car bounced severely, forcing him back into his seat for safety.

Saba's short stature made him peer over the top of the wheel like a kid driving his dad's car in the driveway.

"Saba, where the hell are we going?"

"Downtown. The emir wants to talk to you."

"Why?"

"You will see." He spoke without looking at me, concentrating on the rough blacktop. In the green glow of the instrument lights I could see beads of perspiration break out along his hairy upper lip. He licked them away. I settled down. There was no further information to be had and it was safer to hang on.

The ride took only a few minutes but it seemed like an hour. We narrowly avoided an oncoming truck which Saba didn't see until he crested a low rise. The Mercedes diesel was rifling along in the center of the road, coming like hell. Neither driver had taken the slightest notice of the reflection of the other's headlights, so there was a wild swerve, with great screaming of stressed tires, as both snapped their wheels hard over to miss each other. Saba yelled insults and slurs on the Korean trucker's family tree, his intelligence, and his ability to drive. He turned to me, still incensed, ignoring the road. "Did you see that ignorant bastard? That's what comes of giving driving responsibility to any Korean or Pakistani who wanders in off the desert. It's no wonder we have so many wrecks." I couldn't follow all his frantic monologue, and got Suliman to translate.

Through his diatribe, which continued on long after the trucker had disappeared behind us, he watched me for signs of agreement. Finally, satisfied he'd made his point, he returned his eyes to the road, just in time to see a huge load of reinforcing steel I'd been watching with horrible fascination for a half minute. The Saudis dump it right in the middle of the street where it will be handy to its construction site. There is little legal risk, because if worse comes to worst and someone hits it, the value of four camels will settle the matter even if a person is killed. In our case, it almost cost sixteen camels. Saba swerved at the last instant so hard all of us were thrown around in the interior of the flying green Suburban. I banged my head on the roof then was slammed back down into my seat with spine-jarring force. Saba took it all in stride, keeping his foot firmly down until we reached the outer edges of Jubail. We passed through the police checkpoint without reducing speed. All the cops were sleeping.

The village was quiet and had been since seven-twelve, the time of the last prayer. Our car, now driven more sedately, was the only moving thing we saw. After a few minutes I began to get a nervous feeling of isolation. Except along the main boulevard, there were almost no lights. Where the Aramco flare was shadowed, a deep black darkness covered the sides of the buildings and spread into the narrow, rough streets. The lack of underground waste-water drainage became apparent from the fetid smell of stale, standing water which drifted in through the open windows.

After driving for several blocks into the main part of the little settlement, Saba pulled the car to the high curb. Because of the dark I had no idea where we were, and in comparison to the noise of the mad ride into town, the heavy stillness bothered me. I was debating whether or not to get out when Suliman reached over and pushed open my door. The dome light gave his face a sinister look.

"Come on, Mr. John, hurry."

I wasn't about to act until I knew more about what was going on.

"Suliman, what the hell? I'm not going anywhere."

Before he could reply, Abdallah said something to him in a

low, guttural Arabic, which caused Suliman to begin helping the fat man from the front seat. Once onto the sidewalk, he was guided to the wall, where he began waving his arms around in the air. I thought he'd gone crazy, but in a minute his hand touched a rough length of rope hanging down from somewhere in the darkness. He gave it a hard jerk, then another. All hell broke loose. The rope was attached to a bell which rang stridently in the quiet of the village. The suddenness of the sound startled me, and I managed to bump my head again. Talk about enough noise to wake the dead. First the clanging of the iron bell, then a face popped over the wall and there was a short, shouted conversation. Suliman and Abdallah were waved over to the ornate grillwork of the main-compound double doors. A man with the rank of sergeant in the National Guard showed up, shouting orders to a private who pushed open the squealing iron gates. Then they all got into a heated discussion, some of which I could just make out. Abdallah wanted the sergeant to wake the emir, but the sergeant wanted nothing to do with such an obviously stupid program. Their problem was solved, however, after a couple of minutes, because they'd made so much commotion there was no way Bidoon could possibly sleep. By accident I caught a quick glance of his round face peering out from the edge of the main gate. The shouting petered out as Suliman and Abdallah disappeared into the compound.

By this time, I was looking around wildly, thinking it was all too nutty for words. I'd been left in the car with Sheikh Saba, who had taken absolutely no notice of the confusion. He sat quietly, running his beads as a man of piety and dignity should, looking the other way. I looked, too. For some indication of where we were. Then it came to me. If they'd managed to get the emir Bidoon out of his mayoral bed, this must be the military headquarters corresponding to our city hall, with live-in attachments.

From behind the iron gates, more shouting; this time in three voices. The guard had given up, but Suliman joined the fray. I didn't have time to wait and wonder. After a few minutes, the two appeared, Suliman leading Abdallah, who was carefully folding a piece of paper. Apparently they'd gotten what they'd come for, and it was some sort of document they needed the emir to sign.

We were off again through the romantic desert night until we screeched to a stop in front of a building I did recognize. One of Jubail's three police stations.

We turned off the main drag onto a very dark, very narrow, very smelly, very dingy side alley. Once again it was *The Suliman and Abdallah Show*. The two got out, and with Suliman leading went up a couple of steps. They knocked loudly, the door was thrown open, pouring a brilliant white square of light into the dirty alley, and the two slipped inside. I was left with the dignified sheikh, who continued to take no notice.

After a minute, the door slammed open, then closed when three men stepped outside. They were standing slightly above me, and the orange flicker of the Aramco burn made them glow. One was in uniform with brass markers on his collar and a U.S.-made submachine gun slung over his shoulder. He was a little reluctant as they walked back toward the car, but with Abdallah and Suliman prodding him verbally, he came around to my window.

I was in a high old state. Obviously they hadn't set this up to kill me, but clearly I wasn't there for a birthday party, either. I was afraid they were going to try to lock me up. I could tell now that the armed man was a police officer. Young and low-ranking. A private. But his weapon, not quite pointed at me, gave him lots of authority. Sheikh Saba still hadn't moved from behind the wheel, so there was no opportunity for me to steal the van and make a run for it. Suliman stuck his smiling face into the window, around the side of the cop.

"He," nodding to the man with the grease gun, "wants your passport."

"Suliman, you can go to hell. I'm not giving him, or you, or anyone, my passport."

The officer, reacting to my tone of voice, became more determined. He changed in an instant from an unwilling participant to an active aggressor. Speaking in Arabic, he said, slowly and carefully, "Jawazi. [Passport.]"

I could understand him only too well.

Suliman snapped open the door of the Suburban. The dome light came on and I could see I was facing a slender young man with a rough face, dressed in a baggy olive-green uniform. The submachine gun looked bigger than ever. Light fell only on the lower half of his face, preventing me from getting too good a look at his features.

He spoke again, in a deep voice, with staccato Arabic. "Hand me your passport." He gestured with the barrel of a weapon I knew well from my time in the Army. It was a surplus U.S. model called a "grease gun" because of its resemblance to the device used in filling stations to lubricate automobiles. An ugly thing that would fire an entire magazine of uglier .45-caliber bullets in a flash.

The officer, careful not to get too close in case I might try to grab his weapon, took a step backward. It wasn't necessary. I had no intention of making a play. That damn weapon would turn the inside of the Suburban into trash before anyone could blink. I just hoped the guy wasn't trigger-happy.

The man spoke again, extending his hand. He pronounced the word slowly, so there could be no misunderstanding. "Jawazi." I could tell by his tone he was getting impatient with the stupid foreigner who didn't respond. Suliman started to translate, but stopped when the big barrel waved to silence him. Things got very quiet.

There was no question about having my passport with me. Where I went, it went, too. As a visitor to the Kingdom, it wasn't good form to be caught without papers. Saudi jails are indeed durance vile, and with hundreds of checkpoints located all over the country, you could never tell when someone would stop your car to ask for an ID.

What was going on now was no ordinary spot check, but I still couldn't tell how serious things were. I decided to stall some more.

"What? What do you want?" I tried to appear willing. Cooperative, but disorganized. "What are you saying? What do you mean?" This last brought a look of disgust from Suliman, who damn well knew I understood, and a new movement from the cop. He snapped back the bolt and let it snick forward again. The sound, if you know anything about weapons, carried the decisive smack of a round being chambered for firing. Up to that point I'd been hoping the weapon was for show and all he had was an empty magazine. Now I knew better.

He pointed the blue steel barrel with its big .45-caliber hole toward my forehead and in the poor light spilling from the car door I could see the white tightness of his knuckles where they wrapped around the black-plastic grip. His military training was obvious, so I was certain it extended to the basic rule of arms use, i.e., don't point a machine gun at anything you don't intend to shoot.

He slowly, carefully, repeated the word for passport and

extended his left hand. There was no need for further conversation because it was clear to me he was involved now and was ready to blow me away to save face.

You've probably heard the old adage about the opening of a gun barrel looking like the mouth of a cave when it's pointed at you, but that wasn't my experience. It was small and dark and deadly. I'd seen the business end of a rifle before, but this was the first time I'd been eyeball to automatic, being held by a man who would brook no additional crap.

My comprehension of Arabic improved mightily in seconds. Moving my hands cautiously, I withdrew my packet of papers from a back pocket. As I extended my jawazi he pulled it from my grasp. Not moving the weapon an inch, he shifted his eyes quickly, to see my name, which he spoke aloud.

"Mr. John?"

The uniformed man stepped back, still pointing the grease gun at me, then kicked the car door closed, snapping off the interior lights. Turning quickly, he walked the short distance to the jail door with Suliman and Abdallah, leaving Saba and me in the depths of eye-blinking blackness in the tiny alley. The light from inside the building came and went. It took several seconds for my eyes to readapt to the dark. When I could see, I made out the figures of my two partners walking carefully across the rough, sand-piled pavement, back toward the Suburban.

"What the hell was that all about?" I was half shouting as they came up, partially from a sense of indignity and partially as a reaction to my fear, as well as relief at not having been shot. "I want a receipt for my passport, Suliman."

The Arab looked blandly at me. "The officer said you should come back in the morning. He will give you a receipt at that time."

Suliman's voice said he was lying, but I couldn't tell if he was giving me a partial truth or no truth at all.

There wasn't a hell of a lot I could do in the dark, so I stayed in the car with the Arabs. The drive back to Abdallah's house was as exciting as our voyage out. But there was something eating at my confused mind. With my passport in another person's hands, even an official's, I was unable to leave Saudi Arbia. To board an aircraft leaving the Kingdom, you had to have an exit visa. To get an exit visa, you had to have an entrance visa, to prove you were in the country legally to begin with. I could get another passport if I had to, but only Abdallah, who was my sponsor, could order the replacement of my entry stamp. If I didn't get my papers back, I was going to play hell getting home.

I didn't sleep much that night. It was almost 1 A.M. when I slipped back onto the thin narrow foam-rubber pad. For the first time since moving into Abdallah's house, I wasn't able to put the scurrying rat noises out of my mind.

I'd wondered, when I'd first arrived, why the homeowners didn't keep a pack of cats to decimate the rats. After I had my first close look at what passed for a rat and realized it was bigger than any cat I'd ever seen, I understood.

They didn't bother me too much. One, now and then, would get curious and climb up on the pad to have a look, which could give you a scare if you awoke staring into the flash-picture red eyes, but they seldom bit anyone. Or at least seldom bit anyone seriously.

They were always in the outhouse, though, and I hated to go there after dark. There was no light and I felt exposed when I put my bare bottom over the six-inch hole in the floor.

Before dropping off, I'd made up my mind. In the morning, I was leaving. After a trip to the police station, it was going to be a jitney taxi to Al Khobar and figure out how I was going to get home. I'd had enough. Besides, with the emir Bidoon in the picture, my chances for justice in Jubail were almost nil.

The guys at the cop shop were courteous, but not very helpful. No one appeared to speak any English, and they all had trouble with my Arabic. Worse, they denied any knowledge of my passport or other papers. No one knew anything. Exasperated, I threw a fit, with gestures, loud voice, and slamming the table. What it got me, I didn't need.

Three tough-looking officers gathered around, one pointed back to the cells, then pointed to the front door, the way I'd come into the main room of the station. Their meaning was clear. Shut up and get out, or keep it up and get put on ice. I shut up. Then got out. It looked like Abdallah and Company, through Bidoon's influence, had managed to keep their pressure play private, while leaving room to make it official if the need arose.

An expensive taxi drove me cross-country to the Al Kharja Hotel in Al Khobar, a few miles south of Dhahran, the nearest city with a U.S. consulate. I was going to make a protest and, with the help of our government, get my papers back. Those Arabs were going to be sorry for their hasty actions.

I was indignant. I hated to bring down the wrath of Uncle Sam on my ex-partners, but they'd asked for it. When I got through with them they'd probably be tossed in jail for years. It would serve them right. They had it coming, with all their nighttime strong-arm stuff. The more I thought about it, the more self-righteous I got.

As I sat there in the quiet bustle of the consulate, my mind began to wander. If you'd told me two years ago, when all this started, that I'd be sitting in the U.S. consulate in a small town in Saudi Arabia to regain my passport which had been taken from me at gunpoint, I'd have said you were crazy. But here I was.

Like most situations in life, the whole affair had begun in the simplest possible way. With a phone call.

2 In the Beginning

April 1976

For Houston, it had been a cold winter, with several days of temperatures below freezing, a lot of overcast, fog, and chilling drizzle.

Things hadn't been much hotter at the office. From my desk, looking out over a rolling sea of green trees, I'd been treated to a view of gray clouds ever since my return from Iran. Not that I was sad to see it rain. For seven months, Teheran had been as dry as a gin bottle on skid row. Combined with the altitude, the arid air gave me a daily dose of bloody nose. Humidity felt good.

Heritage Building Systems International, a partnership, was in bad shape. It wasn't our product. That was damn good. We manufactured precast-concrete forms which could be assembled to make buildings of different sizes. From a small house to a large office complex. By U.S. standards, the finished product didn't look great enough to take an architectural award, but it would be durable, have low maintenance costs, and could be quickly and cheaply built almost anywhere.

Tough, quick housing was the sales pitch. And it was true. My partner, George Pinder, who had started one transportable building company and sold it for a ton of bucks, had formed the original firm, International Building Systems.

I got into the deal after my research indicated the '73 OPEC petroleum-price program was trapping millions of dollars in a land short of living quarters. A little more study showed that concrete was ideally suited to the region. Hence the precast idea. Steel forms could be built here, shipped there, then used to mold thousands of

25

identical reinforced concrete shapes which could be locked together to make almost anything.

Buildings using our system had been erected on the rocky, steep sides of mountains in Venezuela and along the tepid brown flood waters of the Amazon, deep in the jungle. The components weren't all that hard to transport and, once on site, they could be joined together like a giant building-block set.

I'd gone to George for some engineering drawings on a project I had working in Iran. He suggested using his system. When I looked it over, I suggested we form a partnership. Heritage would sell in the Middle East, Pinder's International Building Systems would deal with South America, Mexico, and Central America.

That was back in '74. I've often wondered why I didn't listen to my wife, Pat, who wanted me to stay in the real-estate business where we were making damn good money. I suppose there wasn't a whole lot of challenge. Our firm was successful, had good employees, and could, to a great degree, run itself. And I had the wanderlust.

Wanderlust, by itself, isn't a bad thing. Lots of people get it and don't do anything about it. Wanderlust mixed with a personality that wants to see things done, to build things, is another matter entirely. Mine started getting the better of me after the end of the Korean police action. I came back home a changed man. Not so much because of the war, but rather because of the wide, wide world.

I'd been born in '29, one of seven kids, at the start of the Big Depression, in Newark, New Jersey. My dad was diligent and, I guess, lucky. We always had enough, seldom too much, and never, as I recall, a surplus. One thing he managed to instill in us, though, was a need for work. I started my first job when I was seven. By the time I was in high school I was doing forty hours a week for regular paychecks. Dad was tough on us, but those were tough times. When I was eighteen, I got my big break. Like my grandfather, I enlisted in the U.S. Army. I was a sergeant in the Airborne before I knew it, and had learned how to do things "the Army way."

My good times came to a hard ending when the North Koreans decided to annex the southern part of their hilly homeland. We went from sitting about on our khaki backsides to rushing around in green fatigues.

I got a sixteen-month paid vacation in Alaska and later in the glamorous Orient, with all the hot C ration I could swallow, then hit

Stateside with my back pay and the knowledge that there were lots of places I hadn't been and needed to see.

During my time overseas I'd managed to get off the beaten path. A fishing village on the coast, a farming community on a hillside, anywhere there were people going about their everyday business, speaking a language I'd never heard before. It was fascinating, and made me want to see more.

So I did. And found I had a talent for tongues. When I heard people speaking to each other, making love, getting mad, yelling at their kids, their voices were alive. I was able to pick up the rudiments easily. An expanded vocabulary was harder, but I had no hesitation or embarrassment about jumping in and giving it a try. Mix that with a big smile and some hand charades, and I could communicate.

The United States never seemed the same to me. Not worse or bad, in fact to the contrary. There is no place like it and I always want to come home. But once wanderlust takes hold, you see the United States as home—home base—the place from which you can jump off into the rest of the world.

For the first few years after separating from the service I tried to satisfy my desire for travel by seeing American cities. I got as far as Oklahoma, did time on an Oak City newspaper, met some nice people, married my wife, Pat, and went half crazy. Therapy was working on an oil rig and taking what jobs I could find in the oil patch. That was hard labor. Stunning sun, hundred-degree days or ten-below-zero nights. In the oil field, you're out in all of it.

When I started, it was all I could do to stuff my two-hundred-pound lard ass into Levi's. A year later I found myself at one eighty, hard, lines in my tanned face from squinting in the brightness, no gray in my brown hair, and ready to see some more of our earth.

I wrangled a job which combined my two experiences. I went to work with a petroleum publisher who turned out books and magazines. Pat and I were doing fine, having a family, and I was an eight-to-fiver with a yearning for something more. So we picked up and moved to Texas, where I'd been headed in the first place.

Our real-estate business took off, once I took off from the publishing trade, and before long Pat and I were able to vacation to faraway places with strange-sounding names.

But it didn't satisfy me. The tourist turn couldn't quench

my urge to be involved with people as a part of their daily life. Finally, it came to me. I'd always had a mechanical aptitude, I knew I could work outside in hard climatic conditions, and the real-estate business had given me a solid financial base. I was going to become an independent construction man on projects in the Middle East.

What I became was meat for a new breed of opportunist who had grown up as the dollars began to flow in from oil sales to the West. Called "five-percenters," they five-percent you to death. Always presenting themselves as a prince or a king's relative, these sand sharks hang out in the lobbies of the finest hotels, which pass, in Mideastern countries, as business areas. They are armed with contracts, deals, contacts, and a solid-lead, gold-gilt carrot to dangle before anyone dumb enough to look.

I was dumb enough. Not only to look, but to try and bite it, too. For a long time, their carefully phrased, beautifully timed requests for fees played hell with my overseas promotion budget. Until I wised up and got my first jobs by doing what I should have been doing for months. I represented myself to the government of Abu Dhabi, they liked what I said I had to offer, and they bought. My company made its first bucks, I had some great adventures, and my long itching wanderlust was finally being scratched.

After that, because of my combined sales ability and mechanical know-how, I started promoting more overseas projects from Houston. The Abu Dhabi job got me started with George, and in less than four years we'd been to or directed business in Angola, Dubai, Abu Dhabi again, and finally Iran, where I lived with my wife and family for almost a year.

The Iran deal would have made me. As it turned out, all it did was serve as my postgrad course in Middle Eastern ethics. After residing in Teheran, working through people who were cousins to a brother of a nephew of a niece of somebody who could say yes, the prospects looked great. The kids had settled in and Pat was able to get along reasonably well during the times I had to travel. Back home, my partnership with George was bearing fruit as he arranged to set up and conduct plant visits to show an entourage of Iranians how our system worked, and I had the key to closing an $8 million contract to build over a hundred houses in the southern part of the country.

Iran is a beautiful land, covered by semiarid plains, forests, mountains, and, in the south toward Kerman, desert. The people down there are pretty rough as well as very poor. Our housing was ideal. It could take tough treatment and was made from inexpensive materials.

The Iranian deal looked well enough set to have George come over so we could both sign the contracts. Then the other shoe fell.

I knew about baksheesh. Bribery, contrary to the isolationist views of our House and Senate, is a way of life among Iranians and Arabs. They've developed a gamesmanship about the practice. Baksheeshmanship. A deal, for instance, is an opportunity for an expert to see how many different pieces can be fractionated from the whole. Each separate component will have its own amount of baksheesh, thus doubling or quadrupling the take. Who pays is as important as how much, or how often. It's sometimes better to do a lot for a person with real power than for a much higher paying client with less stroke. Finesse at the baksheesh bargaining board is as respected a talent as the ability to play top-flight chess. Only it's more profitable.

Unlike the unrealistic merit-badge manufacturers in our Justice Department, no one over there sees anything wrong in the process. A waiter in a restaurant gets baksheesh in the form of a tip. In construction circles, it's called many things, but "advance commission" is the common term.

Call it what you will, regardless of intentions, businessmen in the Mideast will, if they play, pay. Sooner or later the need to participate in the tradition will arise. When it comes to baksheesh, nothing is impossible. Except stopping the practice. It's so ingrained into the cultural and social conditions of the people they'd miss it if it were gone. They don't know any other way to get things done.

Problems began two days before George and I were to sign the deal on the $8 million worth of housing. Everyone was in line; things looked good.

As anticipated, a request came from our Iranian partner for us to have $250,000 in U.S. bucks tucked neatly into a black briefcase. We were to carry the valuable package to the signing of the contract. When we left, it stayed.

The idea of baksheesh didn't bother me. Neither did the amount, as long as it could be charged through the up-front draw on the project from the loan.

George and I both knew better than to throw in our personal

money. Mideastern deals have a habit of never coming to pass, and once our Iranian contacts got to us for our cash, delay after delay would occur while they thought up ways to get to more of our bankroll. There's nothing shady about this, it's just the cute Middle Eastern way. If they get to someone in business they need to see how much further they can go. It's as big a part of their nature as baksheesh is a social custom.

We tried for a compromise by signing an acceptance contract with the government agent and setting up a personally guaranteed note at a bank, contingent upon the acceptance of the deal. But they wanted cold cash. When it became apparent we weren't going to provide the up-front bucks for the bribe, a curious thing happened.

Before sunset the same day, they had accepted an "improved" bid from an English company. George was furious. He hadn't had my experience of living in the Middle East. He got face to face with the people who had given us the job and waved the letter of intent along with our promissory notes. They were calm and asked for the letter, but he refused. We kept it as a souvenir. Sometimes, on the right occasion, I'll pull the notes out of the company files to show a nonbeliever what a quarter-million-dollar bribe looks like.

No one was very happy that day. But the Iranians were very happy seventy-two hours later when our competitors were successful in flying in the necessary $250,000 cash payment.

To add insult to our injury, the winning firm, showing an outstanding grasp of the Mideastern mind, contacted me through an obscured subsidiary to ask us to supply our original designs, stockpiled materials, and on-site supervisory labor to do the work. The part of me that likes a hustle appreciated their gall, but the other part made me tell them not only "no," but "hell, no."

The poor guys ended up getting theirs. By all reports, both sites got hit hard by the revolution. We later found out they dropped nearly $3 million on the deal. It cost us $100,000, though, for bid preparation, travel, and living expenses in Iran, which definitely hurt our company.

I had to do something, because the Iranian loss staggered us. I tried to resuscitate the deal, working through every friend I'd made, but I could see it was hopeless. Then, one morning, a few days after the final meeting, three Americans working for Rockwell International were machine-gunned down near our apartment by the

Fedayeen, a violent Marxist supported activist group. That was it for me. I shipped the family home, closed up the Teheran office, and went on a three-week flying trip to see if I could shake loose any of the other projects I'd been working on in Iraq, Kuwait, and Lebanon.

Since I planned on stopping in Dhahran, Shiraz, and Abadan, I needed a Saudi visa. After four trips to the Kingdom's embassy in Teheran, it didn't look like I was going to be able to get one. The Iranian Shah and Saudi King were off on another round of their game of mutual harassment. No telex or telephone communications between the two nations were working. So I started thinking of unorthodox approaches.

I BSed my way into an audience with the Saudi ambassador, a short, heavy-set, dark-bearded man with a stoic face, surrounded by four or five scowling aides. Trading on my knowledge of the Koran, I told him I'd had a dream. God said I was to go immediately to Saudi Arabia to develop a program to build a hotel and a great many houses. Scowls vanished, smiles appeared on everyone's faces, and there was a lot of "Allah be praised." The stamp was produced, then put away. I had no sponsor in the Kingdom. Since I was going on business, I had to have a sponsor to sign for me. A formality. When faced with the command of God, the ambassador would sign. Which he did, cautioning me to get a permanent signatory as soon as I was able.

Once I had the right papers, things appeared to be easy. There was a round of good-byes, leaving me with the little matter of shipping home some of our personal stuff and a plane reservation. There were lots of daily flights, all filled by pilgrims making the required journey to Mecca. No seats for weeks. After fretting around for a couple of hours, I went out to the airport and started with the head of the ground crew, went up through operations, and got to the airport manager. My story was long, complex, woeful, and more or less truthful. That was the artistic part. Exaggeration without slipping into an absolute lie. I knew if I could tell the right tale, a seat would appear. I ended up giving English grammar lessons to the manager three hours before flight check-in time, then being escorted down to the boarding area. When the flight crew saw me arrive with a four-man, armed bodyguard they took my ticket and, of course, there was a seat. They also treated me better than some of the other men booked on the flight. A group of Sunni tribesmen, along with some Iranian Arabs down from the hills, were strip-searched to their skin by security, because they were known for sudden flare-ups of violence and old-fashioned reliance on the knife as a tool of negotiation.

There are problems enough with the tribesmen as passengers without having to deal with fights. A recent crash of a Saudi airliner had killed everyone aboard. The cause? Experts surmised that a pilgrim decided to brew tea more to his taste than that prepared by the steward. He started a small fire in his smuggled gas stove. Naturally, he wouldn't leave his plane seat. After all, he'd paid for it and his belongings were there. Before anyone could act, the interior of the aircraft was set ablaze and the plane went down. Saudi air crews know this can happen anytime, so they live in a state of watchful anxiety.

Just as I settled back before takeoff, I remembered I'd packed my health record and shipped it back to the United States. That, I was sure, was going to get me into another mess. I was right.

Two factions were created when the Saudis found I had no proof of my innoculations and vaccinations. Immigration officials wanted to dispatch me back to Iran, since I wasn't a pilgrim or even a Moslem. An Egyptian doctor, who had seen this happen many times before, just ignored their bellowing protests, had me drop my pants, and gave me the whole series right there in the immigration dispensary. Including cholera, a disease which was running to epidemic proportion in the country. By fighting with the protesting officials, I might have been able to avoid a painful session with the Egyptian needle wielder, but later I asked Allah to forgive the misguided. One of the smaller towns I visited had more cholera than people to catch it, so I was glad for the protection.

I connected with a good company as a sponsor, through a well-meaning friend, but the firm was more interested in road building than dwelling space construction. I made a few other calls, but found nothing too exciting. Disappointed, disheartened, and downright disgusted, I took a plane for the States, done in by the baksheesh brigade.

Back once more in Houston, I needed to regroup financial forces. I'd sold my interest in various real-estate holdings. Even with this added capital, the loss in Iran was staggering. Worse, business in the United States was slow. Worse still, the larger construction firms had graduated overnight from hiring small contractors who would utilize materials like ours to manufacturing their own in company-owned plants. It was slim pickings unless you wanted to try for the little jobs, where the freight, not to mention the delay in payments, ate away at profits.

It looked like we were going out of the overseas building business, at least as far as the Middle East was concerned, when the telephone rang. The receptionist got it, switched it to my secretary, and finally it was passed to me. The chain is normal in American business, but it still gives me and some others who want to get things done a real pain.

"John? John McDonald?" The voice was gruff. The sound of too many years spent in too much sun.

"Ah, yeah. Jeff? Jeff Mason?" One thing I hate more than the telephone tag game is having to guess who is on the other end. If a call passes through two sets of hands, there is no reason not to know who it is before you answer unless your staff is stupid or the caller is obstinate. My staff wasn't stupid. Jeff Mason wasn't obstinate, exactly. He just insisted on doing things his way.

"Shit, yes, it's Jeff Mason. Who'd you think it was?" He had a voice that reached out and shook hands with you over the phone. A square shooter.

"How the hell do I know? Whatta you want?" I'd learned through the years the necessity of being direct with Jeff. Things happen faster.

"Lemme ask you a question. How'd you like a little five-million-dollar deal in Saudi Arabia?"

"I'd like it fine." I was excited, but skeptical of anyone who'd call $5 million a "little" anything.

"Knew you would. Now that I've got your attention, let me tell you why I called. If I had a fifty-million-dollar deal my company would be all over it like a bear on honey." What he said was right. He worked for one of the major construction companies. They would consider a $5-million construction project okay, but nothing to get all worked up over. I could tell from his voice, though, that he was onto something. Since I knew Jeff was a precise, methodical guy, I listened.

"Look, I got a friend over in Saudi—"

"Hell, Jeff, it's not like you to call me up just to brag. I got a friend somewhere, too."

There was a long pause. The cracked, sun-bleached voice

started in again. "Shit, John, cut out the jokes. This friend of mine has a friend. Man in high places with the right kind of buddies. Name of Suliman Nasir Rasi. He's heavy in the Saudi Navy."

"The Saudi what?" I knew the country was bordered by the Red Sea and the Persian Gulf and had the Gulf of Aden just a hop and a jump across Yemen and Oman, but I didn't know about any navy. "Have the Saudis got a navy?"

"Have the Saudis got a navy? Does a sailor on shore leave get the clap? Hell, yes, the Saudis got a navy. They spend millions on it every year. How do you think they defend their off-coast oil rigs from pirates?"

"How the hell would I know? Okay, you got a friend, who's got a friend named Suliman Rasi."

"Yeah. And this Suliman Rasi has got contacts with people who have megabucks."

"And?"

"And he is here in Houston, to help develop venture capital and technology for a building project, or a bunch of building projects, in Saudi Arabia."

I paused. The obvious question was why Jeff Mason was calling me on this deal. He worked for a firm so deep in Arabian Gulf business they got paid in riyals, so if there was building to be done, I was certain he knew where to go to find the designers as well as the working stiffs.

"Jeff, I think it's really nice you called me and I really do admire the fact you have a friend who has a friend, who is here in Houston. And I admire the fact your friend's friend, who is here, has a lot of money and wants to do a building deal. Now, why in the hell are you calling me? If the deal were any good, you'd be all over it like green on grass."

"No, hell. He doesn't want to do a whole airport or a nationwide road system. All he's lookin' for is a batch of houses. Or maybe a hotel. Nothin' big."

"Nothin' big. Just, say, a two-to-five-million-dollar job."

"Now you got it, John. Wanna meet him? I owe the guy in Saudi and I thought of you. Won't hurt to talk."

I smiled into the receiver. "You are right, big Jeff. It never costs anything to talk. When and where?"

After I replaced the receiver, I sat back and looked at the ceiling. You never know, I thought. When things look bleak, you never know. I picked up the phone and dialed George Pinder's number. When I'd gone through the obligatory two people, I got him. He didn't know the name, but he sure knew the game.

Suliman Rasi, George Pinder, and I all met for dinner on April 3, 1976. It was a nice first contact. Suliman was a short, dark man, with gleaming white teeth, bright black eyes, and a sparse, coarse mustache clipped in military fashion. He spoke English with an Oxford accent, had neat, small mannerisms, an acne-scarred face, and, as I saw for myself over the next few days, what seemed to me to be a strong taste for whiskey and baby dolls. Thanks to George, we were able to meet both his demands.

George, about two years earlier, had let a group of hell-raisers talk him into going into the nightclub business. The idea was okay, and the food the group produced was great thanks to George's gourmet tastes and supervision. Even so, business had been bad. So bad it looked like everyone was in for a total loss. Until George came through. If serving great food wasn't going to do it, maybe pouring great booze would. Or, rather, great-looking girls pouring and selling great booze might. Anyway, the two restaurants became big money-makers. The repressed Houston businessman, along with his counterpart from out of town who was suffering the pangs of loneliness, found a new home away from home. But Mama was never like the girls at Pinder's places. If Mama had been, the businessman would never have been lonely or repressed.

Suliman took to the club like a starving cowboy to burned roast beef. If he was hungry for whiskey, he was famished for the serving staff. Talking to him was difficult because he would look at me, then his sharp, black eyes would dart off following one of the scantily clad waitresses. I don't think the guy had ever been in a girly joint before in his life. It was apparent that if he had his way, his first visit wouldn't be his last.

All in all, it was quite an evening. Suliman got a little high in the first half hour, then got down to the business of seeing how much he could hold. He managed quite a bit of both the Chivas Regal scotch and the ladies.

We got along swell. George was with us early on, but business called him away.

Between drinks Suliman told me how big a wheel he was back home. His position with the Navy gave him access to a number of perks. And his family background served to introduce him to some of the wealthiest people in the Kingdom.

That was the first time I'd ever heard the word. Kingdom

The way Suliman said it should have tipped me off. Saudi Arabia is a kingdom, run by a king with more powers than any Western feudal lord during the height of belief in divine right. There was no way to know, sitting there in the dim, flattering light of the bar, sipping scotch and tickling tight fannies, what my full understanding of the implications of the word would finally make me do.

Suliman caused me to start a bad habit that night. He was a great one for looking off into space and doing the "In sha allah" or "If God wills it to be, it shall be." For some reason, after my fifth scotch, I started saying, "Judas Priest," in the same kind of fatalistic tone. It sounded religious to Suliman and was drunkenly funny as hell to me; a good inside joke. But when we started talking business, which we did between bouts of being served new drinks and a little grab-ass, I started saying it with real feeling.

First, Suliman told me how, through his backers, he had high contacts with the Saudi government. He was here, he said, in the United States, in direct response to a minister's desire to build a hotel. There would be over a million profit in the deal. For each partner. "Judas," from me, but a little skeptically. I'd heard the tune before.

Second, we got into the housing situation over there, and how it might just be possible to become developer, builder, and seller of a large project. Several other millions of dollars' profit. "Judas Priest!" a little less skeptically.

Third, and for the topper, if either of the first two projects was successfully completed, we'd be the darlings of the government. Therefore first on the list of preferred bidders for any number of other jobs. In short, we could move a partnership between Heritage Building Systems International, and Suliman et al., into the top ranks quick. "Judas Priest!" earnestly. He had my attention. It was big money.

At the beginning, I was a little nervous about Suliman Rasi. He talked too freely, made too many propositions too early, came on too strong. Then again, I knew Jeff Mason, who'd introduced us. Jeff, in turn, knew tons of people on the other side. I didn't believe he'd give me a four-flusher or a freak. As we got closer to closing time, Suliman made more and more sense. Or I was getting drunker and drunker. We finally agreed, at one in the morning, to meet the next day for a round of serious, sober discussion. When I left, he had three of the girls crowded around him and was pushing folded fifty-dollar bills into their very private parts under the edges of their less than ample costumes. I figured someone was sure to see he got home safely.

We set a seven-thirty appointment. He got there at ten o'clock, the classic example of an efficient businessman. I already knew about the Arabic problem with being on time, so the delay didn't faze me. He arrived in my offices, selected a chair in the conference room, eyed the secretary who brought him a cup of black, sweet coffee, and proceeded to document his claims of the night before. Proposals, letters from folks in high places, maps, projections of population growth, articles from magazines with his name in them (or what he said was his name; I didn't read Arabic), rough plans. He had enough paper to cover a table designed to seat twelve comfortably.

Over the following five days, we talked about possible deals, several ways to establish a business relationship, and our next steps. I showed Suliman our latest ideas for the precast forms, took him to the plant where they were made, laid out how the system used a few basic designs that could be modified to build almost any enclosed space, and how different exterior and interior finishes might be applied to meet widely varying end uses.

He was quite open, freely admitting he was an agent only, not one of the principal investors. He wasn't in their financial league. He also was candid about his demands for commissions. We seemed to understand each other.

Finally, we both were satisfied. Him, because he felt he'd found a reliable company large enough to deliver a variety of products but not so large as to go it alone after a job or three, thus ensuring a long-term relationship as well as future profits for him. Me, because if half the things he'd told me panned out when I got over there, he had more contacts than a computer and strength to get us our first project. I knew we could deliver if we got an opportunity. Suliman Rasi was knocking. Once was all I needed.

George Pinder and I checked Suliman through several people but the few reports we got were skimpy. We would meet after each encounter to make notes, review what had been said, and plan our next step. George and I needed to go to Saudi, get Suliman to set up meetings with the different ministries, and see the situation for ourselves.

After a final night on the town, Suliman left for home, while we finagled our affairs so things would run during our absence. I wasn't sure if I'd be gone a week or a month but I swore one thing: I was going to work every opportunity every way I could, and not even think about coming back until I was able to either win a contract or write off the whole mess. I knew I was in for a frustrating time. Doing business with an Arab is not easy. It's hard enough to keep a deal on track after it's been concluded. Making one from a speculative position would be much worse. But I was ready. The potential opportunity was so great I would find a way if at all possible. I was committed to devoting as much of my time as might be needed to this one undertaking. If single-mindedness counts for anything, I had more than enough to score.

3 Of Contracts and Contacts

Later in 1976

The air base at Dhahran had a used appearance to it. Since its start by the U.S. military back in 1943, a lot had been added. Long sidewalks, overhung with Arabic-looking archways containing colored-glass panes, hadn't been in place long enough for the sun to burn the white finish into a sand gray. In a few months more, unless there was constant maintenance, which never seemed to happen in Saudi, the place would look ten times its age.

George Pinder and I stepped off the Air France flight from Paris in single file down the aluminum passenger stairs rolled against the nose door of our 707. Once on the ground, we walked over the concrete of the parking taxiway, a seven-minute hike to the customs entrance of the terminal building between two rows of armed guards. It would take a little while, but plans were already on the drawing boards of several international architectural firms to modernize the facility. Every other major airport in the world offered all-weather boarding protection, but not Dhahran. Then again, Dhahran offered less weather than all the rest of the world's airports. Even though the city is on the Persian Gulf, rainfall is minimal. The choices were hot, hotter, hotter with damp wind, and hotter with wind and blowing sand. Rain wasn't one of the city's problems, but a heavy, salty humidity was.

George and I walked quickly across the blazing concrete apron into the relatively cool interior of the customs, immigration, and health areas. Our luggage was still in the process of being unloaded, so it was a good time to make the immigration table. The flight had only been about half full. Since we were the first people out, we were first in line.

Lines in Arabic countries are not like they are in the West. In England, say, if you queue up for something, you can be certain of getting your turn. The other people will support your right to proper rotation, as they expect you to support theirs.

In Saudi Arabia, it's a little different. First, because there is no discernible queue. If there is room for ten people to stand in front of a table at one time, twenty will try to fit in the same space. And twenty more will form a rank directly behind, pressing as closely as possible to those in front, shoving their arms through to gain attention by waving their papers.

Our being first was no advantage when the rest of the crowd caught up. We were shoved snug against the customs stand, and I swear one guy, right behind me, a dark, greasy-looking, plump little man with watery pink eyes and a mustache, took the opportunity to feel me up. The second time he patted my butt I knew it was no accident, but there was nothing I could do because of the crowd except hope he didn't become too much friendlier.

The airport, like many public buildings in the Kingdom, is a shock to Westerners who see it for the first time. The floor is coated with an accumulation of years of dirt. It looks as if it had never been mopped with soap and water, which is probably true. The same crowding, the same lines, the same battered desks, nothing has changed in twenty years and probably will be unvarying for another twenty under Arab management. There is no word in the language for "inefficiency."

Immigration agents in the Middle East are accustomed to the mob scene played at their stations with each planeload of newcomers. Those in Saudi Arabia are more accustomed to it than most, because of the huge throngs of foreigners who visit the country day after day, month after month, year around. Saudi Arabia is the nation which contains Mecca and Medina, the birth and burial places of the Prophet Mohammed. It is one of the five pillars, or tenets, of the Moslem religion that every true believer must make a pilgrimage from his home to Mecca as a demonstration of his faith. In Moslem countries, there are special symbols to show that one has made the required journey. A shaved head, an extended tail hanging down from a turban, or a green stripe on a robe is usually a sign of having completed this pious trip. The Saudi government spends millions each year to subsidize the cost of the pilgrimage to allow a maximum number of faithful the opportunity of visiting the Kabbah, or Holy Shrine, in Mecca. The same program also opens the Kingdom to visits by agents provocateurs, gun peddlers, rebels, assorted political extremists, and other dangerous characters posing as pilgrims—a fact the royal family recognizes but is powerless, aside from basic police control, to stop.

With all the practice they get, the Saudi immigration officers are supercool about the hordes that fall on them frequently each day. They work with methodical slowness, taking not the first available papers but those proffered with the most emotional show of need. George and I could do nothing but stand there, squeezed from behind like we were. We became first in, last out. Most of the passengers had been Arabic. Since we were Westerners, clearance took a little longer.

The process was confusing to watch. One of the officials would take a person's outthrust papers, start checking them, be interrupted by someone else jamming another passport under his bristling mustache, put down the first papers, take the new passport, start to do something, then be interrupted again by another insistent individual who would hold a document up inches from the inspector's eyes, yelling loudly and shaking the paper back and forth so violently that, I'm sure, it was impossible to read. There was no order. I felt as if I were playing a role in a mad company dedicated to an eccentrically wardrobed production of *Alice in Wonderland*.

After a while, the agents disposed of everyone except the two of us, an Englishman, and a fat woman with a hairy mole on the side of her face. She spoke with a strong German accent, but there was no telling where she was from. The Englishman seemed to be her temporary escort, which she needed. In Saudi Arabia, women are not allowed to appear alone in public buildings, so in Paris, the Saudi airline attendants would not have let her on the plane without an accompanying man.

As she was getting her passport stamped, a rotund Germanic-looking fellow came up, shook hands formally with the Britisher, thanking him for seeing to his wife, then exchanged greetings with the woman carefully, so as not to indulge in a public show of affection, an act which could have landed them both in jail.

Our turn was next.

"Maderaki?" It was a question, not a statement.

"Yes. Maderaki."

"Answer him, George. He wants to know if you're American."

Nod. "Right. Yes."

He stamped our passports, then noted the time and marked it to make it official. Sullenly, he handed the books back. I got George's, he got mine. There was a round of exchanges, all with smiles.

I gave a sigh of relief. Usually, when there is a mix-up of any kind, the people involved end up in the captain's office, where an automatic fine is instantly levied.

Our U.S. passports helped, however, as we were treated with more respect than any of the non-Moslem Europeans on the flight.

Entry ino the Kingdom, for business-seeking Westerners, is always a difficult matter. First, you have to find a sponsor—someone who will vouch for you, affirm that you have business which necessitates your entry into Saudi Arabia, and stand good for your proper behavior while you are there. Suliman arranged for ours through the auspices of a large trading company. The entry visa is vital, because without it, you not only can't get in, you can't get out. It creates a bond between the visitor and his sponsor unlike that found in other countries.

The guard was still sullen. From his appearance, I judged him to be a Yemeni who had come to the Kingdom to make a buck and wasn't too enamored with his work.

Customs inspection was next on the agenda. The crowd moved to a converted hallway which served as a baggage-reclaim area and was now clogging the customs inspection station. Baskets, Morocco-leather saddlebag pouches, wood-crated hunting falcons, Gucci and Hermes grips and attaché cases—you name it, someone in the throng had it by the handle or it was lying on the floor. The place looked like a zany lost-and-found storage room before spring cleaning.

Naturally, my stuff was at the very bottom of a carelessly thrown-together pile of suitcases. People would wade in, tossing and kicking bags out of the way, seeking theirs. Some of the passengers, ruddy-faced from having finished off several "good-bye-to-booze" cocktails before landing, were waiting like I was for the mob to settle. Finally, I managed to snatch my junk and lug it over to the wobbly wooden customs table. Rather than risk another goosing from the greasy Romeo, who was eyeing me with desire, I stood to one side while the traffic thinned. George joined me.

The throng was building again as another plane unloaded, so the noise level was quite high. People were everywhere, babbling in Arabic, German, Pakistani, English, Japanese, and several dialects that didn't even sound like languages. The area was huge, a single fluorescent-lighted, tan-gray-walled hallway, maybe a hundred feet long by fifty wide. Uniformed officials moved here and there, in no apparent hurry. The heat from outside plus that generated by so many bodies was uncomfortable, so everyone was sweating. Most were smelling. Rose water is a poor substitute for Arrid Extra Dry or regular bathing. I leaned over close so George could hear me.

"Did you go through your baggage? The Saudis are sticklers for their laws."

"I did. Down to throwing away that *Time* magazine I bought in Paris. What have they got against *Time*, anyway?"

"Who knows? As long as we're not carrying one. *Playboy*, either, for that matter. They are hell strict about magazines on their no-no list."

A smiling Japanese opened a heavy black case with reinforced corners. Inside was row upon row of carefully wrapped, clearly labeled electrical connectors. The customs inspector had a field day. He opened them all, one at a time, and passed each back to the still-smiling Japanese man, who tried to repack. By the time they were through, the orderly case was in chaos. The Japanese was in tears.

Our turn came. A thickset, long-mustachioed Arab in a rough work robe waved us forward impatiently. He had a bored way about him, but when he saw we were Americans, he perked up.

"What goods are you bringing into the Kingdom?"

George and I shook our heads. "None." "Nothing. Only personal items." I spoke in Arabic and he brightened perceptibly.

Nodding, he fixed us with his sharp, black eyes.

"We shall see."

With that, he seized my case, snapped open the top, and proceeded to rummage around. When he found nothing, he looked disappointed as he made a large chalk checkmark on the outside. He started in on George's two cases. The first held his clothing, the other had a 16-millimeter film of our building system, some sales brochures, and a few business items, including three calculators. One was a complex engineer's model, the other two the simplest Texas Instruments design. The guard instantly bristled, motioning to his superior, who hurried over. They went into a long harangue in Arabic, with much arm waving and voice raising. The chief officer held up his hand, stopping the flow from his subordinate. He turned to face us.

"You are here on business?" He asked this in Arabic, and I had heard the question often enough in the past to understand the meaning.

I shook my head yes, and George, taking the cue from me, nodded.

A voice from my side, speaking English, caused me to turn my head.

"Do you require assistance?"

The man standing there, smiling broadly, was Suliman Rasi.

He turned to the guards, speaking rapidly. They answered, and he slipped each of them a folded bill. Within minutes we were on our way out, to where he'd parked a new white Mercedes sedan.

The whole time I was in Saudi, Suliman drove that Mercedes. Not too well, but with great zest. Once he even drove it underneath a sixty-ton Mercedes truck. Not too good for the car, not to mention the passengers, which included me. No one was hurt, though. It was an official Navy vehicle, but he seemed to have appropriated it for his exclusive use. It was always full of fuel, always freshly washed, and, judging from its performance, carefully maintained.

On the drive to the hotel, Suliman went over our appointment list for the next few days. It sounded great, though I was an old enough hand in the Mideast to know how much value to place in a timetable.

Once you find yourself somewhere east of Suez you have to forget a lot of old ideas. Haste and tight schedules are two primary items to jettison. Nothing in the whole Arabic world, and particularly in Saudi Arabia, works on anything like an orderly schedule. Nothing is ready in time, no one meets when he says he will, no one returns things as agreed, and especially, when it comes to money matters, no one is in any hurry. "Haste makes waste" might be a Christian proverb, but it's a Moslem way of life.

Howard Hughes, the eccentric, reclusive millionaire who also came from Houston, had a basic business rule. He believed in never making a decision or commitment until the last moment, because in the meantime something might have changed and the alteration might affect the deal one way or another. It's probably a good rule, but if Hughes had been placed in a bargaining position with an Arab he would have seemed direct and prompt in making up his mind. By comparison, he would have been. The tendency toward procrastination stems from equal parts of caution, a lackadaisical attitude, a cultural lethargy, a desire to prolong the bargaining, and a sense of the social amenities involved when proper men deal with each other. Throw in a touch of pure avarice, and you have it.

With this understood, you can see why, the next morning when Suliman said he'd meet us at ten o'clock, George and I were able to have lunch before finding him in the lobby about 4 P.M. Seeing him, I smiled, because my faith in the Arabic system had been upheld.

During the next nineteen months, my faith in Arabic methods was upheld so often that the ways of the Western world started to seem strange. But by then I wasn't smiling much anymore.

Suliman Rasi was, as he had represented himself, well connected. Not to the top of the Saudi sandpile, but to people who had contacts at the top. He was trusted. George and I placed reliance on what he said, and, apparently, so did his Saudi connections. Suliman exuded a strong aura of self-assurance, even in the face of total failure.

The month of May went by in a strange, exotic haze of pure procrastination. The only way to break out of the do-nothing syndrome was to express strong exasperation, which would bring on meetings, meetings, and meetings. Which accomplished, as far as we could tell, still more nothing.

I got calluses on my butt from sitting in my stockinged feet for long periods on a cushion on the floor of one or another influential person's home, and blisters on my tongue from sipping the boiled mess they pass off as coffee. In Saudi Arabia, the green beans are brewed at boiling temperatures with other herbal additives. The result is a strong, stimulating drink, ahway, which is as unlike our American coffee as Mercurochrome. I felt I continually ran the risk of offending my host by refusing coffee and insisting on tea. It wasn't much better, because style dictated adding so much sugar and mint to a serving that it tasted like a fruity syrup.

As I came to know the Saudis better, I learned more about their very fine sense of Islamic-ordained hospitality and realized they were being truly gracious in their refreshment service and were far more offended if you drank something not to your liking instead of making your preferences known.

I also learned the proper way to say, "No, thanks, no more coffee." In an early meeting with a government official, I'd forced down one small dose of the scalding brew. Before my cup hit the saucer, the alert host had the pot up and poured a refill. I swallowed that by concentrating on the oily taste derived from the green coffee beans he used and thinking of how I could stop him from pouring me a third serving. Using a Western gesture, I put the cup down and quickly covered the top with my hand. The next thing I knew, boiling-hot coffee was running over my fingers and the host was looking at me with a startled expression.

Our translator explained my American gesture. We all had a good laugh. They showed me how to wave my cup from side to side, gently, making it impossible to refill. This would stop the service, yet still leave the server with full honors for having tried.

Actually, we made more progress in the first few days than we did in the balance of the month. After we covered the initial points of who needed to do what, by when, all work stopped.

One of the earliest meetings was with a real prince of the Kingdom. Now, being a Saudi prince isn't like being the Prince of Wales, but it's a hell of a long way up the ladder of success. There are only about five hundred of them. None are poor or broke.

Our prince, when we were able to see him, was charming. He had strong family business connections. His trading company served as an international importer for several popular lines of merchandise in Saudi, including a respectable amount of heavy equipment, industrial machinery, and business systems. His family's little firm, which was run in his behalf by a devoted group who made side money on most transactions and watchdogged the prince because of his tendency to go overboard in a trade, turned a most welcome addition to the prince's modest salary connected with the Saudi Air Force.

The Saudi Arabian Air Force sounds something like a joke of

questionable taste, but it's not. What it lacks in size is more than made up for by U.S.-trained pilots and, at that time, 152 combat aircraft including F-5s, Lightnings, and Strikemasters, 120 more F-5s on order, and the promise of F-15s in the 1980s. This, plus an arsenal of missiles and two thousand "contract personnel" to train, staff, and maintain the equipment added up to a strong potential.

The prince wasn't too actively at his work most of the time, but his position, backed by the pair of silver pilot's wings, got him his own private jet. Although his aircraft might not be state-of-the-art today in single-engine combat planes, there are only a few in the world any better. Or faster. As an individual's personal mode of transportation it's unique, and it clearly has more status than any racing car. The prince had a couple of those, too, for short hops where his jet would make problems, like going from his castle on the outskirts of town to the soukh, or market, downtown, but he used his trusty jet every chance he got. Which, because he didn't seem to have much to do, was often.

Saudi pilots are, if anything, enthusiastic. Most airline captains hate to land at Dhahran, a military airbase doubling as a commercial field, because they never know when they'll find an F-5 doing aileron rolls at three hundred feet along the main runway. The Saudi idea of neat flying starts and ends with Pappy Boyington, the W.W. II naval ace. He was hot and had the skill to do it. Saudi pilots are hot, but the number of nosed-in F-5 hulks tail up like tombstones at the end of the main runway indicates that some improvement in their skill or judgment is still needed.

Our dealings with the prince were cordial. He showed a quick mind with an easy grasp of mechanical functions, so could visualize the value of our system and see many uses. He readily accepted us as a client of his trading company, agreed to sponsor us with several branches of his government, and, pending a favorable report by each other's bank, entered into an agreement to represent us in Saudi Arabia.

That was in May.

In June, armed with the prince's blessings, and driven by Suliman in his white Mercedes, George and I made the rounds of various government offices. Our designs were right, so we struck pay dirt almost immediately.

My first meeting with a Saudi official was memorable. His office had been designed by someone with little knowledge of Arabic ways. The man sat behind a massive desk, sandaled feet resting in one of the lower drawers, eating watermelon and spitting the seeds onto the expensively carpeted floor. He would talk, without looking directly at me, to Suliman, who would translate. I later learned the man had only been in his appointed office for a few months, having come straight from his tribe in the Rub 'al-Khali desert. A few weeks later, he left behind a furious superior and returned to his people, in order to make the annual caravan migration to the northern oasis. He, regrettably, knew nothing about buildings, but was still the appointed representative.

Our first positive response centered on our ability to build a housing development way out in the middle of nowhere, using untrained third-country nationals as labor. Our system was ideally suited for this, and provided we could arrange to have the necessary heavy equipment and trained operators, it would be easy.

A second, larger show of interest concerned a fully equipped, turn-key hospital. Bids were being solicited by the U.S. Army Corps of Engineers' office in Riyadh. Which was a break, because our building system was acceptable to their officials in Alabama and Virginia from previous jobs. Not only could we do the hospital, we felt we could do it for less than the anticipated bid prices they showed us. We also discussed a housing deal.

Either job would be terrific, and it meant we were on the right lists for consideration to bid on more projects which might arise.

In the process of making contacts, I renewed an old acquaintance with Sheikh Mohammed Abdullah, a man George and I had met early in our rounds. He was quite a fellow. His family had the manufacturing and distribution rights for a number of proprietary products.

With money to burn, Mohammed, along with a dozen equally wealthy companions, civic leaders all, had purchased a swank two-story white villa on the far edge of town. Members of the group met there nightly to drink a little illegal whiskey, then about ten o'clock have dinner, followed by some additional tippling and a little sex, AC or DC.

George and I were invited over one night. For some reason, George volunteered to be the bartender and ended up in a drinking contest. Now, one thing George can do is knock it back. He led the group into downing a full bottle of scotch, priced at seventy-five American dollars on the black market. I stayed out of the fracas to remain sober. Someone had to protect George in case one of the hosts decided to become amorous.

George had a number he did in Saudi which always seemed to gain attention and respect. He would start to describe the two topless clubs he owned, then drift off into tight, descriptive paragraphs about the girls who worked there. Often, he would single out a real or imaginary beauty and pair her with one of the men, delineating her charms with graphic detail. This night, the act proved so popular he expanded it to lay out a potential partner for everyone present, including a seventy-five-year-old man. At the offer of a prospective date, the old fellow got revved up, pushing George for further details. The description of her "very tiny, firm, white breasts" almost drove the old guy out of his head. When we left, he was rapidly masturbating under the cover of his robe.

Within four months, three of the men present that night, promised dates with one or another lovely, telexed their arrival time in Houston. They showed up, too. Before we could get them checked into the Hyatt Regency, they were ready for action. One of them was so eager he severely bit his date's nipple. He had to do without, because she spent the evening in the emergency room at Hermann Hospital getting it repaired.

The sheikhs must have been on a world tour, because after dropping twelve thousand in a four-day stay they left Houston with three of the girls who worked at the clubs in tow. Before the ladies came back, they had been to Las Vegas, Seattle, and for some reason, the Philippine Islands.

George and I left, in late June, with high spirits. We flew to Lebanon, Iraq, Cairo, and finally Kuwait, investigating potential projects. Then to Paris, before going home. By checking with our friendly bankers we learned we'd been the subject of some careful investigation by the Saudis. As far as we could tell, the deals were progressing nicely.

Except for one little matter. We still didn't have a contract. Nothing in writing for anything.

I hate to think of my telephone and telex bill over the next three weeks. Suliman was in daily contact with questions, we were responding with lengthy, detailed answers, he was telling us how well things were going, and we, in turn, were urging him onward, applauding his fine follow-up skills. All on our nickel, naturally, but what's a couple of thousand for phone and telex bills when there are millions in the balance? If you're going to do big-boy projects, you have to play big-boy games, and six-page overseas telegrams seemed big-boy at the time.

The cost of the communication service was nothing compared to the money George and I expended for working drawings, plans, and a new, custom, 16-millimeter motion picture complete with color, sound, and professional narration, showing the Heritage Building System and how it could be used in Saudi.

Megabucks later, George was off again to the Kingdom for a special conference with the good prince, arranged by none other than our incessant correspondent, Suliman Rasi. George was supposed to meet the great prince at his palace, a modest little thirty-room rendezvous furnished without a chair of any kind or a table over twelve inches high.

The palace was a new building, behind a wall which surrounded four acres of land strewn with rusting heavy construction equipment in various states of disrepair. The architecture was so drastically modern the building looked freakish. Princey had dropped over $8 million on its purchase, so no one dared comment negatively, but the whole incident had convinced the family there had to be a tight watch maintained on the man because of his revealed potential to be skinned.

It's not a long drive from the Dhahran airport to the palace, but it was far enough for George to make it clear to Suliman Rasi that we were getting tired of all talk and no contracts. Suliman, between excited stoplight drag races, made his position clear to George. He was getting the short end, too. He wanted some bucks, soon, as an "advance commission." More aggressive than most, he knew there was money in the deal somewhere.

Reassured, George arrived at the prince's palace, but there was no prince. He waited, in a room painted vibrant green, then inquired again. No one had seen the prince all day. No doubt he was off in his jet. No, very politely, no one could tell when he'd return, but, yes, by all means, he knew of the impending arrival of the respected American, so would the American please refresh himself and wait?

Six hours later, still no prince, and it began to dawn on George he had been taken for a short trip through the lily pads, down the primrose lane of lying for the sake of politeness.

After some digging around, he realized the story was like

this: He'd been a guest of the prince before, so he must be important. He is an American. A respected, or at least tolerated, Western tribe. He had arrived, expecting to see the prince, who is God knows where, gone for only Allah knows how long, on an unknown pretext or mission. The prince is alway going off. And he is usually late.

But as a prince, he comes and goes as he pleases. The respected American believes he has an appointment. Not an Arabic appointment, which is sometime between noon today and sundown Thursday, maybe, but an American appointment, which means 10:10 A.M., Wednesday, the twenty-second day of July 1976, and you-feel-bad-if-you-are-late kind of thing.

Now any good Moslem could tell you such an appointment might be proper between man and Allah, provided Allah is willing to wait maybe just a little, because no man is so perfect as all that, but such an appointment between two men is out of the question. Something is bound to happen to one or the other.

Put it all together, the recognition of the importance of the visitor, the missing prince, and the obvious confusion of the appointment, and what else was there to do but lie? If the truth were told, the visitor would be shocked and disappointed. The prince did not remember, so he, the visitor, is not deemed by the prince as being a person of much importance. Feelings would be hurt, and there is nothing to be gained by hurt feelings.

No, better a thousand ways, to say, merely, "You are welcome, you are expected, we anticipate the most immediate return of the prince, have some refreshment."

George, to his everlasting credit, didn't get mad. He just had all he wanted of what was becoming a stupid situation. Putting the best face on things, he smiled, shook hands, and slowly made his way out of the palace. He'd decided to overnight at a hotel east of the small downtown area, then catch the next available flight home.

Suliman Rasi was horrified. He followed George out of the prince's place, waving his arms, crying, and screaming. "What was a brief wait of a day or two after months of work and a flight halfway around the world?"

"A day or two too much," George said, slamming the door of the white Mercedes. "Take me to the hotel."

George exploded when Suliman let it slip that the prince was "possibly still in London." He felt the meeting might have been arranged there, saving him thousands of miles in travel.

The first I knew about the missed appointment was when the phone rang in my hotel in Teheran, where I was cleaning up the last bits and pieces of our lost housing deal. Chris, our manager in Houston, had talked with George, and from the tone of his voice could tell he was plenty frustrated. George's experience had been more with the South and Central Americans, as opposed to the Arabs, so while he was prepared for delays allied with mendacity, he was just beginning to learn how well the Saudis had mastered their art of deceitful procrastination.

I counseled patience, urging Chris to get a message through to Saudi. I couldn't, due to problems in the phone service, caused by yet another Saudi-Iranian face-off. I told him to impress Suliman Rasi with the need for action by making it damned clear there would be no further "advances" until we got something in writing. I also told Chris to let George know that walking out during a negotiation in the Mideast is considered an extreme insult.

Pinder eventually cooled down. By the next morning, he agreed it would be better, since he was there to spend a few more days trying to tie up any deals he could. There was more than $5 million in contracts waiting, if we could only get somebody to move.

Suliman Rasi didn't show up for his appointment the next day at all. On the following afternoon, about 4 P.M., he arrived with smiles.

Yes, he agreed there had been too much time and no contracts. No, he didn't know where the prince was, he might be on his way from Cairo but he couldn't find out from his friends and, finally, didn't care anyway. If the prince wouldn't play, Suliman Rasi, our loyal agent and representative, owed it to us to find someone who would. Someone who had a project for which there was an immediate need for action. Someone such as Sheikh Abdallah Fazza, brother-in-law to no one else but His Imperial Majesty, the great King Khaled.

Suliman was careful not to mention that the sheikh had a rather rough reputation, no longer discussed after his sister managed to get herself into the royal family bed as a wife.

George was curious, but cautious. "Suliman, how soon can we get a deal together? A real deal. I've got to be back in Houston by late this week."

"Tonight. Tomorrow at the latest. He has already heard of you through the government, knows of your aborted relationship with the prince's trading company, and is ready, if you convince him your firm can do the project, to enter into a preliminary agreement."

"When can we see him?"

"Now. Of a certainty. Right now."

Within a half hour they were out of the hotel and headed north toward Jubail, fifty miles away. It was quite a ride. As George said later, "Thank God it was still daylight."

The house was near a small, six-thousand-year-old town. Located at the boundary of the sand-and-rock wasteland, the place boasted a small blue-water harbor which, through the centuries, had been used by pearl divers, smugglers, and honest seamen. The village, called Jubail, had been selected by the Saudi government as the future site of a major industrial development. Although, at that time, little had been done aside from pouring in over $5 million. The money vanished like water on the parched sand, leaving about as much trace. But $5 billion was going to be spent in five years for a gas-production plant, new harbor, housing for twenty-five thousand families, a steel mill, and more.

The dwelling was a low, rambling, dirty-white building with a pink exterior wall protecting a large open-air compound from casual passersby in the narrow unpaved street. Sand, combined with piles of garbage, littered the area. Rats and goats fed side by side in the refuse. Even though twilight had just started, with the sun at the margin of the dun-colored sky, the flare from the Aramco gas burn was prominent enough to cast a light red-orange shadow as the two men walked to the front door.

The majlis was full of people. Several relations were sitting about talking in low voices. They all went silent when George appeared. Most had never seen a Westerner up close. In one corner, a short dark fat man, about forty-five, with a black bristly mustache and beard, sat on a too-small cushion. He was smoking a water pipe. The smell of the burning fruit permeated the room. It wasn't until George Pinder was introduced that he noticed the man's eyes, hidden behind dark glasses.

They were withdrawn, lightly cloudy. At first George thought he was smoking something other than the regulation dried goody in the pipe, but realized he, like many Saudis, was nearly or completely blind. Infection, parasites, and an abrasive climate all helped produce many sight-damaging illnesses, especially in children. Trachoma, a contagious disease combated by soap-and-water cleansing, is endemic. Estimates indicate about 90 per cent of the Saudi population have had the ailment. Many have lost the sight in one or both eyes.

The pipe was passed and George was introduced to a bewildering assortment of Abdallahs, Abdullahs, Fouads, Mohammeds, and Hassans. In Saudi, a nation derived from close tribes, these five names serve over half the male population.

For an Arab, Fazza was astoundingly direct. After only three rounds of coffee and an hour of small talk, they started in on tea, which signified the commencement of serious business discussions.

Suliman had done his job well. The sheikh knew of Heritage Building Systems, our product, and many of the conversations George and I had with the government. He was aware of the hospital projects, the housing development, and the indications made to us for welcoming our future bids.

Fazza, as I was to learn, was a fascinating host. Always careful in what he said, circumspect when discussing himself and his wealth, he seemed eager to conclude a business arrangement.

He claimed to have several million American dollars, or the equivalent, made through trading, buying, selling, and negotiating. Our later bank evaluations of his position, while sketchy, in no way disagreed with what he told George on their first meeting. Fazza wanted to qualify George quickly to see if there was potential for profit in a contract with him.

By eight that night, after an elaborate ceremonial dinner on the floor, they came to the bare bones of an agreement. Heritage would fabricate the necessary forms or molds, and the Saudi partners would buy them. Heritage would deliver the forms to the dock, then provide technical advice on their installation at a site developed by the Saudi partners according to detailed plans we would provide. The facility would be an open-air yard equipped with a rock crusher and several small portable concrete batch-mixing machines.

The forms, consisting of movable outside walls which, by using four ratchets, could be drawn in toward the center core for filling, then back out again to remove the completed building module, were simple to operate. They were also portable. Five days after casting all the structural units needed for one job, the same setup could be trucked to another site, miles away. From the original molds we would supervise production of precast pieces, to be used for our joint venture construction contracts. The end result was a building of practically any size, from a ten-by-ten cube to a twelve-story office tower.

The initial manufacturing site was the first step. But an assembly line, even an open-air one, was of little use unless there was a market for the products. Joint venture number two. Fazza could get a contract for a housing development, provided we did the hard part and supplied him design, pricing, and management. He had influence in the right places and the timing was good as well. More homes were a part of the reform program set off by the $35-billion surplus profit from oil-embargo price hikes resulting from the boycott. The King, Khaled, was taking no chances. Arrayed against him was half the family, who had supported the old King, Faysal, until his crazy nephew drove even his most ardent supporters to regicide.

Khaled has the National Guard, like a federal police, called the "White Army." The men are levied from trusted tribes, well armed with modern U.S. equipment, and number about thirty thousand. The rest of the family has the Army, along with what passes for a navy, and well-equipped air force. It's all under Khaled's command, unless he takes a notion to command it against his relations. Then it's choose up sides, see who has the firepower, and be on their team. Being caught out on the "other" side after one of the periodic flare-ups is not considered too swift. People have been known to lose their heads over this matter of allegiance. Literally.

Khaled decreed there would be housing for the masses. The masses of Saudis, of course, not the masses of Arab workers who'd flocked in from ten other Moslem nations and who were doing the scut work of the Kingdom.

He also declared an approved plan of education. Aramco, as a part of its deal to hang on to even a portion of its concession a little longer, agreed to build, staff, and equip enough schools so every child in the entire Kingdom would have access to one. It was a nice thing to do. The schools were there, the teachers were there, the books, blackboards, Korans, pencils, and paper were there, but until Khaled, very few students were there. His order changed all this. He passed a law giving each father who kept his male children in a school a certain sum of money. The amount was more than a boy could make herding goats, or working in a store or factory, so the father had incentive to send his sons to school. They are still working on the problem of the girls. Progress is slow. Besides, no one can have everything. Khaled's plan worked, though. The previous literacy rate of 15 per cent is sharply improving among town and city residents. The desert-dwelling Bedouin tribes are another matter, requiring patience. Their nomadic urge is, for now, uncontrollable. New forms of schooling are being tested for these people.

The houses for the masses idea was made for Fazza. A sister in the King's harem gave him a certain amount of cachet. He knew where a decreed housing project was going to be started, thus where we should locate our plant. That he could get the contract for the construction of the houses, George didn't question. After I met him, neither did I. It was clear. He could.

Working in English, using the honorable Suliman as translator, George sat cross-legged, writing on a clipboard. Fazza sipped coffee, sucked on his water pipe, and occasionally stood up to embrace a new arrival, kissing the man on the lips and both cheeks then bumping noses lightly, in the tradition of his tribe.

The kissing bit was always a problem to me. George and I had both been warned about the possibility of transmitting venereal diseases this way, from lesions on the lips. I don't know if the warning was apocryphal or not. I do know one of the hot spots in the Kingdom for venereal diseases is Mecca, and it always struck me as odd that a Westerner going there ran a risk of catching something with hardly any risk of having much fun getting it.

After a few meals in Saudi Arabia, I stopped worrying about diseases transmitted by kissing. What I wouldn't catch by hunkering down with a bunch of guys, eating with my fingers from a communal tray where everyone else was eating and licking their fingers, wasn't worth considering. I never got into male lip touching, though. It always made me uncomfortable.

George drew up a basic agreement, made it general enough so it would hold water yet specific enough so it was more than an I'd-like-to-do-something-with-you-someday type of document, and got Fazza, with Suliman as translator and witness, to sign it. Those three pages of handwritten yellow legal-size paper sure changed my life.

According to Chris, who was still relaying messages to me in Teheran, George was excited. It didn't take more than a minute for me to catch his enthusiasm. We made our plans quickly. He would leave for the United States to take care of some of his South American business. Chris would telex me a copy of the agreement. I, in turn, would fly to Saudi, meet with Fazza to establish the contact, then spend some time selling our building system to whomever the sheikh could get me in to see.

After a difficult flight, I stepped off the plane onto the concrete apron of the airfield in Dhahran at about 2 P.M. on August 15, 1976, excited, enthusiastic, and exhausted. The mop-up operation in Iran had been emotionally trying, but this was balanced by the potential that seemed to be opening up in Saudi Arabia.

I spent the first day in the white, fourteen-room Al Manura Hotel, built next to the Persian Gulf, and felt better next morning when I met Suliman in the lobby for the drive to Jubail.

Getting comfortable at the Al Manura took some doing. The guest accommodations all faced the street, where, from six-thirty in the morning until nine at night, the symphony of horns made New Year's in Times Square sound like a rest home. I think Arabs have interlocked their car horns with their feelings of manhood. Using a loud horn continuously makes a man aware of his strength. An insecure Arab will start honking first thing in the morning and keep it up for ten minutes after turning off the ignition at night. The streets surrounding the hotel must have been populated by very insecure Arabs, because the din was deafening.

The fourteen rooms each had a private bath. But there were never more than seven bars of soap at any one time. There was also no hot water. The big tank on the roof was pumped full every evening. By midafternoon the sun had beaten on it long enough to make it bearable, so that was the ideal time for a shower. There was only one problem. A room was furnished with only one towel, which, used or not, was picked up early every morning and laundered. It was always returned shortly before dinner, about 6:00 or 7:00 in the evening. Getting the sand and squished flies off meant either a warm, midafternoon shower with a long drying time or a flash rinse in the stored water, cooled by evaporation to less than body temperature. I complained about the towel shortage one evening to the Ethiopian hall porter, who was anxious to please. He ran out of my room and after a minute, I heard, through the thin partition wall, an English voice. "Hey! Where in the hell are you going with my towel?" The porter appeared before me, smiling broadly, and bowed as he presented me with a towel, still soaking wet from my neighbor's bath.

Suliman, as usual, arrived in time for a meal. His knack was uncanny. He always showed up right at lunch or dinner, and always stuck me or George with the check. He did have one redeeming grace, though. Once a week or so he'd spring for a big supper. It was a way of saving face.

The trip took a little over two hours in the white Mercedes. Suliman was a better driver than most Arabs I'd ridden with, so didn't cost me too many gray hairs.

My first impression of the street on which Fazza lived was that someone, for reasons of his own, had built a sub-division in a garbage dump. The amount of trash and general crap piled against the walls and running out into the narrow lane was astounding. No effort was made to burn the waste. It was simply tossed over the wall, outside the house compound. Out of sight was out of mind. Except once in every several weeks when the trucks came and workers shoveled the mess up to cart it away. Then there was lots of hell raised over the cost.

Suliman didn't seem to notice, although, after stopping the car and climbing out, he walked carefully around the riper heaps as he made his way to the main entrance. His flowing robe and headdress protected him from the flies.

I sat in the car for a minute, but the bugs were so bad I finally decided to get out. At least I'd be able to move around. I found I could move all right, but there was no place I could go to avoid the stench of decaying matter.

One other thing struck me. There was almost total silence. I could hear a voice or two, along with the wind, but there were no underlying sounds of a freeway, a busy street, or hundreds of air-conditioning units. The lack of noise added to the feeling of being out in the country.

Suliman rapped at the green wrought-iron gate protecting the entrance to the courtyard, and in a minute a barefoot servant came scurrying over the rough mosaic floor made from small, sand-spattered black and white tiles. They were obviously expecting me, because when the man caught sight of Suliman, we were instantly ushered into the majlis. We stopped at the door which faced out onto the courtyard long enough to honor custom by removing our shoes.

Inside, I found myself in a ten-by-twenty room. The gray tiled floor was partially covered by vivid green, U.S.-made, nylon-shag carpeting. A heavy coating of plaster had been hand-laid over the concrete blocks used to build the walls, and a coat of bright-robin's-egg blue more or less painted on the rough texture. The ceiling, covered by a brown rush woven mat, had two modern, white, recessed fluorescent light fixtures hooked up at each end. Between the glowing lights, ceiling fans hung down a couple of feet, turning slowly to produce a warm draft. Two small air conditioners were loosely jammed into holes cut through the eight-inch-thick wall. Like most of the units I saw in Saudi, they were almost never turned on.

Aside from several cushions, a low table, a few water pipes, and one battered TV, the room was unfurnished. Odds and ends, including a bottled-water cooler and a large transformer used in converting United States appliances to Saudi current, were dumped along one wall. An antique sink was not too securely installed just outside the courtyard door. Used for washing hands before meals, it was surrounded by an assortment of small towels, a water bottle, and a tall filigreed brass pitcher containing the mandatory rose water or other perfume.

At one end, there was a narrow, four-foot-high, shuttered window decorated by elaborate hand carvings. Normally the master of the house would seat himself in front of this barred aperture, to sip tea and talk with passersby.

Following Suliman's lead. I seated myself on a bright-orange, foam rubber-filled cushion, only to immediately arise again when the door opened. Mustache and beard neatly trimmed, flowing white robe barely covering his naked feet, and being led by his young son, Sheikh Fazza entered, smiling. He kissed and embraced Suliman, shook hands with me, made sounds to the child, and plumped himself down. The obligatory coffee arrived. I passed, preferring tea, which he ordered for me.

Our meeting followed the general trend. Yes, I'd had a good flight. Uneventful. No, the drive up went quite quickly. A good two hours of polite messing, interspaced with long pauses, sips of refreshment, people coming in, passing though, then going out without seeming to take notice of us, or Fazza of them, and Suliman translating every word.

Suliman's translating alway bothered me. I can't say he deliberately changed the meanings of things too often, though he would if it was to his benefit, but I'm certain he softened or blunted a point when it suited his sensitivities, to add what he felt was more polite refinement to the conversation.

Aside from moments indicated by custom, as when bargaining over a price for instance, Arabs are soft-spoken and indirect. In a land where tradition supports the concept of blood feuds and murder over insults, an individual is well advised to speak gently. This is one reason Westerners have problems dealing with Arabs, who, to avoid any clashes in conversation, say one thing, appear agreeable, then do something else entirely. They haven't lied. They've just been carefully polite.

Finally, at a motion from Fazza, the boy, a cute, slim, curly-haired kid named Fahad who obviously adored his father, brought a green-plastic envelope briefcase and placed it next to the sheikh, who rummaged through it, selecting papers by touch and comments from his son.

George Pinder had warned me about the sheikh's blindness. After removing several sheets, he passed them to Suliman, speaking rapidly. The younger man looked quickly at the first one, then laughingly handed it back. Fazza smiled, too, as he replaced it into the case.

Suliman scanned the documents he had left, passing them over to me. "He mixed up his papers," he said, in his English accent. "The first sheet he gave me was the deed to a house somewhere."

I smiled, and the sheikh, assuming I'd been let in on the joke, grinned hugely.

The pages I had were filled with tight Arabic script. It was hard for me, looking at it, to decide which end was the start and which the finish, much less what it said.

I looked inquiringly at Suliman.

"What's this?"

"A contract."

"Any particular contract, or just a contract in general?"

He smiled. "It is an exact translation into Arabic of the agreement our partner, Mr. Pinder, made with Sheikh Fazza."

"How do I know that? I can't read Arabic."

"Because I tell you."

"You passed it right to me. Unless you saw it on another occasion, you didn't have time to read it."

"It is not required that I read it." He was looking at me as if I were a simpleton.

"Oh." A long pause. It's funny how soon my conversations in Fazza's majlis lapsed into long, semihostile or suprised silences. I decided to try again.

"You don't have to read it, because Fazza told you it was an exact translation."

He beamed. "Right. Now you see it."

I didn't see anything. Even funnier how many conversations I had in Fazza's majlis that sounded like a part of the Mad Hatter's Tea Party.

Trying to be helpful, Suliman handed me his gold Cross ballpoint pen.

"I'm supposed to sign it?"

"Of course. Then we will have the deal documented in both languages. As you know, Mr. John, only a contract written in Arabic is valid under Saudi laws."

"This agrees with the original George drew up?"

Suliman was back to an impatient scowl. To him I was acting like an idiot again. Sheikh Fazza sat, impassive, hubbling his hubble-bubble pipe, looking pleased. His son listened attentively. As his father's trusted, confidential secretary, he had an earnest graveness beyond his years.

My mind was racing, trying to understand exactly what was coming down around me. On one hand, it could be a swindle. But one only a fool would set up. There was no way I was going to sign a contract in a language so foreign it didn't even use recognizable letters, until I could take the document to someone, get a written translation into English, then compare it with the telex George had Chris send me just before I left Teheran.

Maybe it wasn't a swindle. There were times, I knew, when lying or cheating by a Moslem was not dishonorable. It was merely good business. Direct cheating or lying to gain an advantage, especially after a pledge had been given, is often practiced by even the most devout, as no few Westerners have, much to their loss, learned. In fact, to many Arabs, our unorthodox, unnatural code of honor is a source of amusement. Not to mention opportunity. In my mind, there was a question as to how far the teachings of Mohammed extended toward infidel nonbelievers from the West. I had a hunch the limit of the extension was extremely variable. And at the discretion of the extender.

There was a third difficulty. If Fazza was being straight, and if this paper was an exact translation, and I balked over signing, there was going to be hell to pay. Talk about an insult. I might get out of his tacky living room alive, but any chance of a deal would be dead.

More to buy time than because any solution had suggested itself to me, I turned to Suliman.

"Would you ask Sheikh Fazza who made the translation?"

He looked at me quizzically, then faced the old man and spoke slowly, with careful diction.

"He says it was done in Dammam. His attorney had it made."

I had an inkling of an idea.

"Ask him if he trusts his attorney."

From the tone of the fat man's answer, I could tell he was not too enamored with members of the legal profession, preferring the more traditional rulings by a religious leader. Suliman also explained that Fazza was at a disadvantage in legal matters. He had no attorney among the members of his immediate family.

I focused on Suliman's eyes. "Tell the sheikh exactly what I say. Don't freewheel. Okay?"

"Okay." He nodded at me.

"Say first that I do not read Arabic. Say second, I do not have the original document, as drawn up by my partner, George Pinder, with me. It is in my hotel. Say next, I will accept the sheikh's word this document is exactly like the one he and George agreed to. Then ask if he will give me his true word he is certain they are exactly the same. Repeat the word 'exactly.'"

There was a long exchange. I hung everything on the concept the fat rascal was not lying. That he was honestly extending me the same honor he would to a true believer, and that he would be offended if I didn't sign. But I threw in a ringer. When I saw he wasn't fond of lawyers, I hoped it was possible to cast a nuance of doubt. If he gave his word they were exactly alike, exactly, then I was in the soup, because I'd made up my mind I wasn't signing until I got a good translation.

My other ace in the hole was Suliman. It was lucky he didn't know I'd brought the copy of the original agreement George had sent me, because then I'd have him to contend with, too. He could read both and tell me anything.

It got quiet again, with the sheikh thoughtful. I could see his mind work, and gave a mental sigh of relief. He wasn't going to tell me it was exactly the same unless he knew it. I was right. He was treating me like a civilized man, even though I was not of the one faith.

Suliman faced me again.

"Fazza believes the statements to be the same. But of course, he is not absolutely certain."

"Tell him I have a way we both can be sure. I will take this document to another attorney." "Attorney" is a rough word to translate from Arabic. The same role does not exist in the Moslem culture, as questions of law are argued on the basis of religious tradition, which changes from tribe to tribe, or, more important, from interpretation to interpretation of the word of the Koran. The Western system of civil advocacy does not prevail. "I will have him translate it back into English. Then we will meet again, here, with the sheikh's permission, compare all versions, and sign."

There was another sputtered exchange. I could see from the fat man's expression that my suggestion was not the best news he'd ever heard, but in the end, he agreed.

Twelve hours later I was back. With a new respect for the sheikh. The Iraqi attorney I'd found in the town of Dammam had done a quick but apparently sure translation, and it agreed, as close as something will after having gone from English to Arabic back to English, with George's original. I was being treated as a member of the human race, not an outsider. I trusted the Iraqi attorney because he confided in me his lack of love for Fazza, who, he said, owed him eight thousand dollars for legal work done a few years back.

I had a special surprise for our next meeting. After checking the document, I'd stopped by the hotel to pick up my 16-millimeter projector. I set it up in the majlis, projected onto a blue wall, and showed Fazza, and a flock of his pals, the film we'd made on our building system. Fahad explained each scene to his father.

The group wasn't just enthusiastic. They were frantic. I showed it again. Fahad, with Suliman's help, described the action carefully, asking me to stop it several times. Fazza called on Suliman to translate parts of the script, then would nod. On the third play, he seemed to know it by heart.

Word of this unusual distraction got around, and by the fourth time through the projector, I wished I'd had a popcorn concession. It made the problem of the translated joint venture agreement disappear. We both signed the Arabic version and Suliman began taking notes from Fazza about who would be contacted to show the new film. It began to look like a long August.

Later that evening, I got one of the rides of my life. Fazza decided, about nine o'clock, that I should be a guest in his home. It's hard to express the honor this bestowed upon me. To allow a nonbeliever, and a Westerner, to be a houseguest was virtually unheard of in Jubail. This necessitated our driving into Dammam to get the few belongings I'd left at the hotel.

Full of bonhomie, we all trooped out to Fazza's green Mercedes. Suliman jumped into his car, said something about picking me up in the morning so we could start the round of governmental visits he and Fazza had agreed upon, and roared off in a shower of sand.

The sound of his exhaust fading away down the narrow road back toward Dammam died just as the call, "Salat," sounded for evening prayer. There I was, standing in the silence of the desert's edge. The Aramco flare was in full fiery bloom, flickering orange high in the air. I felt very alone.

Prayer over, Fazza, pointing and steering an imaginary wheel, indicated for me to get into the car. I did. In the back seat. He got in front, the position of honor. We both watched as Fahad, the ten-year-old, climbed into the driver's seat of the green Mercedes 300 Sedan, where he sat on a six-inch foam cushion. The boy was so short he could scarcely reach the gas pedal and see over the top of the dashboard at the same time, but apparently he was used to driving, because before I could move to take control, we were on our way, engine gunning.

We got to the hotel, but we sure as hell didn't get back. Not in the Mercedes, at least. I climbed out, went to my room, picked up my stuff, and was checking out when the excitement started.

Fahad, taking Fazza somewhere else, got to flying down one of the narrow dirt lanes they call a street and raced to a photo finish with another car at a corner. When he jammed on his brakes, the Mercedes slid straight ahead on the sand strewn pavement through a wall made of mud bricks.

That's when I learned what a heavy guy Fazza was. The car, after knocking down a man's wall, knocked down the man, who was enjoying the relative cool of the evening by taking tea in his courtyard. He wasn't hurt, but he was plenty pissed off, doing a lot of screaming.

Normally soft-spoken Arabs get loud when they get excited. When they get emotional, too, wow! Part of the brouhaha, I knew, was to be in a position to effect a better settlement, but even so, they all carried on like a pack of nut cases.

Naturally, the cops came. Along with a local detachment of the home guard, wandering military, a couple of civil dignitaries, all the neighbors, and anyone else who could hear the anguished screams. Some crowd. Not content to merely stand around and marvel at the damage, they all chose sides and took part.

The injured man dragged officer after officer out to the road, then to the Mercedes, which was steaming water and making gurgling noises, then pointed to Fazza, who was calmly waiting for the pandemonium to fade.

The police knew the sheikh was blind and the boy drove. Fahad, the world's only ten-year-old chauffeur, seemed unconcerned by the crowd. His worry was not for the damage to the wall or the resident's dignity, but the wrecked car.

For the record, you can't put a Mercedes 300 Sedan through a mud-brick wall with impunity. It raises hell with the paint job. Not to mention the body work and mechanicals. It was a complete write-off.

The situation had its serious side, however, because an accident in which there is an injury, any injury, means instant jailing for the driver.

Fazza comforted the boy and, tiring of the commotion, spoke to the constabulary. I don't know what he said, but it must have been strong, because they all backed away. He talked to the homeowner, then, with the newly arrived constable, whose presence started the screaming all over again. Quite a crowd had gathered, and the people gave a collective gasp when the injured man appeared wearing an oversized, sloppily tied bandage around his head.

Months later, I found out it took Fazza all his influence, plus an eighty-thousand-dollar bond to keep his son out of the slammer. He also ended up paying dearly, although slowly, for the damage. It cost more to settle the incident than if the man had been killed.

I never saw the Mercedes again. The next day there was a brand-new dark-green Chevy Suburban; Fahad at the wheel. With the seat all the way forward, he could see out and accelerate at the same time. I rode with him on several occasions, and he proved to be as good a driver as most adult Arabs. Which is not to say great.

In the next weeks, I showed the film to more than fifteen governmental honchos, including a group during a four-day trip to Riyadh. For my mental well-being, I also took over most of the driving chores, much to Fahad's disappointment. But Fazza's mumbled requests to Allah as he sat next to me were better than jousting with constant heart failure. Almost every drive was interrupted by a call to formal prayer. I'd stop the car and sit behind the wheel while everyone else climbed out and knelt on their mats. Then, prayer duty over, we'd reload the crew and be on our way.

It was an interesting time. I met many brilliant men in the Saudi government service, had some serious interest shown in the project of opening a plant, and felt progress was being made. We were down to being one of three finalists in the Saudi government's official selection of a simple, low-cost building technique. Win the competition and we were all very, very rich.

On the other side, I was fascinated with life in the house. Fazza hadn't been kidding about being wealthy. As time passed, I visited his properties with him, including a concrete-block-manufacturing company, a terrazzo firm that made tiles, a grocery store, an auto repair garage, a curio shop, and lots of land.

Later, people questioned my interpretation of his holdings, but it was quite clear to me at the time that Fazza called all the shots on the various endeavors. The manager of the block and tile company would come in weekly, for instance, to pick up cash for the payroll. The two would sit endlessly going over who should be paid what, screaming, almost crying in anguish, and generally creating a ruckus in the majlis. In the end, Fazza would have a chest full of money brought in, fork over, and the two would part on the best of terms.

The sheikh exhibited what I would later find to be a national trait. Whether due to a general mistrust of banks, or just because they like the feel of money, the Saudis prefer to do business with cash. Especially coins. The largest riyal piece is worth about thirty-five U.S dollars, and even big transactions, involving hundreds of thousands of dollars, are made with them. Which means the buyer and seller, or their representatives, stay up most of the night verifying amounts. There are primitive counting devices, but by and large businessmen seem to prefer to handle the coins and clink them around.

I was offered the use of a car on one occasion, but I refused when the owner opened the trunk. It was filled with packets of riyal notes, in preparation for a big deal. I didn't want the responsibility of having all that change in my possession. The owner had a hard time understanding my concern over my cargo.

4 The Deal and the Arabian Nights

Through September 1977

There is an old military joke:

"What was the first thing you did when you got home?"

"Made love to my wife."

"Then what did you do?"

"Put down my suitcase and did it again."

My late-October homecoming wasn't quite that frantic, but I was damn glad to see Pat. I was happy to see the kids, too. It was just nice to be home, living in a house with tables and chairs, a lawn out front with wall-to-wall green grass, and a store down the street which sold cold beer. It's the little things that count.

Pat and I are close. When I'm home, we spend a good bit of time together. She is the kind of person who finds satisfaction in her family, but who always, because she does things so efficiently, has time for herself, too. In the weeks we were separated, she spent many hours alone, so being together again was a vacation for us.

Pat is a woman of varied interests and since I take my work home, she was able to question me about the Saudi situation and intelligently form her own conclusions. She'd lived in the Moslem world, knew a huge amount about our end of the construction business, and could see where events were leading. She was more than supportive, but concerned for me. Especially my health. The Middle East, away from the Europeans' area in the larger cities, or the Aramco compound, isn't the healthiest place in the world. I never did get really sick, though. One bout of food poisoning and a twirl with sheikh's two-step, of course, but nothing serious.

There was a lot to do in Houston. I was asked to consult on the real-estate business as it needed input and fresh direction, I had to put together an architectural drawing team with structural and electrical engineers, and last but far from least, try to answer back correspondence while I wrote an action plan to move things along. A developing relationship with one of the foremost companies in the field of precast concrete also proved helpful.

Wow! It wasn't inexpensive. I had high-powered engineering talent working on the hotel project and designing an Arab-resistant, goof-proof steel form with the capability of being operated on a level hunk of ground by a semicrippled halfwit with ten thumbs without there being a chance for him to get hurt or break the mechanism, and still make a good casting when he was through. Which might be a while.

In addition, we had undertaken, at Fazza's insistence, the complete design of a fifty-bed hospital. We were responsible for everything, from a supply of tongue depressors to bed sheets to X-ray machines to an additional building for nurses' quarters.

For this task, Abdallah Fazza had drawn a commission from the Saudi government. The major construction firms ignored the deal, since it was too small for them to mess with.

After some searching, I found a former Navy M.D. who had a dose of adventure in his soul and paired him with the wife of the man, Jeff, who'd first introduced Suliman Rasi to me. She was a registered nurse. I felt this medical team would pass the arduous checking necessary to be cleared by the Saudi government for admission into the Kingdom. This process is painstaking, including an examination of parents' backgrounds for possible Jewish ancestry. Their assignment was to go over and estimate the requirements of the hospital firsthand. At the same time, they'd have the chance to eyeball their future employment location. They went all right, but after seeing things up close, they cut their trip from three weeks to four days. On returning, nothing could persuade them to go back.

More than $118,000, expended for drawings, airfare, design, and other professional services, had been invoiced, over a period of six months, to our partnership. But no money was coming in from the desert. Suliman, who had 5 per cent surcharged "commission," constantly assured us payment was on the way, but somehow, no bucks ever seemed to make it across the big sea.

I was pumping plenty of personal cash into the deal, drawing on new, improved lines of credit from banks, and halfway scrounging around for an investment group to help handle the interim financing while we set up shop to do the hotel.

I'd also regained my place on the list of fine friends of International Telephone and Telegraph, not to mention Ma Bell, by the daily stream of electronic contact with my counterparts in the dunies. Since there was a nine hour time difference, I did a lot of 3 A.M. phone answering. Telexes, telegrams, telephone calls, you tell me a way to send a message over there, or from over there to over here, and I used it. Over and over. It got so a dial tone sounded like a cash-register bell. But in for a dime, in for a dollar. There was a deal there. I could smell it. It was mine, if I worked wisely, delivered on time, and maintained my standards of product quality.

Quite aside from the lure of filthy lucre, I had another reason for putting so much of myself into the projects. If I did this right, spent the time training workers, and gave them the proper technology, when it was over, and George and I had split our $5 or $6 million bucks' net profit, I would have helped add a new capability to their country. Many families, homeless or next to it today, would, through the years, find shelter and happiness in the houses that would continue to be made from our forms long after we were gone. That might sound funny, or a little quixotic, or even a bit on the corny side, and I guess it is. It's still true, though. I'd seen too many Arab kids in too many countries living too poor a life-style. Same for their parents. The revenues from the oil could help them, if there were some way to spend part of the proceeds inside their own country. George and I were going to leave behind one way.

About this time, Suliman began getting the real shorts for money. I never did figure out his complete deal with the Saudi Navy, except to understand that his commission followed the general principle of passing cash from the main tribal hoard to selected men who were on the "in" list. He was "in."

When he was flush Suliman threw money around like a sheikh on a spending spree. But it appeared to me that he lived from day to day, apparently without much laid aside for the dog days which always come.

A sample of his number with the Navy was his annual six weeks in London each summer. What he was supposed to be doing, I don't know. What he told me he did, in bits and pieces during many conversations, was enough for a book. He would, by his account, start in like a skyrocket on day one, and finally, in a flash of blinding color made from uninhibited behavior and an Arab's sense of fun, starburst with enough brilliance to light up all London. Then it was one last drink on the plane and step down the stairway back to the straight and narrow.

His finances never seemed quite up to his stated excesses, and now, months after the events of his summer sojourn, he had the dollar hungries. I figured that out later. Much to my cost and consternation.

In November, Suliman started pushing George and me hard to make a return swing through Saudi. Immediately. He had this deal, that deal, our deal with Fazza set and ready to expand, it was imperative we get there quick, before everything fell through. A typical five-percenter's hustle.

George and I had seen some of this mentality at work with agents in the Middle East before. The idea is to promise you anything, get you on the scene, then hope that your presence, combined with the wild number of business ventures and adventurers you'll find in every first-class hotel lobby, will lead to something. If it does, then the agent is a great fellow. If it doesn't, he is caught in a crack. Even so, he isn't out anything tangible. The black mark on his psyche isn't noticed.

I believe Suliman got to using the economical means of Saudi Navy long lines to call us daily. He was sincere, concerned, and straightforward. We had to get there. It was the right time to settle all our business.

Normally, we wouldn't have had much concern. When a partner in a venture pushes too hard, all that is usually required is to contact the money man straight out, to ask the true status. In this case, it wasn't so easy.

Our money man, the good Sheikh Fazza, was blind, spoke no English, and lived miles from the nearest telephone or telex. The only way to get a message to him was by personal delivery or Trans-Ocean Camel Express.

After two weeks, Suliman began to call twice a day, still I think, because he disliked spending his own money and was often short of cash, using the Saudi government's nickel. He became more frequent and frantic. When were we coming with the plans for the Moon Plaza Hotel? He couldn't stall them off much longer. When would we arrive with the forms? The money and arrangements were ready. How about the hospital deal? Did we just want to let go of it for good, etc.? Anyone with less experience would have been packed and long gone before his third week of bombardment. Not George and me. We were both like the man who learned not to sit on a cold stove by first making the mistake of sitting on a hot one. One time teaches you a lot. And we'd had our one time several times before.

What we did seemed so logical at the time. We wrote a letter to Fazza asking him for the straight skinny. Were we needed there or were we not? If we were, we'd be there. We backed the letter, written in Arabic, with a telex to Jubail, agreed to abide by his response, and settled in for Thanksgiving.

I had a nice time with the family. The kids were healthy, Pat was in an especially bright mood, and her dinner was fine. Just fine. It is a memorable day in my life, because it was the last calm before the sand storm.

The telex hit the next week:

Please come to Jubail at your earliest opportunity to conclude matters that are in readiness here.

Regards. Abdallah.

Sheikh Fazza had spoken. And we had agreed to go. Even if it was December 16 and it meant being gone during Christmas and possibly not making it back until after New Year's.

We went through Gay Paree. To me, it's an easier trip than via London. Not that the trip is an easy one no matter how you fly, because from Houston it takes at least a day and a half in the strange, unsettled, restless limbo of airplanes, airports, odd meal hours, and alcohol known to all world travelers.

For some reason people who don't do much business traveling think it's glamorous. They are entitled to their opinions, no matter how poorly founded. There is, however, one redeeming feature, but it is transitory and short-lived. Just before cutting loose to board, I get a sense of freedom. My only schedule is that of the airline, I expect to hurry up and wait, but I'm free of all daily details, family concerns, everything. Like I say, it doesn't last long, but it's as effective as an adrenaline shock for a little while.

Our visit to Paris was short. Burdened with drawings, proposals, sketches, Christmas presents, our clothes, and a general assortment of other crap, we ran through Charles de Gaulle Airport because we were late and just had time to make the Saudi connection. So much for Paree, hello Dammam. An intriguing comparison.

Nothing had changed. Not the weather, the beat up look of the place, the scene at customs and immigration, nothing. Same old Saudi. Same old Pinder and McDonald. Same old shit from Suliman. Only this time we'd fallen for it. How badly, we wouldn't know for a few days.

Part of the preliminary drawings had already been shipped to Suliman, who, though slow, got them around to the Ministry of Industry and Electricity, a euphemism for the bunch who controls the purse strings. The first reports were positive, and on this encouragement, I'd gone ahead and knocked out the next two steps: transfer of the preliminaries to working plans and estimating the hotel package. I'd added a third team, bean counters, to total up all the little goodies like the cost of operating the air conditioning, the lawn sprinkler system, laundry for 240 rooms, carpet durability in main traveled areas, and other esoteric oddities which go along with running a hotel for a profit as opposed to operating at a loss. We even altered the drawings to meet last minute-site changes.

What I had with me was one of the best packages I've ever seen, complete from the earliest steps through the end of the first year's operations, all translated into Arabic.

Abdallah, the blind fat fox in flowing robe, welcomed me like a long lost brother. I sputtered out my rusty Arabic, endured a garlic-breathed hug-kiss-nose bump, hugged back, and was actually glad to see him. Later I learned to fend off the kissing, when I wished, by shaking hands firmly and gripping the other man's forearm in my left hand.

I wasn't so happy to see Suliman. Not mad exactly, but I wanted to build a fire under his ass after the slow way he'd followed up on the preliminary drawings and my questions. We didn't have a row. That would have been un-Arabic, standing in the airport. Later, however, in his car, driving out to Abdallah's house, I got about as offensive as a person can on the edge of the desert and not start a blood feud.

He was so repentant I felt like a pukka sahib at the peak of the British colonial period dressing down a wog houseboy. I should have known better, because it did no good at all except to relieve my pent-up feelings.

Abdallah and I discussed money and the six months' worth of overdue invoices. George didn't help matters. On the plane he'd gotten me all riled up, ready to fight, by saying, "I'm gonna tell that shitty Suliman bastard..." But when I got started he went right into our good guy-bad guy routine, saying, "Aw, hell, John, don't be so damn hard on our ole pal Suliman." Same with Abdallah Fazza.

It was like payday at the tile factory,with screaming, arm waving, dirty looks, hurt expressions, and general histrionics. No one won, although Fazza agreed to fork over his share of the expenses we'd run up to bring the project this far along. That settled, but with no cash in hand, we set up shop for a few days.

George and I located in our old favorite, the Hotel Al Manura, in wonderful downtown Dammam, just fifty short, treacherous desert miles from the home of our benefactor and partner, the sheikh Fazza. It cost us fifty bucks, as a tip to the majordomo, to be considered for a room I wouldn't have stayed in back home if they'd paid me fifty. We deliberately planned to keep our headquarters away from the sheikh's house for the first few days, because that was the only way I could see to get him separated from Suliman in our presence. Separated they had to be, if I was going to get the answers I'd been wanting to several questions.

It worked. In a couple of days we finagled a private conference. Or as private as a conference can be in the majlis of an important sheikh's house. Which is not too private. At least Suliman wasn't there. He didn't find out about the meeting until later, which made him mad as hell, but the soup was out of the can by then.

Abdallah Fazza, his son, and a translator he hooked in from Aramco, met us. Coffee time. Tea time for me. Chitchat. "My how he's grown." A frown from the kid, but smiles when he saw the presents we'd brought. It was Christmas Eve, and we had a gift for everyone, young, old, male, and female alike. We'd even thought of including a camel or two, but there was a shortage of Purina Camel Chow in the Houston stores so we passed.

I really made a faux-pas during this meeting. My interpreter noted to Fazza that he was about to be married. It would be his third wife, and she was in what corresponded to our junior high school. Naïvely, I told him that was great. And mentioned how much help she would be to his other two wives. "After all, having a teacher in the family will help with the kids."

There was a long pause. "You do not understand, Mr. John. She is a student. A girl of twelve years. We will be married after her next birthday." I looked at the man, who was well into his thirties, and went on to other matters.

More small talk. Then down to it. I would speak looking directly at Fazza; the translator, watching me intently, would translate; the son, concentrating, would ask to be certain his father understood; Fazza would answer, looking, with his sightless eyes, at me; the translator, looking at him, would translate; and I'd get an answer. Long dialogue, lots of action, little information. What we got was enough.

Question, through the above process: "Were things far enough along for funding?"

Answer: "No."

Question: "Why, then, did the fine sheikh send us the telex?"

Answer: "What telex?"

Question: "The one that brought us here during Christmas."

Answer: "What the hell are you talking about?" But more polite. Genuine puzzlement.

Additional response: "I thought you came here because you wanted to see how things were progressing. That's what Suliman told me."

Aha! Our friend Suliman of the Royal Navy. Direct question: "Did you send us any kind of telegram, telex, or make a phone call? Did you get our letter?"

Answer: "No." Blandly. Too blandly for it to be a lie.

The expression on George's face when he heard the translation still lives in my memory. I started to laugh, while he got even hotter. He was sitting on the floor, holding a plastic bubble-gum machine we'd brought as a gift, and almost threw it into the blue plastered wall. Mad? Judas Priest, he was mad.

I couldn't resist. Leaning over, I said in a low voice, "Merry Christmas, George." Fazza and his son, hearing the familiar phrase, joined in, and there was a chorus of "Merry Christmas, George." The poor man almost lost his mind.

By the time we left to· start the drive back, George had settled down, but every time I'd whisper "Merry Christmas, George," he'd get red in the face and I would go off again into gales of laughter. Finally, he saw the humor in it all and laughed, too.

We had an interesting Christmas Eve. A friend, who was employed by a competitor of ours in Houston, was honchoing a desert camp not far from Fazza's house and he'd invited us for the holiday. Somewhere he'd scrounged up a few shots of scotch for George and three cans of beer for me and him. In addition, Bob had Somali housekeepers with raven-black skin who could make me cry with delight over the way they cooked chicken. The rest of the camp had frozen turkey. We had pepper chicken and a hell of a nice time.

Next morning, we got up about ten o'clock. No hangovers. No family, either. No kids peeping in to check the gifts, no kids getting me up at first light to walk through a cold room to the tree, with its lights and stacks of presents. Not much of anything.

I was on my second cup of tea, in the main dining room of the Al Gosaibi, which is more elegant than an Army mess hall, but less neat than a skid row cafeteria. We were both silent. We'd come over the ten miles from our hotel, the Al Manura, because the food there was worse than at any mess hall or handout stand I'd ever seen.

"Merry Christmas, gentlemen." The voice, with an intriguing Continental lilt, was female and coming from around a large column against which I had my back. George and I turned, peered around the edge, and found a smiling lady dressed in the blue uniform of flight stewardess. In a few words, we agreed to sit together.

She was there because a group of Saudis had chartered an entire 707 from a European airline for a trip from Rome. Maria, who said she was married to a motion-picture producer, and seven other lovely ladies, were lodged in a cabana on the hotel roof. They were accompanied by a full complement of officers, including a pilot, copilot, and flight engineer, and had been promised excitement, fun, frivolity, and pay equal to three months' wages for the one-week trip. She invited us up to meet the gang, and we spent a cosmopolitan Christmas day.

The airline people started talking about none other than our original intended partner, that intrepid pilot the good prince.

Remember him? He of the private jet? Well, he was a sponsor of this party group. The night before, at a celebration in honor of the crew, he'd given the girls diamond bracelets. One for each. The ladies were expecting propositions next, because they were fine-looking as well as vivacious. But not that night. Our prince was after the pilot and copilot to join him in a unisex ménage à trois. He was crushed when they said no. The stewardesses thought the role reversal was funny. For years they'd had to find tactful ways to turn down flight crew members' advances.

The next day, George said he was going home. There wasn't enough for two of us to do anyway, and he kept wanting to be back in time for New Year's with his friends.

He went to Houston, and I went to Jubail. To visit Fazza. Who was upset when he learned George was gone. To keep me in closer touch, Fazza asked me to move in with him. Since the hotel was costing $150 a day, I said fine.

One more round trip and I was situated in a ten-by-ten bedroom on the outside rim of the house. My bed was the usual foam-rubber pad, there were no tables or other furniture, but it was free. I was a part of a real Bedouin's household. As I mentioned before, it was a different experience.

During the many weeks I was a guest in Abdallah's home, I never saw the women's quarters. Etiquette dictated I never ask; he never volunteered, and I never got in. As a matter of fact, while in his house, I only saw a few women. One had a South Sea Island look to her and was very attractive. It was her job to clean my room each day after I went out. From her style, I knew she wasn't Saudi, so assumed she was a sort of slave who stayed on after the recent law abolishing slavery was passed. The rest of the women I recognized as Pakistanis, who lived on the premises with their husbands and did various services around the place.

The first woman of Abdallah's immediate family I saw, through the half-closed door of the women's entrance, was old enough to have been his mother. Mrs. Abdallah never did appear. I did hear her rather strident voice, daily, demanding something or screaming at the kids.

A daughter of one of Fazza's neighbors was another female I met. About seventeen, not in the least, as far as I could tell under her ghishura veil and robe, gone to fat, dark-eyed, black-haired, and with a good chance to be Miss Saudi. If they had such a title. I got to know her by osmosis during several visits to the soukh. Abdallah, Fahad the boy chauffeur, me, and any of the other family members, males only, who wanted to go, would all pile in and rip off down the sandy road.

Once parked on some narrow dirt street, the group would split up, Fahad staying protectively close to his blind father. On at least three occasions, the neighbor girl managed to time her walk through the soukh to meet me. Accompanied by a friend, who scurried off at the sound of my voice, she was risking a beating from home for even glancing at a man. I worried about the public nature of our supposedly chance encounters but rapidly realized no one watched. It was the soukh. No one cared. They were all too busy with their own doings.

Some doings. The soukh is as much a state of mind as it is a place. It's a neutral meeting ground, common market, and commodity catch-all rolled into one. It's noisy, smells of dirt floors and generations of humans, and is a perpetual parade of people in motion.

In the old days, long ago, the soukh was a compound where merchant caravans could camp and set out their wares. Camels, used to pack the goods, were penned in the center, where hard bargaining over livestock occurred.

Now, the livestock is gone and the open-air nature of the market has changed. Today, there is a series of beat-up, falling-down buildings with plaster pealing from their mud bricks. Inside, every square inch of space, apart from narrow walkways for buyers, has been claimed by a vendor. Rights to an area can go back through more than ten generations. Goods are piled on the floors, along the walls of what were originally corridors, on tables, on carts, and anywhere else there is space.

Some form of strict but unwritten law defines where one person's store starts and another's stops. There is no standard size or layout. Plots are scattered randomly through the buildings, fitted in like some crazy mosaic of merchandise, grouted with the people who have come to browse and buy.

Chuffing diesel trucks and buses, engines unmuffled, roar

around the buildings, a base note to the sharper brass sounds of car horns. The aroma of burned oil hangs oppressively.

Voices, raised in bargaining, are timeless in their sound in the hot, humid air. It is people dealing with people, as they have in the soukh for hundreds of years. There is a subdued excitement, a feeling of anticipation, hope, lust, and Allah knows what permeating the atmosphere.

With all the confusion, though, there is almost no theft. The penalty is too high; crimes too publicly punished. A convicted thief loses his right hand, so may never eat with people of breeding again, as the use of the left hand is a mark of venial behavior.

At night when the market closes, the vendors simply throw a cloth over their wares for protection from the dust, then go home, assured they will find things as they left them the night before. And day after day, year after year, they do. There is no questioning the effectiveness of the laws of the Koran in maintaining order. The punishments are tough, carried out with efficiency, and seem to serve as a deterrent.

The sellers in the soukh are all individuals and their places of business show it. The shops, narrow stalls, specialize in eccentricity. One, for instance, carries toothbrushes, kerosene lanterns, and leather gloves. That's all. Next door, the inventory is elevator control panels, ballpoint pens, and Tampax. Not much order, but it makes for interesting shopping.

To buy without bargaining is to demean not only yourself but your salesman. It shows you have no real interest. Besides, why would any sane person buy or sell at the first price? To gain. To gain what? Cash. That's the final fuel of commerce. All soukh transactions are conducted for cash, with great concern shown in counting and re-counting to verify amounts or debate over exchange rates.

Between my mystery girl's total lack of English and my limited Arabic, we didn't communicate too well, but there is another language she seemed to speak just fine. Her eyes, looking through the slits of her ghishura veil, were really hot. I'd heard of hot eyes all my life, but I never saw any until the first time she locked me into a staring match. What I could see was enough raw passion to kill. At the time, I'd been away from home for about ten days. I'd be lying if I said she didn't fascinate me. The job, and the trust Abdallah Fazza had placed in me, however, interested me more. I didn't rebuff her, just hid behind my language barrier, and played innocent.

It sounds insane, but I had a feeling for the little lady. Most of it was brought on by the understanding of what was, to me, her plight. I don't know if she felt despair or not. After all, it was her country and her customs. But it bothered me to think of her being married off with no choice.

The marriage lottery with her as the prize would start with her father's brother's oldest son. If he turned her down, the next oldest was in line. If they all passed on her, they would start to look outside the family.

The marriage itself was not a religious ceremony. Only a Koran-based legal formality, and she didn't have to be present or consent. Once married, the best she could hope for was that her mother-in-law wouldn't boss her too hard, and that her husband liked her enough to keep her. If not, her dear old dad would be honor-bound to buy her back for a few camels or the equivalent in cash or trade. Then, because she was female and a drag, the lottery would start again.

Judging from her obviously passionate nature, I assumed no one had practiced the common operation which removes the clitoris. It's losing popularity, but something like half the population still inflicts this terrible custom on young girls.

I tried not to let my personal feelings for her mix into the sexual urges I was having. It was hard at times, and it got harder.

Her next number was unforgettable.

It was a regular Saudi day. Hot in the morning, hotter still in the afternoon, the sky a clear burnt umber with occasional patches of blue. No clouds, but sand, sucked up by a passing windstorm, hovered high in the stratosphere, reflecting sunlight with a gold-orange brilliance.

About 10 A.M., I wandered out of my narrow, confining room up onto the flat roof where I frequently went to look over the desert and the town. I left the fan on the high ceiling turning lazily, stirring the warm, humid air. I had never associated humidity with the desert, but we were close enough to the coast to allow for a constant sea breeze. Not cooling, but damp. Ten miles farther inland, the ground was parched, cracked deeply where sand hadn't filled the open spaces.

The courtyard was quiet. Servants, up early, had washed it down, leaving the alternating black and white tiles sparkling. That had been three hours ago, so now there was a dull, dusty coating over everything. They'd be back, about noon, to do it again, as they would later in the evening. From far away, there was a sea smell on the hot wind.

Across the bright courtyard was another low roof, forming an open balcony. The two-story portion of the home, which housed one of our neighbor's harems, as I called them jokingly, rose alongside the open space, so it was possible to walk directly from the females' counterpart of the majlis out onto the low-walled parapet. It was open and bare, allowing me to see well into the upper courtyard. This was hardly acceptable under the terms of the Koran, which forbade anyone being able to see into another family's quarters. My appearance on the roof acted like a signal, because before I could turn away a young girl appeared carrying a large jug and a short, three-legged chair. She looked my way only once, arranged the stool, placed the clay bottle on it, and stepped back inside. She returned in an instant, followed by Miss Hot Eyes, who was wearing a thin, gauzy white robe. The folds blew easily in the breeze. Averting her eyes, she turned toward me, and with a shiver-shrug slipped off the gown. The younger girl took it and placed it out of my sight. I wasn't looking at the robe anyway.

She was terrific. My view was cut off by the edge of the roof, so I couldn't see her feet or legs below midcalf, but the rest was stunning. I'd always heard Arabic girls were short-waisted and heavy-legged. If that's the norm, she was quite abnormal with a long, thin waist, slightly rounded belly, a swelling mons, and then, clearly defined, the darker soft folds of her sex. She was clean-shaven, as are most Saudi women who live at home, and it gave her a little-child look.

The smaller girl stood up on the stool, lifted the bottle, and poured water onto her mistress's olive-cream body, slowly, so that it made glistening streams over and between her nicely rounded, full breasts, then along her tight, firm flanks.

She turned, obviously enjoying the sensation, and my eyes followed a trickle of water down the hollow of her backbone to the undulating cleft of her pert bottom. Both girls were giggling and I could hear their voices clearly across the distance separating us.

It was almost more than I could stand. Then act two began. She started to raise her arms, to allow the water to spread along the sides of her rib cage, and, as she did, began a slow, rolling movement of her hips. I've seen cooch dancers and I've seen strippers, but that fine young thing could show anyone I'd ever seen how. My imagination had not done her justice.

She was dazzling. Sexy. And I was about as hot as her eyes. I'm a morning man anyway. I like the effect of daylight on the finer parts of a woman's anatomy. I got my fill in about two minutes. The look-but-don't-touch bit bothered me, though.

After she'd thoroughly soaked herself, run her battery down gyrating, and posed in every conceivable position including bending over with her fanny toward me, legs slightly parted, she began to dry off. The younger girl assisted her, and in another minute she was back again into her gauze shift. I was close enough to see her dark nipples, erect from the chill of the water and the cooling effect of the breeze, stand out like two black olives, jutting the thin material up and out.

Then they were gone, leaving me with a stiff problem and a beautiful memory. I knew my problem would go away if I ignored it.

I came off the roof into the narrow hallway, wondering if the show had been for me. The girl had not once looked directly my way, but the main feature started as soon as I appeared. Her helper had peered straight at me, to be certain I was attentive. Judas Priest, I thought, what next?

What next was a short, swarthy, always-polite Pakistani servant waiting right outside my door. At first I thought he'd come to lead me to the fairy princess, but no luck. He had, however, seen the special performance. From his quick glance at the bulge in my pants, I knew he'd seen its effect on me, too.

He pulled me back into my room before speaking. "Mistah John, sir."

"Yes, Daoud?"

He was in his late forties. We'd had a couple of conversations during the long evenings, sitting out in the courtyard on the tiles. Some of his friends joined us once in a while, and one night he'd heard George and me go on about booze and dollies. All the Pakis we met seemed to like our American brand of humor and easy companionship.

His home was a small village north of Hyderabad, a town northeast of Karachi, on the Indus River. He grew up in the humid lowlands, reared in Christianity by a passing missionary who tried to swap soul for bread. The preacher got some lip-service conversions, but left only confusion in his wake. Daoud was a mouth Christian, an active Moslem, and had been around enough to be anything any situation required. Including mine, at that moment.

"There is very bad news, Mistah John." The "there" referred to the neighbor across the court.

"How so?" I was going to play innocent. I liked Daoud, but couldn't tell if he should be trusted. I didn't think I'd done anything, but most strict sects of the true faith forbid any man from seeing any woman not his wife nude. I might be in trouble for just watching.

"The girl is young. How do you say, not wise in her acts. She brings danger for you if her father, her grandfather, or any of her brothers find out."

I was a little embarrassed. "What the hell am I supposed to do, close my eyes?"

He smiled. I always liked it when he smiled. He was a warm, friendly man and his even white teeth were a bright streak across his almost mahogany face. He also had those luminous hazel eyes so common among Pakistanis.

"That would be a very good idea. But difficult to do."

"You damn well bet." By this time I was back to normal, all appendages in their accustomed places. "Do you think it will happen again?"

"Who, on this side of heaven, can say? It has never happened, since I have been here, two years, before. It is very dangerous, Mistah John."

My turn to smile. "It would be more private if you just sent word to her to come over with a case of scotch."

He smiled, too. "But no more serious."

I knew what he meant. The offense had been committed. I'd looked upon her. That wasn't enough to get her stoned to death, but more than sufficient to flare up a blood feud between me and her brothers. Daoud, a sympathetic man, knew it, too.

Daoud had come to Saudi like thousands of other Moslem Pakistanis. Work was hard to find in the old country, starvation common. After the fracas with India, the monetary and commercial systems went to the dogs. There was plenty of money in Saudi Arabia, and, if an immigrant were educated, as he was, at least enough to read Arabic and do simple sums, there was work. Lowest level, of course. Saudis tend to want to do little or nothing but boss. Which leaves a lot of bottom-echelon positions open for any outsider who can get papers and show up on the job site. Most Pakis I met were dreaming about using Saudi Arabia as a stopover while they tried to find a U.S. sponsor.

He began to nervously clean the room, dumping ash trays and picking up laundry.

"Did you enjoy your view of the sea?" Discreet indirectness.

"Only the end."

I didn't think he knew enough English to get my pun.

"Why didn't you close your eyes?" His question was simple.

"Alas, I, too, am only a mere man."

We stood a second, both of us, looking at each other. It was so quiet in the house I could hear the fan in my room turn the air.

"You have a problem. I, possibly, have a solution."

"Oh?"

"As you know, I am Pakistani. Not Saudi. Not strongly Moslem. As you also know, I am married."

I thought I'd seen his wife. A short, heavy woman who wore a gold ring in her left nostril as a decoration, and had long, stringy black hair which hung down to her waist. She was not veiled, and wore the bulky metal slave bracelets, so I knew she wasn't a Saudi.

"As you know, I, too, am married."

"But my wife is here. Yours is far away."

It took me a second to grasp his meaning. Then, as it came to me, I felt the old panic coming on. I didn't want his wife, or any other woman besides my wife. Sure, I'd had my usual fantasies when the hornies took me over, but that was then. Now, cooled off talking with him, all I could see was that sex might get me into one hell of a mess, so I'd better not mess around.

But Daoud wasn't going to have it. He wouldn't let go.

"You have offered to provide me with a letter of recommendation to your country, Mistah John. I now offer you personal comfort without danger of the neighbor men. We must be, of course, discreet. These barbaric Arabs refer too much to the Koran, as subsequently interpreted by later leaders of the faith."

The rules from the book are clear. A man must not lie with a woman not his wife. If they are both unmarried, that's easy enough to arrange, as the man may enter into a "temporary" marriage with the woman, which can last, by mutual agreement, for five minutes, five days, five months, five years, or any other specific time. Obviously, since a woman can have only one husband at a time, a married woman cannot enter into a temporary contract with another man. Sexual relations with anyone aside from her husband are forbidden. If she succumbs to the charms of another, and is caught, she is an adulteress. Her father, or a brother, shamed by the wayward ungodliness and disgraced by having a wanton in the family, can be called upon to kill her. Which they often do, in private.

Sometimes the shame of it all becomes too much to bear and the killing gets done in a fit of passion, right out in front of God and everybody. A grandfather, enraged by his granddaughter's use of Western dress, Western ways, and Western sexual freedom, created an international incident at the Riyadh airport when he publicly killed her. She was with her Lebanese boyfriend at the time, who must have feared for his life. He should have. The old man, carried away by the emotion of the moment, could easily have forgotten himself and whacked off his head, too. In this case, all the newspapers carried the story on the front page, complete with pictures. Westerners said, "God, isn't that awful. A grandfather killing his granddaughter." Saudis said, "Now there is a great, good man, who knows the wisdom of the old ways." I'm afraid the girl got a taste of woman's lib. Then really got liberated.

As for Daoud's wife, she was married, but her brothers and father were far away. If she were found in flagrante delicto with a man other than her husband, namely me, some well-meaning Saudi would come forward to volunteer his services as the Scourge of Allah. No matter what Daoud wanted, they would probably kill her by tying her up, stuffing her into a linen bag, and stoning her to death. Or at least beat her senseless. The Saudi who did it would feel justly righteous. If his daughter were far away and behaved with shame, casting shadows on his family name, he would only hope there would be someone to stand up to do the same for him. Makes sense.

What didn't make sense was my present situation. Daoud was determined to get me laid. I was determined to pass. His heavy wife wasn't my style.

"Daoud, I appreciate your offering me the gracious company of your fine wife, but I don't think it would be appropriate. Under the circumstances, that is. If someone found out, they might kill her."

"I think not kill her if it becomes known she had my permission. She would probably only be whipped."

"Well, I'd rather not be the cause of her getting whipped."

"I assure you, it is all fine. In her village, where I bought her from her father, friends of the family are better treated than here. She is very experienced."

"I'm sure she is."

I tried to brush past him, but he was partially blocking the way. He clutched my arm with his small rough-skinned hand. His brown fingers ended in nails white from the pressure of his grip.

"I understand and appreciate your concern. And your reluctance. She will come so both our hearts will be strengthened."

He released me, and shaking my head I went down the hallway toward the majlis. The only woman I'd seen around Fazza's house I'd even be remotely interested in was the South Sea-style former slave. Judas Priest, what next?

What next was straight business. A lot of it. Suliman and I attended a meeting with a government official shortly after noon, I played my now-famous almost Academy Award-winning film for another group, and I held a prolonged business conversation with Abdallah Fazza in the majlis just before dinner.

Since a pair of good old desert boys had dropped in, we all sat around until about ten o'clock smoking and drinking. They had their hubbly-bubblies and syrup coffee grounds, I had my Cuban H. Upmann cigar and umpteenth glass of boiling-hot instant Lipton tea. I followed the conversations as closely as I could, but even with Suliman providing added translational aid, it was difficult, although my Arabic was improving. Finally, tired by the concentration, I excused myself.

After an always-tense visit to the unlit outhouse, which also served as our shower, I stood for a moment in the dark. The Aramco flare wasn't as bright as it had been, and I could see the stars to the north. The sky looked a little different, with the dippers lower toward the horizon, but pretty much the same. There was a bright moon shining through the stratospheric sand particles and everything had a soft golden sheen.

It felt, standing there away from the noise and confinement of the house, like an Arabian night was supposed to feel. Or, at least the way I think an Arabian night should feel. A light, damp breeze wafted by, tickling the hairs on my arm.

One day, I would go with Abdallah, as he often promised, to see his people in the desert. I wanted to spend some time out there, away from the town and out of sight of the orange flare. I knew if I would, I'd be able to come a lot closer to understanding many things about the Saudi national character which now seemed inconsistent or inexplicable. Filled with the night, the strangeness of the scenery, company, and my general situation, I sighed once, muttered a low, "Judas Priest," and went to bed.

Not to sleep, as it turned out.

Daoud wasn't going to take my no for an answer. I might as well admit it, I was intrigued. Not by the thought of Daoud's stout wife with the stringy hair, but with the girl across the way. There was no chance she would slip over. And there was no way I'd slip into Daoud's wife. Celibacy may be abnormal, as the Saudis believe, but it can beat some alternatives.

I lay on my mat in the darkness of the small, bare room, running over the state of our business deals again and again, reviewing what had to be done the next day, and feeling an erection creep up on me. I heard the closing of the big steel gate locking the courtyard and flinched when the bright floodlights were turned off. I could just barely hear Fazza giving Daoud final instructions for the night. The house became silent.

From my position on the floor, sounds came to me in a funny way. The doors had an inch or so of space beneath them and noise seemed to roll like marbles down the corridor. All I could hear was deep snoring broken by an occasional fart, from one or another of the sleepers in my wing.

Two more hours of tossing, drifting off lightly, then snapping back to full wakefulness. A great start for a great night.

My eyes snapped open when I heard the popping sound a sandaled foot makes when it grinds a large grain of sand against the tile mosaic of the floor.

In the space under the door, looking out into the lighted corridor, I could just make out two big toes. Not clearly, but enough to be sure someone was there. The Aramco flare made faint pink-orange patterns on the wall of my narrow room. There was enough light, when helped by the sound, to tell someone was turning the handle of my latch. I waited, tensely. It must have taken fifteen minutes for the damn door to start to open, and I lay quietly, mind racing. The thought came again and again: this whole affair was like a story in a girly magazine.

At the first movement of the door inward, the action stopped again. There was another interminable wait before it slowly started moving once more.

I was uptight enough to have a heart attack. I didn't know if it was Daoud's wife, a robber, the girl next door, although that wasn't too likely, but you can't blame me for hoping, or, worst of all, Abdallah or Suliman, who, having heard I was in a sexual state of anticipation, decided to pay me a visit to relieve my anxiety. The last struck me as funny, but it didn't seem wise to laugh, so I lay, stiffly waiting.

Finally, the door opened enough to allow whoever it was to peek around the edge and see me. It was hard, in the glimmering semidarkness, to make out her features, but it wasn't the girl from next door. Nor was it Daoud's wife, because this lady didn't need a shave. Then, unexpectedly, she stepped into the room, leaving the door open behind her.

I let out a sigh of surprise. It wasn't Daoud's wife, nor the girl from next door, nor my host, nor anyone else I'd even considered. It was the very nice, South Sea Island-looking lovely who cleaned my room.

From ten feet away I could tell she'd doused herself with perfume; the smell preceded her. She looked at the wall over my head.

The still-open door scared me. It was bad enough for her to be in my room, but worse with the door open. That was inviting detection.

I spoke softly, in Arabic, telling her to come in and close the door, for our mutual well-being. She seemed reluctant, so I got up and shut it gently.

I turned to face her. She was watching me closely. Still in Arabic, I asked, "What is your name?"

There was a long pause. Long enough, because I'd spoken in such a quiet voice, to make me wonder if she'd heard. In an even softer tone, she said, in obviously rehearsed English, "I am Daoud's madam."

That threw me for an instant. Then I thought I understood. "Ah, Daoud has two wives." I was speaking as quietly as she.

The lady shook her lovely head. "No. Only me."

I started in again. "Who, then, is the short woman, with the..." That was as far as I got. Apparently tired of listening, she quickly undid the buttons of her dress and with a single movement had it snaked up and over her head. She seemed unconscious of it, and dropped the garment where she stood.

She had me very conscious of her now. Very conscious. In addition to the dark hazel eyes, which I could not see, and the pearly white teeth, which I could see vaguely, she was unbelievably lovely. High, taut breasts, dark nipples, a tense stomach with a certain roundness, and the flickering orange-red-pink light reflecting off her brown skin leaving shadowy hollows just begging to be explored.

"What did you ask?" She finally spoke again, in Arabic.

"I asked who is the heavy lady. The one with all the bracelets."

She had surprise in her quiet voice. "That is Daoud's mother."

Now I was out on the edge. The one I thought he was trying to put off on me was his mother. The one I wanted, and had mentioned once or twice to Daoud as being desirable, was his wife. Judas Priest, he must have thought I was the most direct, macho S.O.B. in Saudi. A guy with enough nerve to tell him to his face how lovable his wife was.

The situation began to become clear. Daoud had thought, because of my big mouth, that I wanted his wife, therefore would recommend him to the U.S. of A. So when I gave him the letter, he took it as a part of a quid pro quo. He got the paper, I got a freebie roll with his dearie. Sweet deal. Especially because after being away from home for so long, I could have used a roll in the hay.

I wish I could say I thought of Pat and the thought kept me from it. I wish I could say I was strong, and avoided the situation. I did think of Pat, mostly how damn mad she'd be if she ever found out. And I did gather my strength to resist. But neither decided the outcome. Plain old fear did. I might have liked to, but the thought of getting caught, which obviously had her half scared, petrified me. As much as I would have liked to get on with it, the idea I might be the cause of her death and bring problems into my own life made me less and less able to get up to it. I got back down on my mattress bed, and spoke to her in low tones. I lay down, away from her, because I knew if I touched her all my resolve would fade into the sunrise of the lust I was just barely able to repress.

We exchanged a few more words and she sounded puzzled. Then, and I think I detected a note of relief in her tiny voice, she said, "You do not wish to enjoy me?"

"You must thank Daoud. But you cannot stay. Besides, if I do enjoy you, I am afraid the other servants might hear and talk. It is too dangerous."

She did a most female thing. Freed of what she seemed reluctant to do but was going to do anyway, she opened the door a crack so I couldn't miss seeing her body as she slipped back into her thin, one-piece dress. She was good-looking, and I kicked myself, mentally.

In a trice she was gone. I was thinking of what I should have said. And done. It took me a long while to drift off to sleep. The last thought I remembered fascinated me later when I awoke. It was ten o'clock in the morning and I was still wondering if she would have been any happier doing her duty if I'd been a Pakistani, therefore familiar, rather than an American.

That night, and the previous afternoon, made up my mind for me. It was after New Year's, I'd been in the Kingdom over three weeks, and it was time again for me to head back home.

My final act was to visit the bank in downtown Jubail in the company of Abdallah Fazza and Suliman. They were to arrange a letter of credit for Heritage Building, through their fellow bank in the capitol Riyadh, to Irving Trust in New York, and from there to Texas Commerce Bank in Houston. Once that was done, we would, in turn, start work on the steel forms, so we would have everything ready for delivery to the manufacturing site they would prepare by June. Everything looked smooth, all signals said go, so I flew back to Houston.

On the plane I was struck by how much the people leaving Saudi seemed to drink, and how much the people flying in tended to consume just before landing.

One final Saudi snafu for this visit. They closed the aircraft door, but the Air France pilot couldn't get clearance to start his engines. Saudi Immigration had missed its count of exit coupons and was unable to get its total in agreement with the Air France figures. We sat in radio communication, with the stews rechecking.

I went back to the galley in the 707, looking like a man in dire need of a scotch and soda, and said, sweetly, "Ma'am, would you please unlock the liquor cabinet?"

She looked at me, took pity, and showed her compassion by doing just that. There was a tangible feeling of pressure on board, and the booze locker would clear it up. Smiling, she undid the closures, removed her key, and without a word, moved forward to leave me alone. I took a couple of scotches, gave three oil-field hands a few assorted bottles, and resumed my seat after mixing a medicinal draft with soda and ice. My, my. How good and cold.

The stewardess was really bright. Or had been around the course before, because by innocently leaving, no one could accuse Air France of serving liquor on the ground in Saudi.

I returned, as usual, by way of Paris, bought Pat a gold necklace, and found, to my surprise, when I saw her, I didn't have a guilty conscience because of my big-time sex scenes.

Home was never better. The kids were all fine. I had been missed, and I was glad to be back. There was a lot to do, but we were closer than ever before.

In February, I received a telex from my Saudi partners. The hotel deal was near enough to a contract that they felt we'd better go faster with the manufacturing site to make the precast units. There was also a growing possibility we'd be called in to finish our bid on the hospital package.

All I needed was their financial participation. Which came in a month, through a letter of credit in the amount of $450,000. This was much of the cost of making the forms to the special needs of the conditions in Saudi, shipping them over, and erecting them on a site they would furnish. The money was to cover a part of our expenses to date, most of the cost of manufacturing, shipping the forms, and some commission we'd set in for Suliman.

A letter of credit is an interesting thing. It's an agreement between banks. One holds the money, and the other, at specified points according to the letter of agreement, dispenses it. Both banks get a fee for their troubles. The letter of credit is a good way to do business with someone in another land who uses another currency, and have both parties reasonably assured of getting paid.

We posted a twenty-thousand-dollar bond to ensure our part of the deal and drew down cash as the job proceeded. Having the money there renewed my confidence, even though it wasn't enough to pay for the whole forms package and other expenses we were running up on the project designs.

But I was happy, because the four hundred thousand-plus was the first dough I'd seen in the deal aside from George's and mine. It made me feel a lot better. It also got me working harder, to make the shipping date we'd agreed upon. The Arabs might be lackadaisical about time, but I sure as hell wasn't going to be.

Suddenly there were potential deals everywhere. The seven-story hotel, the hospital, and a call I'd made on the Ministry of Industry and Electricity began to show promise of a contract for a series of housing designs which could be put up by untrained labor.

Everything turned hot, including Suliman, who was breaking under the pressure. He would call, in a panic over some minor point, and urge me to get over there right then or the whole mess would blow up. I'd calm him down as best I could, but a day later he'd start all over again.

I went back in June for three weeks, then again in August for three more, but added nothing to the gains already made on previous trips. It's a temptation in the Mideast to go for too many projects. To do so will almost always result in disaster. You have to pick the ones you feel you can win, then stay with them. The deals were progressing, taking so much time I had to postpone working on some potential jobs in Iraq, Lebanon, and Kuwait.

The name of the good prince started coming up again, too. I was still more than interested in working with him, but we never did occupy the same space at the same time so we could talk.

The only notable occurrence on my September trip was the fulfillment of my dream to be Lawrence of Arabia. I was invited to a tent encampment of a desert tribe of Bedouins who were somehow related to Abdallah Fazza.

I'd returned from a meeting in Riyadh and was sitting in the majlis doing manly things when a new guest appeared. From the way he was dressed, as well as the way he was treated, I could tell he was someone special. Careful introductions were made all around, and he turned out to be a visiting nephew of a cousin of Abdallah Fazza's uncle or someone. He was another card-holding desert dweller. His camp was fifty miles away and he gave us reasonable directions, considering the lack of road signs and the sameness of the terrain.

Fazza was a great one for face. He showed me off as often as he could, because I was both a novelty and an important asset. I represented technology. At times I felt like I needed a banner to go over one shoulder, white satin with red, white, and blue letters: "American Technocrat."

There was no one in the majlis who could translate, so I was relying on my limited Arabic, trying to follow the chain of thought and get along. The desert tribe had a good year, they were glad to be back near civilization, and a celebration seemed in order. The conversation went on for a while, then Fazza suggested I be invited, to allow the sand sheikhs an opportunity to see and feel a real live Western engineering type. When the guest asked, using second-grade Arabic, if I might attend, I jumped at the opportunity. It was a chance, it developed, to present our hotel project to one of the top decision makers, who would also be present. Business and pleasure combined in one grand night of fun.

I could just see me surrounded by dancing girls, dressed in my white thauba and kafiya headdress, sitting on thick carpets and being fed by a nubile maiden. I knew that was a crock, but I was interested in going. My closest visit had been courtesy of MGM in a musical and I was positive there was more to the event than that.

We settled on a night and arranged transportation. Fazza would leave early the same afternoon, to talk tribal matters with the dunies. I would follow later with Suliman in his white Mercedes. He'd act as my translator. Abdallah Fazza assured me I'd be a big hit. The fact that I'd even bothered to try to learn Arabic marked me as a man of taste. The gesture would be appreciated.

It was more than a gesture. I was going to be back in about a year to run a crew composed of two hundred men. When that happened, I had to be able to communicate or there would be chaos.

The appointed day for the event came, and surprise of surprises, Suliman was on time. More or less. He was only a half hour late. That was shock number one. Fortunately, I was ready. Shock number two I wasn't ready for, but there it was anyway.

Suliman had a passenger. A young, fuzzy-bearded man-boy in his late teens or the first part of his twenties. He was introduced to me as his Royal Highness with a name sixteen syllables long. It drew great signs of respect, and was not repeated, because after hearing it once, everyone knew precisely who he was. I met my first true prince of the royal house. A son of the royal family, in fact of the branch now in power. He was a biggie. Figuratively speaking, of course. In person he was about five five, and there was no way he would scale out at more than 120. He had pale skin, with a light coffee-and-cream color, coarse hair as black as a raven, a sharp nose, and cheeks pocked by the usual acne. I'll say one thing for him, he did have a regal manner. A little shy, but regal. He spoke no English, and like Suliman was dressed in a pure-silk thauba. His was embroidered with the upper-class standard gold threads.

There was a loud farewell, the three of us jammed into the Mercedes, me in back with my roll of plans, them in front, and off we took. Normal Saudi drive. Casual demeanor in the face of terror. I thought driving was bad when we shot down the highway, but somewhere, way, way out in the sandy boonies, we took a turn onto a track which almost wasn't there, and it got wild. Sand everywhere. Scrub brush, too. Large pale-white rocks, big enough to hole the engine pan if they were hit wrong. Which bothered no one. Suliman and the prince conversed occasionally, and once in a while one of them would direct a remark to me. I was sore-handed from hanging on and my leg was cramped from slamming on the brakes for him, so I didn't respond very smartly.

On the way we passed a small Toyota pickup truck, sitting parked in the middle of some sand dunes, with two brown, ratty-looking camels in the back. They completely filled all available space and had crapped everywhere. My cohorts didn't seem to notice.

After a while, for no reason I could see, we slowed. The twin white plumes of dust and dirt we'd been rooster-tailing behind the car as we sped along dropped. We were all dusty inside because the windows had been down. Naturally, Suliman hadn't turned on his air conditioner, so it was hot. Wowie, it was hot. The air, a hundred miles inland from the coast, had taken the opportunity of drying itself, exchanging moisture for heat. It was past four in the afternoon. God knows what it was like at one or two o'clock. I knew I didn't want to find out.

We went along slower and slower, the engine making a low rumbling sound as we fishtailed up hill and down sandy dale. All at once, I became conscious of several men's voices. Merriment was apparent. I thought we'd arrived at the encampment. Wrong. We'd arrived at what is commonly known in the United States as a circle jerk.

The white Mercedes regally motored over a low rise and there, on the hillside facing us, no more than five yards away, were ten to fifteen men. All ages, ranging from late teens to grandfatherly. They were sitting around on the ground, close to one another. Everyone had his robe up at half mast. They were showing off their sandals, naked legs, and hairy genitals. Each had someone else's penis in hand and was stroking vigorously. I judged from the sounds they made that they were enjoying it immensely.

I was stunned. It was the first group grope I'd seen in Saudi, although I knew many of the men were bisexual. There had been an almost constant series of innuendoes and incidents which I could have taken as an invitation to a homosexual liaison, but usually nothing overt or too hard to handle.

I took my eyes off the pumping fists as it didn't seem seemly to stare, and found the prince's eyes watching me closely. His attention was diverted for an instant, and one of the men waved. He waved back, then returned his gaze to me.

"Do you find their behavior shocking?" Suliman said it with a leer.

"Not too." I was being supercoool. "It's strange, to me, because there would be nothing like this in the United States. But they all look old enough. Besides, they appear to be enjoying themselves."

"You do have a fine outlook, Mr. John. Of course they are enjoying themselves. What could be more natural?" Suliman started into what I was supposed to think was a translation of my conversation. He was up to his old trick, though, of elaborating and adding to what I'd said. There were too many chuckles and glances involved to be a straight exchange.

I was tempted to tell him what could be more natural, but kept quiet. Maybe in the desert what I saw was more normal than having sex with a female. It wasn't that way for me, but I was the guest.

What I didn't like was the way Princy was looking over his seat back at my crotch. Checking to see if the mutual masturbation scene turned me on, I guessed. It didn't. I wasn't put off by it, but it held little sexual fascination for me.

We drove slowly over the little rise and the group dropped from sight. The only sign of them was an occasional gleeful yell or yelp. I guess out in the rocks and sand you pass time as best you can.

A half mile from the playful group we came upon the three tents of the family.

A Bedouin tent doesn't look much like the ones in movies starring Errol Flynn or Burt Lancaster. Something is lost in transition from the MGM back lot to the middle of the desert. Mostly what was lost is shape. And size. The nomads' tents are much lower structures, made from a single sheet of black canvas, supported internally by irregularly arranged poles, so there are numerous peaked protrusions poking out at odd angles. Entranceways are dictated by the direction of the prevailing wind. There're lots of places where the tent material doesn't touch the sand, leaving many openings. Everyone in the tribe, however, comprehends where the front door is and uses it with great formality.

Inside, the dwelling is surprisingly sumptuous. Wind-billowed walls give a feeling of desert romance. The tightly woven carpets, for which the Islamic world is justly famed, abound in a profusion of wonderful colors, patterns, and sizes, covering up every square inch of ground. In some places the rugs are two and three layers deep, ends overlapping. Designed for desert use, their hand-knotted, tightly woven construction is impervious to sand or rocks working through. When you put them over the earth they make an ideal floor. When you put them over a scrap-wood floor laid on sand, they become palatial.

Once inside the tent it's easy to see where so many customs now accepted in the more ordinary Western-style Saudi homes started. The tradition of the majlis, from the idea of one tent for one family. When the whole lot, from Aunt Sukka to great-grandfather Abdallah through baby son Mohammed, use a single tent for shelter, they all use one room. A part of it is curtained off and allotted a private entrance to make a special area for the women. The rest is left to the men of the clan plus visitors who stop by.

The open-door policy is the only practical one, because there are no doors at all in the first place and no way to close them if there were. A thin drape can be hung over the main entrance to serve notice to honest passersby that the master of the house is otherwise engaged and not receiving, but the roomy part of the tent, the counterpart of the majlis, is open to kingsmen and fellow tribesmen twenty-four hours a day, 365 days a year. Enemies, too, are included. Friend or foe, a guest is offered a share of even the most meager supply of food.

The open-courtyard concept comes from this nomadic life. The men spend hours sitting together outside, by themselves as a group, shaded by a gazebo-like structure of poles and wind-tattered strips of cloth.

I'd already seen that they had fun ways to amuse each other during their long sessions in the out-of-doors but I assumed they had their more serious meetings, too. The courtyard in Saudi homes is used the same way the sun-shade shelter is by the nomads.

The custom of removing shoes before entering the majlis is also derived from desert traditions. The rugs will keep sand from working up through from below, but they only serve to trap sand brought in from the outside and accidentally spread on top, hence the small area near the entryway where everyone takes off his shoes and dusts himself down. This helps keep out some of the ever-present sheep manure, too. A good idea because of parasites carried in waste matter.

One problem with the tent, which no one much mentions or seems to notice, is how they smell. Cooking is done outside, but eating, smoking, sweating, and other human odor-producing pastimes, including bedwetting, are performed inside the confines of the tent. After a few years the cloth walls get ripe. It's not a bad smell, but it's not Chanel No. 5, by a long shot.

The flies are bad, too. Great clouds of the flying black critters. They're known to transmit certain diseases, but there is nothing to do about them except swat. And after a while you stop even that.

I never would have imagined swarms of flies in the middle of an arid wasteland. They follow man and domesticated animals, and are a pestilence of such a common nature that most desert dwellers seldom bother to shoo them. The robes help, leaving only the face and hands exposed to attack. Score another one for proper design in clothes for the Saudi climate.

Tonight, though, for our party, things were a little better. A special tent, the property of a high official of Saudi Arabia, had been erected. White silk with gold threads, twenty by thirty feet with a ten-foot ceiling, it had been put up just for this little soiree.

So there I was. Sitting on a cushion, legs crossed, dressed like a modern Lawrence of Saudi Arabia in a summer-weight Brooks Brothers suit, swaddled in a king's ransom of Oriental rugs, being served lukewarm goat's- or camel's-milk punch by a couple of Pakistanis, surrounded by my fellow men, a rough lot of rascally, dark-skinned Bedouins sporting coarse beards and mustachios.

Judas, that bunch looked sinister. But they were quite nice and made me feel right at home. I was the only one not in a robe. Fazza liked it that way as it made me appear even more exotic to his cohorts.

It was a Saudi shindig. After all had refreshed by washing and perfuming their hands outside in basins placed alongside water pitchers on the sand, we went in. Next was a brief ceremonial purification by the traditional use of myrrh smoke. A brightly smoldering sliver was passed from one to another, billowing a gray-white stream of smoke. Each guest waved it about, then fanned the smoke into his headdress, wafting it around like a light fog. The aroma reminded me of my time as an altar boy.

Next came a small glass of pear nectar. Canned, not cold, but wet and welcome.

Dinner was served in a single, gigantic course, heaped on large trays. Gritty dates, gritty boiled rice with raisins, a gritty vegetable mix of undetermined origin, and a couple of trays of freshly slaughtered goat, which had been burned over a fire so it was charred on the outside, blood-red rare inside.

I don't know how the desert tribes keep their teeth past the age of thirty. It seems to me the grit would wear groves in them. Sand is everywhere, so every meal is like a picnic at the beach. A lack of tables to keep things up off the ground only compounds the problem. But since a table would look goofy tied to a camel's back when they moved camp, they did without. Reason behind another custom. Everything a desert dweller owns has to be able to fold, break down, or come apart for packing.

Tradition was followed exactly. The host had assigned his second in command to visit with the guests of honor while he personally supervised and shuttled the servants. When every guest was satiated, he would finally eat. Always last.

During the meal, one of the Pakis dumped a whole tray of meat. Nothing was said. No fuss, no commotion. The host rolled the mess up in a rug, quietly doing all the work himself, and dragged it outside. He was back overseeing in a minute, ensuring that the meal would be a calm, tranquil time. I'm sure the poor Pakistani got his butt thrashed later, but no one present even appeared to notice the problem.

As the food was served the sun went down and the party got going. The guests started talking animatedly as the servants lit

Coleman gasoline lanterns which sputtered and gave off sharp hissing sounds. Light from the lamps reflected off the shiny golden tent fabric, the greasy faces of the guests as they stuffed themselves, each using only the fingers of his right hand as any right-thinking person would do to show breeding, and the brilliant reds, blues, tans, and blacks of the rich rugs.

There is more to eating with the fingers than is at first apparent. The trick is to roll up a ball of rice, throw back your head, and drop it into your mouth. The rice tends to stick to your fingers, so you end up sucking it off. Not tidy. Somehow, a Saudi gentleman is able to keep the rice from sticking. Less sucking. More tidy.

I was seated next to Fazza, who was, in turn, next to the host sheikh. Suliman was on my left and the boy prince who'd ridden down with us was on his other side. Everytime I'd catch his eye he'd give me a shy wink.and a coquettish, silly smile.

The host gave me a lot of smiles, too, which, combined with the desert night and a feeling of isolation, made me a little apprehensive. He was a tough-looking older man with sharp, dark hawk eyes and a grin that gave him a death's-head appearance. Because of the spots on his sun-freckled skin and his yellowish coloring, I judged he had a liver problem.

During the feasting there were endless rounds of tea, cups of the Arab sweet coffee, and refined conversation. I'd been hoping for dancing girls, but a girl dancing in front of all the men was the last thing anyone there but me would imagine appropriate for a party like this.

It was a pretty strong affair. The tent, the middle of the desert, the calm, genteel air of the diners, the food, their Rudolph Valentino dress, the strange smells, the whole scene.

Seeing I was through, my host signaled me. Armed with my rolled-up proposal for the Moon Plaza Hotel, and followed by Suliman, we went outside.

A neat hundred thousand dollars' worth of carpets had been spread as the floor of an open-air pavilion. A dozen hissing Coleman lamps were scattered around the edges, providing sharp white circles of light. Overhead, the sky was deep black. Stars were bright, multicolored points. Men, who had finished their meal, were sitting in groups on the rugs, talking and taking their ease. It was hot, so everyone was damp with sweat. A few water pipes were gurgling.

Suliman led me to one bunch, and after a while slipped me into the ring which had formed around a lamp. It was time to talk a little business, so, as custom dictated, we had come away from the tranquillity of the dining area, where, if need be, we could give vent to emotion.

My host asked to look at the proposal, so I passed it over. He studied the drawings carefully, then settled back and began reading the text. Occasionally he would make a comment, which, even with my limited Arabic, I could understand. He admired the completeness of the report and the fact that it had been translated into his language.

Finally, he handed it back to me, saying, with a smile, "You shall have the twelve million riyals."

Suliman translated, but he needn't have. I could tell perfectly well the old man had bought the project. As a ranking official, he had the power to make it happen. Our meeting took a total of five minutes and we adjourned to the tent.

Tent, hell, I thought. Let's get back into town where I can call George and tell him the good news. But that would never have done, so it was back into the tent and back to gracious living.

As I sat I couldn't help but wonder how much of the twelve mil would eventually work its way into the pockets of my fellow revelers. It didn't make the slightest difference to me. All I wanted to do was get started. There would be more than enough for everyone when the job was done.

After three more demitasse cups of instant tea, just to be social, I was ready to go to what I laughingly referred to as "home." Looking around for Suliman, I spotted a white-robed younger man, an aide to the high official, coming through the remnants of the crowd toward me. Making a hand signal which we interpret as "go away," but in Saudi means "follow me," he spoke his little English with an urgent attitude. "Come. We are going for a drive."

I got up and moved with him, trying in my broken Arabic to explain, "No, I'm not in the mood for a drive." When I saw Suliman in the back seat, I figured a further business talk had been ordered and he was along to translate.

Some business. I should have known better. Especially when I spotted the young prince, with two associates, being directed toward the car. The next thing I knew, the back door was opened

Suliman got out, Princy got in, and the high official's face, cheek to cheek with Suliman, was looking in the window, wolf's smile in place, but with a tinge of sly amusement. It was obvious they were out to get the prince laid. A driver climbed inside behind the wheel. He had a bottle, Styrofoam cups, and some ice. Where he'd gotten it, I didn't know. Or care.

"Have a drink, Mr. John."

I shook my head, but he persisted, with untypical Arab aggressiveness. Still saying no, I settled back. Princy edged over toward me, expectantly, but I gave him a hard look which slowed him down. The driver, not satisfied with the turn of events, cranked the engine into life and roared out of camp, throwing sand everywhere.

Now that bothered me. Inside the confines of the encampment, I was safe. It's a rule of Bedouin life. But suddenly I wasn't inside any longer. I was bouncing insanely across rocks and sand dunes under a silver moon in a car with two men who had sexual ideas for my entertainment. I was getting excited, all right, but not the way they wanted.

This is a good place to make something clear. I don't have any feelings about the homosexual side of the Arab male's nature one way or the other. I don't find it bad or good, merely a matter of geography and custom. If I'd grown up in a country where there was almost no opportunity to meet in private with a more or less consenting member of the opposite sex, and there was no stigma attached to homosexual activity, I have a hunch I'd be positively in favor of homosexual diversions.

Different strokes, different folks, different ways to do it. Suits me. What didn't suit me was the sometimes heavy way some Arabic men went about soliciting my favors. I am more than willing to take a nice no from a lady, so I feel they should be willing to take a nice no from me. Some wouldn't take no, nice or otherwise. That's what gets me upset. Sex is a personal matter. Very personal. I think I have the right to select the person with whom I'll enjoy it. Off the soapbox, back to the matter at hand, in the back seat of the nutty white Mercedes, bouncing through the rocky, silver sand dunes.

Our driver spoke only a few words, to say how lucky I was to be able to view the desert at night. I would have agreed, but we were banging around so much as the car jounced over the rough ground I could hardly see out. Hanging on took all my attention.

Finally we stopped at the bottom of a low rise. Here it comes, I thought, put-out or get-out time. Getting out was out of the question. We were way the hell and gone in the middle of nowhere. Just the three of us, all pals in one cozy car.

The young prince slid over and put his head on my shoulder. I slid him back as gently as possible.

He said something in a plaintive tone which caused the driver to turn in his seat and face me.

"What is wrong, Mr. John? Relax. He is trying to be friendly."

A scene from my senior year in high school flashed back to me. Me and my girl in the front seat and a friend, two years younger, with his lady in the back. They couldn't get started making out. Awkward deal.

"Have a drink, Mr. John. It'll help you relax."

That, too, was familiar. In high school we all believed if you could get her to take a drink, you could get her. Worked as often as not. Although it probably was due to the fact that she had decided to play long before she decided to drink.

"If I take one drink, will you start up this junk heap and drive me home?"

He got busy with the cups and ice. No sooner than I had the drink in my hot little hand, I had the hot little prince back. He took my acceptance of the whiskey as an acquiescence to his advances. I put him down again, this time with a little more force. Which really started the hell-raising. Princy went into a screaming jumble of words. The driver tried to calm him. From what I could decipher, he was saying he'd have me in jail for manhandling His Royal Personage.

Trembling, our chauffeur finally got him to shut up, then turned to reason with me. "What is the matter with you, Mr. John?" He sounded disgusted and scared.

Maybe it was my recollections of high school or just a stroke of luck, but I replied without thinking. "I've got a terrible headache and I want to go home."

There was a long silence, then a straggled conversation. The man behind the wheel started the engine and we motored back to the encampment. When we found it, all the lights were low and the men were lying about together in sets of two, four, and six, doing what came naturally.

The driver had a hushed conversation with Suliman, the prince, and the high official. Suliman spoke to me before he followed them into the main tent.

"I am going to try to patch things up. Mr. John, you must learn to act better. The royal prince could have you killed or jailed for touching him. In formal situations, you wouldn't be allowed even to talk to him without bowing your head. He was just being friendly. Now I'll show you my friendship by trying to patch things up." He followed the other two into the big tent.

I sat in the car. In a way I was worried, in a way I wasn't. Inside the camp I felt safe. The official, Abdallah Fazza, and Suliman all knew I was the key to money they hoped to make. They weren't going to let anything too serious happen to me. On the other hand, if Princy was as powerful as Suliman said, maybe they couldn't stop it.

I waited. And waited. One or two men looked longingly in through the window at me, but I'd been receiving that kind of glance all night.

It was an odd sensation for me to have my body sexually appraised. I'm not fat, have a fairly good physical self-image, and for my age am in good shape. It's one thing for a guy at the University Club back in Houston to look me over in the shower, assessing my state of obesity or fitness after a tennis game, but it was another to have someone look me over as a potential sex object.

Two or three in the tent earlier that night had given me up-and-down stares reserved in the West for a knockout lady. One point is sure. I developed a whole new appreciation for the women's liberation movement. Being a sex object isn't very neat at all. Especially, as far as I'm concerned, when the interested party is of your same sex.

After an hour, Suliman came out. He seemed relieved.

"I have fixed it. I must get Abdallah, then we will leave."

He was gone again and I was alone again, in the midst of the silver sand sea.

The frivolity continued until the wee hours. At least ten-thirty. Which is late for the peoples of the desert. They arise with dawn, to move about in the coolest part of the day, shelter up during the heat of midmorning, then come back alive in the later afternoon. By eleven they are bedded down again, except for the guys on duty who are looking after the sheep-goat-camel herd-flock. Dawn comes early.

The Saudi official gave a final salutation in the name of Allah, and men straggled to their cars in small groups. The clear, hot night air was filled with the sounds of starting engines. One at a time, headlights punching dark holes through the black night, the Mercedeses, Land-Rovers, Suburbans, and other assorted machines slued off through the sand dunes toward the narrow two-lane road.

Churning through the bright desert, we drove past a herd of a hundred or so noisy camels. Everywhere, goats and sheep were bedded down for the night. The lumps were hard to see in the glare of the headlights. When we reached the paved road I relaxed. It was hard for me to remember that the sandy dirt path we'd driven on had been, not more than twenty years ago, considered a main artery. The only traffic then was an occasional Aramco vehicle or a camel.

Settling back, I thought of the evening's events. Final approval on the twelve million riyals made me smile.

Suliman spoke quietly. "You hurt his feelings." He said it slowly, concentrating on missing an oncoming truck. We did, but only by a coat of sand-blasted paint.

"How?"

"He paid you the honor of noticing you. Thousands of his subjects would be thrilled to be so honored."

"A notice like that I don't need. It's a cultural thing. I don't have sex with men."

Suliman nodded. "At home, of course not. You would be called queer. But here, there is no problem. He is very much attracted to you."

Back to the diplomacy game. I didn't want to offend a member of the royal family, even if it was a remote member. On the same hand, I wasn't interested in a sexual union to ward off a possible attack on my contracts.

Abdallah was openly peevish, almost hostile. He kept demanding a translation from Suliman. I didn't blame him. Tomorrow, he was going to have to do a lot of apologizing in my behalf to make things right. I was sorry to have inconvenienced him. In this instance, I felt it was better him a little than me a lot.

I closed my eyes in the bounding car. Suliman kept on until, raising my hand, I stopped him.

"Suliman," I spoke in a low, serious voice, "please. I really do have a headache."

We drove back to the house in silence.

A Thousand and One Arabian Frights

Through November 1977

I broke my stay in Saudi in September. I was lonesome for my family, all business seemed to be progressing smoothly, and I wanted out of the Arabic world. The constant pressure of living in a culture so alien-strange was taking its toll. The crowning blow came on a Monday, early in the afternoon.

My contacts with Americans in Saudi Arabia had been limited on this trip. I was immersed in business dealings with the government, a guest in Fazza's home, living away from the main-stream of American travel, and had little time for visiting.

I knew, from previous chats with "old hands," how serious the Saudis were about carrying out their mixed legal-religious obligations, but I had never come into personal confrontation with the system.

That Monday morning I'd been in several meetings with key people from two major construction firms. All were U.S. citizens, and I was feeling very "back home." The talks went well and, enthusiastic, I started walking in downtown Dammam. No particular place in mind, I was wandering, looking at the sights, such as they were, and enjoying people involved in their regular routines.

Dammam is not a big place. It's built right on the seacoast, and the thickest part of the town is along the waterfront. As you move back, away from the blue waters of the Persian Gulf, the buildings thin out, being slowly replaced by rolling sand dunes and green date palms which, in turn, after fifty yards, give way to the edge of the arid, rock-covered desertlike mainland.

The Saudis have made an effort to claim about a mile of additional coastal footage by contracting with the Dutch to fill in a vast shallow area with sand dredged up from farther out. The water in that spot was no more than a couple of feet deep, so it was possible. What resulted is a large, open area. In another year or so it will be the heart of a new city.

Now, however, it's an unofficial recreational facility. Kids and young men have lined off a bunch of soccer pitches using rocks and cans for boundaries. Its like a sandlot football field back home. Not too regular in shape, but good enough to play on. And play they do. I watched long enough to see several guys who were plenty proficient.

It looked funny, though, and drove home the strangeness of the land. The kids and youngsters raced back and forth, barefoot, holding up the edges of their robes to free their legs and give them running room. They looked like a cluster of women frightened by a mouse. The thauba is a fine garment to beat the heat but not too suitable as athletic wear.

Standing with my face to the gulf, a tall red radio tower was on my right. To the left, an even taller TV antenna. Other than these and a mosque tower, the visible landmarks of the city are almost nil.

Buildings, with few exceptions, are five or six stories maximum, made from low-quality masonry or even dried, sun-hardened mud. The majority are only one- or two-story structures. All are in dubious repair. The brick-and-mortar exteriors were covered, long ago, with a single, lonesome coat of paint, most of which has peeled away in the hot, humid climate, leaving spots of chipped gray showing through washed-out robin's-egg blue, dirty white, and off-pink, three frequently used colors.

The streets are narrow, usually unpaved, and filled with chuckholes. In many areas there are no sidewalks. Outside faces of buildings come right to the edge of the street, with no extension for a walkway.

When it rains, the water meanders downhill, uncontained by gutters or subterranean drains. It doesn't rain that much, though, except for the month of January. Even then, the total amount of precipitation is certainly not enough to cause a demand for an underground drainage system. Although the surface runoff does make septic tanks and the sanitary sewage system overflow frequently, which, in turn, is probably the reason January is a high point on the cholera calendar.

I usually tried to avoid the streets without sidewalks. It's a scary feeling to be trundling down one, up to your ankles in dust, and hear an impatient car horn suddenly blare behind you. When it happens, there is no place to go. The natives just back up to a wall, press against it to make themselves thinner, and allow the vehicle to roar past. And they do roar by. Saudi drivers don't back off down narrow streets; they stay on the loud pedal. Two things occur as a consequence. First, no car's suspension, even a Mercedes', can take being slammed over potholes at thirty or forty miles an hour. As the front wheels hit the washouts, the vehicle is jerked from one side to another. The erratic motion is enhanced by having the driver steer violently, in a mistaken belief he is avoiding some of the worst obstacles. The second is the amount of dust the passing wheels kick up. It's not my idea of a good time to stand, gut sucked up and back against a wall, while a Saudi drives a wide car, bouncing from side to side, through the canyon of walls. Then, you're no sooner over your fright, and sometimes a little amazed to still be alive, when the rolling dust covers and chokes you. One or two incidents like that, and I learned. I tried to avoid streets with no sidewalks. Which limited my direction of travel to the areas of the city where many people congregate.

I'd been by the large, battered mosque next door to the cluster of government buildings several times, but had taken no particular notice of it except to be curious about the size of the crowd milling around.

Today was no exception. I was walking casually. There was nothing much out of the ordinary. As I approached the mosque, I was struck by the sound of a large group screaming and chanting. They were making the same kind of noises you hear in a bullring, excitement mixed with tension and bloodlust. There were so many people pressed into the exterior courtyard they were overflowing out onto the street. Men—they were all men naturally—many holding their young sons' hands, were standing on tiptoes at the back of the throng, trying to see over the heads of earlier arrivals. When they stretched, necks straining to get a better view, their robes came up their dark calves, revealing callused, dusty feet and leather sandals. It was impossible for me to tell what was going on. Could have been anything from a bingo game to a donkey auction. But everyone seemed tensely expectant.

I ambled along, still relaxed, interested in the proceeding enough to look in through one of the openings. Since I'm half a head taller than most Saudis, I could see into the interior of the courtyard adjoining the mosque, but all I could recognize was a small sea of the backs of red-and-white-checkered kafiya cloth head covers. The men inside were looking in the same direction.

I hadn't actually stopped when I peeked inside, just slowed considerably. I felt a hand grip my arm, pulling me gently into the crowd of yelling people, then another hand, and before I could resist, I was being shoved through the packed mass into the open space. Somehow, bodies parted ahead of me as I was forced along, so I was moving toward the front ranks.

There was a tangible air of excitement around me. The interior was bright. Freshly whitewashed stone walls were punctured periodically with open spaces in the form of arched windows, which let streamers of brilliant sunlight through to fall on the kafiyaed heads of six or eight hundred people who jammed the grounds. I was passed along quickly by howling, bearded, laughing men, not roughly, not gently, just remorselessly. I'd never seen a Saudi crowd in such holiday fervor. Not even at a soccer game.

A stone wall ran from the mosque to encircle a courtyard on all four sides. I was pushed along into this private area. The mosque proper, showing architecture indicating it had been influenced by some Holy Land Christian church, filled the background.

The enclosed space, except for a twenty-foot semicircle in the middle, was crammed with yelling, chanting men. Six or eight people were standing alone. On the ground was a formless bundle.

I was frightened, because I felt I knew what was going on. I'd heard of it from other Americans. This was a day for sentences to be carried out. The crowd, spotting me as a Westerner, had dragged me in so I could see justice being done.

What I saw done that day may or may not have been just. I wasn't given the details of the cases. But it was enough to wake me from a sound sleep soaked in sweat for weeks afterward.

As soon as the men stopped shoving me forward, I managed to grasp something of what was being shouted. The bundle on the ground had been a woman. When I realized she had been stoned to death, I was glad her body was wrapped in the white sheet. From the few red stains I could see seeping through, I'm certain her remains wouldn't have been a pretty sight.

I'd seen people in the street earlier throwing stones, but I wrote it off to a Wailing Wall ceremony. It had been for real. The woman, and I never did get the story right, was accused of either having committed adultery or of having adulterous intentions toward a neighbor's friend. Convicted, she was sentenced to death. They rolled her up in a muslin mattress cover, then had her fellow townspeople throw rocks until she stopped breathing.

My attention had been fixed on the body under the sheet, so it came as a surprise when the crowd sucked in its breath like one pair of giant lungs. I looked up to see a white-robed man hold up a long, wicked-looking black steel butcher knife. He waved it at the rest of his crew. Two men had been holding another, and now they hustled him forward. He was so petrified he could barely move his legs. They dragged him.

Another white robe appeared, waving a wide leather strap, which he quickly wrapped around the captive's forearm. He pulled it tight, grabbed it with both hands, bracing his arms, and nodded to the knife wielder. The two men holding the third set their grip.

I knew the penalty for theft was the loss of the right hand. Third offense, of course. And I knew they cut off the hand. I had heard it was done in a hospital under surgically clean, supervised conditions. I was about to learn it wasn't always quite that way.

The man with the knife, a look of grim determination on his face, grabbed the offender's hand. The strap holder tightened up even more. Instead of severing the member with one chop, the executioner started slowly cutting and slicing away, whacking at the white bone until it snapped. I could hear the grating and cracking clearly over the noise of the crowd.

The prisoner was screaming and begging, the men were yelling, some were chanting, red blood was pouring past the tourniquet strap, and the smell of the packed place was unwashed people, fresh slaughter, and exhaust gas from passing automobiles.

Finally, after what seemed an hour, the executioner made one last cut with a sawing movement and the prisoner's hand came away, free. He held it up for a moment so those in back could see, then casually dropped it. It fell into a partially open position, already looking gray-white, on the rough black paving stones of the courtyard. A little blood came from the ragged edge of the severed wrist, but not as much as might have been expected.

I thought it was over, but it wasn't. For the next act, a man stepped forward carrying a can. A plain old square, shiny tin one-gallon jelly can, blackened on the bottom from being over an open fire. I couldn't tell what was inside, but it was hot. Boiling almost, smelling like kerosene. It was apparently oil, an unguent, or some medicine in water. When they dunked the prisoner's stump, it was all the three of them could do to hold on to him. The thief went wild with pain. Eyes rolled up in his head, his yelling was strangled, and his whole body shook.

Three more men came through the crowd, which noisily parted for them. They took over from the original trio, put the prisoner onto a stretcher, and wheeled him off to a waiting ambulance. I could hear the rising-falling wail of the siren outside in the street as the watchers dispersed. Two of the original group of executioners picked up the remains of the woman in the stained sheet, the third gingerly lifted the severed hand by a finger, careful not to allow blood to drip on his clothes, and they went off, into the enclosure.

I was alone. It was over as quickly as it had started, the crowd gone in darting steps, the courtyard quiet. Except for the blood-stains there was no sign of what had taken place. But in the eye of my mind I could see the poor man struggling and in the ear of my brain I could hear him screaming out his agony.

I stood for quite a while, shaken. It sure as hell wasn't the first time I'd seen blood. My turn in the Army had taken care of that. But Judas Priest, I'd been unprepared for the barbaric act I had been forced to witness. I wasn't sick, I wasn't stricken, I didn't want to throw up. I just wanted to get the hell out of Saudi Arabia and get back home where I understood what to expect and what was going on.

Abdallah Fazza, Suliman Rasi, and the rest of the people involved in our deal weren't too happy about my decision to pack and go. No one tried to stop me, but I could sense a certain coolness. I met with them on my last evening in Fazza's majlis, to go over what needed doing before we could proceed. The three of us came to complete agreement, set deadlines, and that was that. Or so I thought.

I arrived back in Houston on September 24. Pat commented I'd lost weight, but her home cooking quickly restored it and added more.

From that day through December 12, Suliman Rasi besieged me with batteries of telephone calls, cablegrams, and letters. Question after question, about the very things we'd agreed upon in our final meeting, flowed in. No one over there was able to handle the simplest query from government officials or private industry.

I met with George to discuss our situation. The deal still seemed promising but, clearly, someone was going to have to go soon after the New Year and stay until the major projects were completed.

George volunteered to be the one to relocate. He was the logical choice, because of his years of experience with the building systems and the fact that my family still had scars from our Iranian sojourn. We finally decided he'd leave sometime in the next nine or ten months, as soon as the funds came through and we'd completed work on the forms.

We were both back in Saudi before Christmas. On the twentieth, Suliman called. He was in a state of raw panic. The deal on the hotel was falling through, the deal on the housing was breaking up, Fazza was backing out of building the erection site for our forms, and whatever else could go wrong was, had, or was about to.

I wasn't too eager to be away for Christmas, but on December 22, George and I, suspicious, left, armed with our second extensive array of Christmas presents for the members of our partnership, their wives, and children. We arrived on the twenty-fourth, early enough to discover we'd again fallen victim to exaggeration.

We stayed only long enough to assure ourselves the business was on track, then came back. George departed ahead of me. I held over to handle a couple of important meetings arranged after our arrival.

I pulled into the driveway of my home in Houston twenty-six days after I'd left. It was the thirteenth of January 1977.

By February, we'd completed the preliminary drawings for all engineering of the steel forms. Converted to metric sizes and scaled for Saudi Arabia's ten-foot ceilings, as opposed to our eight-foot heights, they looked longer and thicker than the ones we'd been accustomed to. Later when we tried them, they worked well.

Three hundred fifty thousand pounds of steel and they operated like a Swiss watch. The simplified design had gone a long way toward making them Arab-proof. All we had to do now was send them over and dig into the next portion of cash to set up the precast manufacturing plant. Jobs would be booked for years in advance.

That's what I thought. It didn't work that way. I went back and forth to Saudi so many times in the next few months that I began to feel like an airborne yo-yo.

Potential new contracts flowed in faster than I could handle them. The hotel was coming along, an engineering-construction firm was interested in buying 150 houses made from our modules, Petromin, the Saudi government petroleum organization, was discussing three hundred houses, and another two hundred were in negotiation from other sources.

Fazza was a happy man. The business, due to our imagination and guidance, was prospering even before it opened. He'd been given a sum of money from the government to develop the manufacturing site for the forms factory, so he was ahead going in.

One thing worried me. On my trip in June, and again when I returned in August, no site work, as far as I could see, had been done, even though we'd helped locate a half dozen contractors who could do the job. Site preparation, as well as its development, was the responsibility of the group Fazza had put together. When I asked about the apparent lack of progress, excuses, supported by assurances, sprouted like weeds. They had our instructions. Negotiations were underway. Work was imminent.

I reminded everyone involved that George and I were going to arrive at the end of the first week in November, about the sixth or seventh, with the forms, ready to swing into action. That was met with cheers and more promises. They would be ready.

I also went round and round with Fazza, who continued to show me off, over expense money. He swore he'd have me a check on my next visit, but it was always on the next visit, no matter which one I was on. In less than a year, George and I had spent $118,000 of our cash on travel, telephone, telex, and working drawings. This was due from the partnership. The four hundred thousand for the forms would be collectible by late November, if all went well. Then we'd be on our way to big bucks.

One final incident occurred on this trip which sticks in my mind as being typical of my Saudi period. It should have told me something about what was to come, but it was so obliquely funny at the time I didn't take it to heart.

One of the main points I'd been bugging Fazza about was a stone-crushing plant to make aggregate rock necessary for the concrete modules. He, and several of his people, had been over the matter many times. I'd even supplied him with detailed designs and had taken the time to describe what we needed. He'd promised to have it ready, and I demanded to see it.

To my utter surprise, Abdallah showed obvious pride. He set a field trip-site visit for early the following morning. That, I thought, was more like it.

Abdallah got up next day at eleven for breakfast. Good old Daoud, man of compliment wife, brought me the news the second the sheikh hit the majlis. After eating and spending a half hour with his hubbly-bubbly pipe, Fazza was ready. Fahad at the wheel and off we went. In the wrong direction. The cassara, which is the proper name for an aggregate crushing works, was to the northwest. We went south. "For gasoline," I learned. Abdallah was taking a ten-mile drive to stop at a station where gas was eleven cents a gallon and there was a tea shop.

It was a typical Saudi filling station. An acre of unimproved, raw land set back about two hundred feet off the edge of the blacktop road with a rutted driveway leading to a twenty-by-forty-foot concrete pad sprouting three pumps. As we drove up, the attendant was using the gas nozzle to hose down the pad area and clear it of trash. Forgetting the fire hazard, there was nowhere else in the world a man would use twenty to thirty gallons of gasoline to clean eight hundred square feet of concrete. Gasoline was cheaper than fresh water in many places. The practice did have its drawbacks, however, as shown by the high number of burned-down gas stations I saw.

After a lengthy tea break, we were ready to go again. Fahad at the wheel and off we roared, back the way we'd come. Finally, on the far southern outskirts of the city, we arrived. The site of our wonderful cassara.

Six Pakis came running up, then started groveling and kissing Fazza's hand. When I was introduced, I got the same veneration. The men lived in a small mud-brick hut off to one side, standing out in the bright open, sun hammering down. The grand tour included a peek inside the door which was two old rice sacks nailed to the top of the frame. Filth, flies, fleas, and six plain mats for sleeping. I made a mental note on improving the living quarters because sickness would cut into productivity. Besides, workers need to live better than that, no matter what. Good living conditions and good work went hand in hand on all my jobs. This one wasn't going to be the exception.

Da dum. We needed a fanfare, Fazza was so proud. A hundred yards away was the mighty rock crusher.

That miser had somehow gotten hold of an old dilapidated truck, had it jacked up, pulled a rear tire, and attached a belt to the wheel. The belt looped over the pulley of one of the most beat-up, clapped-out, light-duty rock crushers I'd ever seen. It was German made, so after at least twenty years' use it still worked, but not well. With thirty guys to feed it around the clock and take away the aggregate it produced, we'd have about 10 per cent of what we needed.

I started to scream about what had happened to our plans and all the careful instructions, but stopped. It would be better to attack this in private, not in front of his employees. Abdallah Fazza, oblivious to my reaction, kept trying to get me to compliment him on his ingenuity. It was clear he didn't have the slightest idea of how large an operation we'd been talking about. It was clearer still his ignorance could lead to big troubles.

Did it ever. Looking back, I still believe at least a part of our problems stemmed from the overall lack of sophistication in a number of areas—financial, mechanical, and social—existing among leaders in the Kingdom. It isn't any wonder. In less years than my lifetime key Saudis have gone from a nomadic desert life tending herds to being dominant figures in boardrooms of major corporations. Or into deals like ours.

That's a more difficult change than it may sound. The desert existence isn't hard, it's the hardest. Survival is a daily goal. To survive, anything goes. Until they become experienced, Westerners don't believe or appreciate this facet of Bedouin character. I call it their "water-hole survival mentality." The Saudi Arabian admires a reflex action which cashes in on any opportunity. And our deal was an opportunity ripe with potential for cashing.

On April 13, 1977, the letter of credit was released by our bank in Texas. There was a hassle over some points but we finally got enough to do our part of the job. We did it, fast. The completed forms were delivered to a new company site we'd developed on the outskirts of Houston for final testing on July 10. They worked. Exactly as planned. There was quite a celebration that evening, because we were on the last lap. Or so George and I thought.

In the next sixty days, I was as busy as a cat taking laxatives. Three of my nine lives were digging, three were doing, and three were scouting for new territory. I was hopping back and forth to the Kingdom like a commuter. On September 10, while in Saudi Arabia I formalized the government registration of the project, which meant we could ship our part of the bargain by next available boat. We'd already done the required packing, so on September 29, when we saw the forms safely loaded aboard S.S. *Gutentels*, at the Port of Houston, we threw another wingding celebration. This one was all the sweeter because, by working night and day, we delivered our cargo in time for it to be one of the last loadings prior to a dock strike.

Telexes flew back and forth, confirming and reconfirming that all was ready. As far as we could tell, the site was prepared and the foundations for the form supports in place. George and I had our tickets for November 1. We'd be there in plenty of time to take delivery and set up the operation.

Then the balloon broke. An urgent message from a project in the Peruvian jungle reached George late on the evening of October 25. He tried to cope with the difficulty by phone, but it was no good. Since he was a master at solving construction problems, his body on the premises down there was the only thing which could keep that contract afloat. We discussed it at length, deciding I should proceed to Dhahran. If I got there on the sixth, I could meet *Gutentels* and wrap up our part of the bargain. We had a tentative contract with a small English firm to supply the necessary labor, so I'd even have access to an experienced crew in case I needed them. I'd be back in a week if everything went well, or considering it was Saudi Arabia, by Thanksgiving if all moved at the camel's pace I expected.

I have coined a saying about dealing in Saudi Arabia: Look for the best, expect the worst, and don't be dismayed by complete and utter disaster. That's what I walked into. Complete and utter disaster.

The forms arrived. When they hit the port, the partners, who had agreed to hire a crane to off load the huge metal units from the delivery trucks in Jubail, began to agrue about paying for this part of the project. While we screamed at each other, the forms were lowered to the dock, where demurrage, a quaint custom prevalent in the transportation field, started. This is a rental of the wharf space to hold the items just unloaded, starting ten days from the instant the weight of the item touches land. It stops when the goods are removed from the area. In between it goes up quick. There's a limit on how much time dock space may be occupied. At some point, the auction man turns up.

I knew about demurrage. The Saudi partners knew about demurrage. Which is why I hadn't shipped the forms until their telex assured me the site was ready. Which, of course, it wasn't.

Twenty-five thousand dollars later, it still wasn't. I was. Ready, that is, to do something, to stop the ever-increasing demurrage charges. I went out to the docks frequently to inspect the equipment, worrying about the effect of salt air on the uncovered, exposed steel. All the critical parts were in sealed containers, but I was concerned about the main shapes rusting. Fortunately, they were designed to take a lot of abuse, and the small amount of surface oxidation they picked up would strip itself away during the first few minutes of use.

I found the port security wasn't very tight, but since the forms weighed tons each, I hoped no one would steal the damn things while I tried to settle with my Saudi partners. What there was to settle, though, puzzled me. Fazza was being obstinate about paying for the crane to move the forms off the trucks after arrival on site. He was also bucking about the demurrage charges, of which there would have been none had he done what our written agreement called for in the first place. This wasn't the first place, though, it was Saudi Arabia, and it was going to take time, which was beyond me, because so far as I could tell, everyone should have been eager to get the forms off that seven-mile wharf and put them to work. That's how little I knew about Arabic business practices. In spite of the best advice from bankers and shipping-company personnel, Fazza remained obstinate.

To keep things alive, I began checking on the forms more often, hoping my presence would make it appear there was some action and nothing had been abandoned.

On the evening of November 26, 1977, the day after another of my visits to the unprepared site and to the port, I sat in the majlis and announced my plans to go home until after January. If I thought I had troubles before, I was sadly mistaken.

6 The Start of the Sheikh Down

Into December 1977

The seats in the U.S. consulate in Dhahran were among the most comfortable of any public area in Saudi Arabia. A combination of governmental protection of local businessmen and the location inside the Kingdom of a chair-distributing firm which imported some horribly uncomfortable yellow plastic cheapies may be two of the reasons why the populace still prefers a foam-rubber cushion on the floor.

Seeing the consulate, set back in its compound off the road, gave me a thrill. The brilliant flash of the Stars and Stripes, flapping in the damp, hot wind, offered a haven. Inside, it was like home—if you happen to live in a post office. There was a lobby, long lines, and several windows where people dealt with disinterested American officials over the problem of acquiring visas or other minor matters.

Our ambassadorial staff exists inside the Kingdom only at the pleasure of the King. Not too different from embassies and consulates in Western nations. What was different, though, was the fact that the Saudi government, in the form of armed police and soldiers, had upon occasion, entered our facilities without request or consent. They would do so again. Contrary to international convention, our consular offices were not considered to be sovereign U.S. ground. More, no member of our staff could leave the Kingdom without specific permission from the Saudi government.

In the light of subsequent events in Iran, these points are interesting. If one Arab nation forced us into this arrangement, why not another? It's a tough question for our State Department.

How long I sat I don't know for sure, but it was long enough to go back through my mind over the whole damn mess. One thing came from my reverie. I was getting a little mad: at the way things had gone; at the way I'd been treated last night, what with the .45 caliber grease-gun holdup and all; and with the consulate people who didn't look all that busy but were clearly too occupied to see me.

After what seemed hours, a real live woman, dressed in a skirt and blouse, who walked and talked American, but was English, came through the swinging doors marked "Staff Only" to single me out of the waiting crowd. Watching her bottom twist put me into a better mood.

She listened sympathetically. An interesting experience throughout the Middle East is the close kinship Western men feel toward Western women. And vice versa. Much of the shyness found in dealings between the sexes back home vanishes. They are more like men friends in the States, in many ways, than are Arab males. We think more alike. They need our protection to even walk down the street. Nothing disrespectful. Quite the contrary, it's the ultimate of respect and friendship. Men who have their wives in Saudi also feel it, so seem to understand and take no offense. It's natural and stimulating.

I watched her walk away after getting my story, and felt better. The gentleman assigned to my problem was another story. He looked like a fraternity pledge at an Eastern college. Pink cheeks and all. The British woman had explained my predicament to him and he ushered me into the inner sanctum.

I followed him to his oversized office. The excitement offered him by my plight was a change of pace from facing infinite rows of tobacco-stained teeth wrapped in sincerely tight smiles as he was presented with endlessly boring visa applications requiring him to ask the same repetitive questions ad nauseum.

No sooner than we were both seated, he showed his glee by shouting into the neighboring office, "I've got another passport seizure, Bill." Who Bill was I never learned. What I did find out was fascinating.

I'd gone in expecting the Seventh Cavalry in a bugles-and-sabers charge with me riding along in the lead column to reclaim my passport, I guess. What I got was a calm discussion.

Yes, there were problems with passports. Of course, the consulate would see to having me issued a new one immediately. I was an American overseas. If I made the proper application, the law would take care of the rest. They had to give me one. Be glad to do so. How had I lost it? Taken at gunpoint? Really! At this juncture my own government's official looked at me strangely and moved his chair slightly farther away. Gunpoint, eh? Would I care to explain? Very bland, the way he asked it. I explained. The man listened, eyes wide and staring at me carefully from behind his horn-rimmed glasses. About twenty-eight, he had the Ivy League, Foreign Service-as-a-career look. His name was Roger, and he added so many "buts" and "excepts" to every sentence it took him five times longer than it should have to say anything.

I could tell he'd heard similar stories before. He'd also given the same answer before. Not bored. It was still a break in his otherwise drab routine. The consulate would look into the matter. Naturally, they couldn't get involved in a concern between a private citizen and either the government or natives of the land, but he could assure me that taking my passport at gunpoint was quite serious and the U.S. Foreign Service was not without friends and influence. What I didn't need was for him to tell me it was serious. I knew it. I'd been there. It had looked quite serious to me.

A new passport would take only a few hours. If I'd leave an address, or better yet, a phone number, he'd be happy to contact me, or I could stop by later. All I had to do was fill out some forms and supply three photos. They'd even arrange my flight home. Hot damn, I thought, reminding myself to be ashamed of all the nasty cracks I'd made about bureaucrats.

Then he brought up the killer question, now referred to as McDonald's Paradox.

I could get a new passport. My American citizenship could be traced easily, with only a little investigation by the State Department back in the United States. A couple of telexes would do it. The visas and entry stamps? Another matter. Entirely another matter. How could they tell what visas I'd received? Those were the records of another government. Then how could I get an entry visa for Saudi? Had to come from the same Saudi sponsors who'd vouched for me in the first place, or from outside the Kingdom. But I couldn't go outside the Kingdom to get one, without already having one so I could prove I was there legally, thus qualifying me for an exit stamp. It was the exit stamp I needed in the first place. Without one, I would be unable to buy any kind of transportation home. I couldn't even walk across the border. I had to have one to leave.

Was there some problem in going back to my Saudi sponsors? Was there!

I decided to try another track.

"Look. I'm here, right?

The man studied my face, slowly, as if he were assuring himself. There was a pause. Then he spoke. "Right. You are here."

"And I can get a passport. To replace the one they took from me, right?"

This time he only nodded agreement. From the lines in his forehead I could tell he was thinking hard, following me exactly.

"Good. Now if I'm here, and you can check on my status of citizenship, you can also check to see I don't have a record. That I'm a legitimate businessman."

Smiling, he nodded and spoke. "Right. That means we can have you out of here by early next week."

Two minutes and we'd gone from immediately to next week. "Then you can get me an entry-exit stamp?"

He shook his head. "That's just what I was saying. They damn well won't let you on a plane without an exit-approval stamp. And it takes an entry stamp to get an exit stamp."

"And I can't get a new entry stamp from my sponsors because they're the ones who took my passport."

He nodded. Fortunately for both of us, he didn't say, "Right," again. I probably would have hit him. Really excited now, he called someone on the phone. After asking a few questions and listening, his smile returned. He hung up, stood up, and earnestly shook my hand, reassuring me he'd have everything resolved in a few days. Two. Three at most.

Two minutes later I was back on the street with a handful of forms and a better picture of the nature of my dilemma. It was growing from a scary incident on a dark night to something of serious proportion. A problem in getting out of Saudi had been the furthest thing from my mind three hours ago. Now it was a principal worry.

I wasn't broke, but my immediately available resources were limited. It's expensive to stay in an Arabian city. I had my choice, though, as the three resort hotels, the Al Gosaibi, the Al Manura, and the Al Kharja, are all within a twenty-minute traffic-filled jitney cab ride from one another.

My suite at the Al Kharja Hotel consisted of a ten-by-twelve room. There was a washbasin—shower pan in one corner connected to running water, not intentionally hot but usually above drinking temperature. Not that you'd ever dare drink from a tap. The water lines stayed full of air and always spurted rusty brown when the faucet was turned on. That and a commode, in a small attached enclosure, resting on a black-and-white tile floor, were the fixtures. A small scrap of rough cloth, which at one time must have been dyed red and blue but was now mottled gray, tossed down as a throw rug, a narrow iron bed utilizing galvanized construction wire for springs, and, marvel of Western marvels, a chair and table were the disposables. Opulent Oriental furnishings. The door was so thick it looked like a surplus item from Fort Knox, with a lock that locked enough to keep Attila the Hun and accompanying elephants out. The view from the window was the back court of some of the most poverty-ridden people on this earth. Over all, there was a faint yet distinct smell of sewage. Not due to leaks, but, rather, as is common throughout the Middle East, to improper venting of sanitary facilities and a lack of check valves, resulting in back pressures that bring up foul smells. Especially in the hotter months.

The price for this white-walled, sybaritic, rat-infested, flyspecked retreat: $130 U.S. a day, please, no weekly rates available. Indian and Lebanese innkeepers in the Kingdom, while having the mannerisms and suspicions of their Western counterparts, lack a corresponding veneer of courtesy. They come on surly early, then get bad real quick. Saudis disdain this line of work. Aside from ownership, which allows them to attack the cashbox every night, they stay away.

Restaurant prices were comparable. I was adapted to native food, a good thing, as the so-called American-style dining establishments were super-American. Which is to say the food was mediocre to poor, the service lousy, but the prices enormous. Two tough eggs and freshly slaughtered sheep meat for breakfast, with a couple of inch-and-a-half-thick slices of what passed for toast and some sticky jam, ten bucks. Coffee went with the meal, but, Judas Priest, the stuff was stale instant death made from lukewarm water and goat milk. When a diner took a seat, he was automatically charged for the whole meal. A wonderful repast.

Prices were better in the open-air market or in several Arabic restaurants. They looked bad, though, and it was impossible to order in any language other than Arabic. I never failed to be the center of respectful attention when I ate in one. They were obviously not accustomed to a Western clientele. The most expensive eateries, priced even above those featuring an unsuccessful version of "continental" cuisine, were the enormously popular Chinese and Korean establishments. They catered to any nationality with money.

So there I was, the morning after my visit to the consul, sitting on my bed, right in the middle of my extravagant suite, sipping on a glass of Lipton's to wash down a hunk of pita bread and a chew of dates I'd bought the evening before, counting my resources. I had over a thousand in cash, a wad of traveler's checks, my credit cards, and some bank letters of introduction and communication. I was in no immediate danger of starving.

Finished with my elaborate breakfast, I ate two Planter's Peanut Bars for dessert. Planter's were my favorite candy in the desert. So called "tropical" chocolate is so loaded with parafin to keep it from turning into a runny brown goo in the heat that it tasted like a candle. After I had crudely showered and shaved, I went down to the lobby. The two reception salons, furnished like a rundown Y.M.C.A., were crowded by people looking to make a deal, any deal, with anyone who would stand still long enough to listen. An *I Love Lucy* rerun, sans commercials, was blaring from a Japanese TV set in one. The other featured Arabic music.

Out on the busy street, standing in the sunlight, I found the noise of the traffic preferable to the babble of voices inside. The taxi drivers started their horn symphony, composed of intermittent beeps intended to attract the attention of any Westerner they saw on foot. They tooted along beside me for a little way, then gave up.

It was a nice day, so I decided to take a walk. No sense going to the consulate, because I'd done all my paperwork and dropped off the required photos the evening before. I was about to step away when the sound of my name being called stopped me. I looked around over the top of the crowd and spotted Suliman Rasi, Abdallah Fazza, boy in tow, and the son of Abdullah Saba, one of the partners.

Suliman worked his way through the small crowd of people, starting to talk before he reached me. "Ah, Mr. John. We hoped we'd find you here."

I was surprised to see them but didn't want to show it. "Where else would I be? This is the hotel where I said I'd stay."

"Ah, yes." He was standing next to me now, breathing a little hard from the movement through the throng. "But we weren't sure you were in Al Khobar at all."

"Where in the hell did you think I'd gone? Home?"

Subtlety did nothing for the man. He never could understand sarcasm.

"Home? Of course not. You have no passport."

That got me mad. Damn mad. "You bet your buggered little ass I don't have a passport. You and the rest of your pack of bastards had it taken away from me. At gunpoint."

He looked as innocent as only an Arab telling a falsehood can. "There is some mistake, Mr. John. That night the policeman needed your identity papers because you were being unreasonable. We can work it all out now."

Ah ha, I thought. Finally. We've got $15 to $20 million worth of contracts in the bag if we can just get started. They've come to their senses and we're now going to get back to business. About time, too. I was still hesitant, as my experience told me there was more going on than I knew.

Back in the States, that sort of thinking would be hard to understand. I might have had trouble in following the logic. I was used to it now. My months in Saudi had attuned me to the non sequitur and the sudden change in conversational direction. I looked over at the waiting men. Sheikh Saba had joined the merry band.

"Look, Suliman, I want my passport back. I'm madder than hell about all this. But I'm still willing to work with you and the gang."

I didn't let him know I'd been to our consulate and made application for a replacement.

"About your passport, Mr. John. It is merely in the possession of the police. They prefer, at this time, to have custody of the document, instead of you in custody."

"Me in custody? Now, why in the hell would they want me in custody?"

"Because you have broken your bargain to key people in the Kingdom. You owe them money and refuse to pay."

"Owe who what? Like hell I do."

"Ah, then that is the problem. You do not feel you owe for some part of the erection of the forms on the site. And the site preparation, as well. We should have a meeting and talk this out like civilized people."

By this time we'd all walked back into the salon. The conversation turned to who wanted Pepsi, tea, or coffee.

After refreshments, we returned to the main discussion. Our voices quickly got louder. Seeing everyone looking at us, we moved to a smaller, more private room. With Fazza, Suliman, Fahad, Saba, and the other boy seated in various places on the floor, there wasn't any reason to waste time, so I slipped into my best Arabic-English mix without first being polite.

"I want my passport back. The one you had taken from me the other night at gunpoint."

There were blank looks. When an Arab wants to look blank, he really can. Not stupid, blank. There is nothing whatsoever to see in his eyes or on his face. I had five expressionless faces looking at me. There was no attempt at denial or any argument, just the total, complete blankness. When Suliman Rasi spoke, it was as if I'd never said a word.

"Mr. John, we have a problem."

I decided to go along with the tide. "What's that?"

"We are saddened men."

"Why so?" This rhetorical question-and-answer game could, as I well knew, go on for an hour. It's the price you pay when you want to get to the point with a Saudi.

"Have you not been a guest in the house of Sheikh Fazza, as well as the guest of Sheikh Saba? All we wish you to do is stay a few more days."

"It has been my honor to have been their guest." That, like in straight Arabic, for their benefits. Both of them smiled contentedly. Behind their smiles, I could see coldness and agitation. Why? I wondered.

I found out fifteen minutes later, which is how long it took to twist the conversation around to the crux of the matter.

"... We felt cheered," Suliman was going on—I'd been half listening, nodding now and then, wishing for a glass of tea—"when you arrived and the forms arrived, as you said they would. It was heartening to see all the stories we had heard about Americans and their haste in a business deal was, in your case, not so." The veiled insult perked up my ears. We were starting on the critical point. He watched me, then when he saw no sign I was going to interrupt, went glibly on.

"We waited for you to erect the forms, as you said you would do. As we agreed you would do. You did not. Days passed, still you did nothing. I spoke with you about the charges the forms were gathering on the docks. But it was your money, so if you wanted to sit idly by and wait, it was your business."

I looked at Suliman so hard and carefully I could see blackheads in his pockmarked skin. He showed no sign he was telling the most barefaced lie I'd ever heard. My Western thinking kept me expecting him to wind down his crazy horse crap, but he didn't. Instead, the more he talked, the more he believed his own story and the more excited he became. His demands went up in direct proportion to his voice.

Ten minutes later, I'd heard enough. My blood pressure was climbing. I screamed at him and at Fazza about the thousands of dollars we were all losing by not having the site ready and the forms in our possession. All faces were blank masks because of my rudeness. They looked that way because they were setting me up for a royal Saudi screwing.

I was as tight as a coil, and Suliman was speaking as if he hadn't heard me. "...So we were wondering, why haven't you lived up to your part of the bargain? Why haven't you set up the site and installed the forms? After coming this far with the deal, surely you can see we are close to making a profit. It makes no sense for you to stop now. We are here to ask, 'Why, Mr. John, why?'"

At that moment I felt like "Why, Mr. Johning" him, all right, straight in the mouth. I held my temper. To hit someone in Saudi is dangerous. To hit someone with influence is much worse. Jail time, for sure. Long jail time.

I forced my voice into a reasonable semblance of calmness. "What in the hell do you mean, Suliman? You know as well as I do our agreement called for me to deliver the forms and for your team to have the manufacturing site ready. There has never, accent on never, been the slightest question about that. You dingdongs haven't even decided where the site will be, much less laid down the concrete bases. You and Abdallah prepared our joint-venture document. You know your responsibility."

Vacant stares all around. The small room, with all of us in it, and the highly inadequate air-conditioning system wheezing out a wisp of cool air as the sun got higher in the sky, was beginning to feel stuffy. Humid stuffy. I caught a whiff of sandalwood smoke on the robes of my guests.

"What are you trying to pull? Don't you see how you're screwing up this deal?"

"On the contrary, Mr. John, what are you trying to pull? You know quite well the agreement calls for your firm to deliver the forms and install them in working order— "

" —on a site developed and prepared by your, accent your, group, to the agreed-upon specifications," I finished for him. My voice was no longer cool.

It was some scene: five Arabs all looking at me blankly, all dressed in their business, everyday robes with headdresses, sitting on the floor in the small room, with me on the only chair.

"The contract," Suliman's voice was the same as ever, "as you call it, says you will install the forms. You have not done so. There is, however, a simple solution. We will assist in the construction costs, as per our agreement."

Suliman was thinking about his cut in the deal now. If it ended here, he was out money. He needed to patch things up, so he called the others around him, translating what he'd just said. They came mentally unhinged. They formed a Marx Brothers-style huddle and, talking at the top of their voices, occasionally looked at me to see how much I was overhearing or understanding. Suliman spoke again.

"Although you are in violation of one part of your agreement, Mr. John, there is no reason to be in violation of all. If your firm will put up, immediately, the sum of five thousand U.S. dollars and locate a company to prepare the site, you may proceed as if nothing has happened, install the forms, and be ready to reap the equal share of profits our agreement entitles you to."

The last was delivered as cool as a north wind out of Alaska. He didn't even bother to look blank. He smiled as he said it.

I smiled, too. "Suliman, you are a dirty motherfucker." I paused to let this sink in. My thinking was, if I were able to insult him enough to goad him into some outward display of emotion, I'd then be able to argue with his logic. It didn't work. In fact, he didn't seem to be upset at all. Maybe he was considering the idea. Maybe the phrase didn't have the proper impact due to cultural exchange. I don't know. I tried another tack.

"Let's go through this one more time. Are you aware of the terms of our agreement, Suliman?"

"Completely. As I helped draft it, I know its contents."

"Right. Then you know as well as I do there is nothing in the deal about our being responsible for any of the cost of preparing the site. There is a clause in the deal which specifically says this partnership, Fazza, yourself, Saba, and Bidoon Ismek, all agreed you'd hire and pay for a local contractor to develop the site for the erection of the forms. We furnish the forms, you furnish the finished site. We furnish transportation of the forms to the site, you furnish the unloading on the site. We furnish the expertise, and you furnish the labor. Six parts. Three for each. I've got the forms here. Part one for me. I'm all set to get them to the site. If there was one. I'm ready to furnish the training and supervision for their use. Part two and three for me. You haven't made the site ready. Part one of your fuck-up. All Fazza has done to date is try and palm off the on-site unloading costs onto my company. Part two of your failure. I don't know if you have the labor or not. We're not far enough along for that point to matter."

I paused. He jumped in.

"Oh, no, Mr. John. The agreement, in the Arabic version, says you will build the forms, set them up, and supervise their use. There is nothing about our furnishing a site."

Mere words cannot describe my feeling at that instant. I've read that a hundred or so times in various books, but honest to Judas Priest, it was true. I was speechless. There I'd been, arguing with them for weeks over the site, discussing the particulars, pressing for its completion. I knew what the agreement said, in English as well as Arabic. Back in the States, I'd had it translated twice to be sure. With the exception of some minor phrasing about Allah, they agreed to a comma's worth.

It's not an uncommon Mideastern negotiating gambit. Tell any lie you wish but tell it loud. If you can screw someone, do it big.

Suliman's delivery, so calm and sure, was convincing. I had a moment's doubt. Could they have genuinely misunderstood? Maybe George and I had made the error. Then I remembered. The telex. They had sent me a telex which stated the site was ready. That was my okay to ship the forms. George and I had made an error, all right, but it had nothing to do with who was going to set up the site. It was one more lie from them, like all the rest. I decided on a frontal attack.

Smiling, I got up and strolled over to the low table where I'd tossed my battered brown briefcase. I rummaged through it and produced the flimsy copy of the telex. Without letting go of one edge, I slipped it at reader distance under Suliman's nose.

"Read this, you camelfucker." I was still hot. So was the room. The tension in the air caused everyone to sweat and our smells began to permeate the slowly circulating air.

Suliman read it. He smiled to the end, then looked serious.

"Who sent this to you, Mr. John?"

"What the hell do you mean, who sent this to me? Abdallah did, you bastard. That's his name right there at the end of it. Like on the other ones you and he sent." My blunt forefinger was pointing to his name on the lower left side.

I turned to Saba's son. "Ask Abdallah Fazza if he sent this telex." My Arabic was elementary, but good enough for him to get the point.

There was a spate of fast jabbering from Suliman to Saba's kid. Too much for me to follow. Then they asked Fazza something. His denial needed no translation. "No. I sent nothing." The fat sheikh turned his sightless eyes toward me. "I did not send this, Mr. John." In a sharper tone, he snapped at Suliman. Too little division there. They were going to stick together.

It was like talking to a roomful of loonies. I'd had enough. More than enough. I leaned down close to Rasi's face, where I could smell his goat breath, and spoke slowly, nose to nose.

"Suliman, I have copies of the agreements. They call for you and the Saudi partners to prepare the site. I know what they say in Arabic. In English, too. This telex" —I waved it in the air— " came from you, with their authorization. You wanted to get those forms here for some reason even though things weren't ready. You know that, I know that, and so do they. Now you're trying a shakedown. Or maybe a sheikh down." My voice was rising. "It's not going to work. Somewhere in this zany land of Oriental Oz there is a court of law, and with these agreements and this telex, you and your crooked buddies haven't got the chance of an ice sculpture in the middle of the desert. The court will find for me, and when it does, I'm going to sue you guys for so much it'll take a private pipeline direct to the

Ras Tanurah oil fields to generate enough cash to pay back what I win. You got that?"

There was a long silence. Abdallah Fazza asked for a translation and Suliman obliged. There we were, me standing, bending down, Suliman, mustache bristling, sitting, our noses a half inch apart, and me practically yelling. He didn't bother to wipe away the spittle flecks which accompanied my pronouncements. When Fazza spoke in Arabic, I was pleased I could understand enough to get his meaning.

"What does he say? Will he pay the money?"

An argument that needs to be translated after every hot exchange is ridiculous. The whole damn thing became too funny for me to worry about. I straightened up and started to laugh. First a chuckle, then a semihysterical belly whomper. The others looked at me as I had been looking at them. They thought the strain was too much and I'd slipped a cog. Still laughing, almost to the point of helplessness, I gathered them up with much waving of arms and shooed them into the hall. Suliman was the last to leave. On his way out the door, he was still bland.

"We must talk more, Mr. John. Later. As a foreigner trying to avoid honoring an agreement with Saudi businessmen, you are in very serious trouble." In the hall, my partners were doing a doomsday chorus.

"You bet we'll talk, Suliman. In court. Where it counts." I slammed the door, and let the scared look I'd been holding back plaster itself across my face. Eyes wet with tears from the release of nervous energy, I slumped against the wall. In the background, through the thin partition, I could hear the men walking away, down the narrow corridor, talking among themselves. Suliman's voice was the loudest. He was filling them in on our conversation.

I didn't sleep well. That was unusual, because if there was one thing I thought I was accustomed to, it was sleeping with distress or turmoil around me. Before retiring, I went carefully through the documents in my briefcase, reassuring myself on each familiar point. I don't know why Suliman's outrageous commentary made me doubt my own certain knowledge, but it did. I've thought about that a lot since then, and I've come to the conclusion I have a very American trait. I'd associated with Suliman for months, on many different occasions, and although I knew he had his faults, I'd considered him friendly. When a friend says I'm wrong, I listen so I can evaluate the situation. Few of us have ever had a friend blatantly and consistently lie about vital, important matters. It's bound to make anyone question his position.

I questioned mine. No matter how I looked at it, we'd done what we said we'd do, by the time we said we'd do it. They hadn't. One fact I knew: even though there were copies of the papers I had with me in the United States, I was going to keep the ones in my briefcase by my side, at hand, with one eye on them at all times. That's probably why I had a wild dream about chasing paper contracts down dark narrow streets and never catching them.

Nerves got me out of bed early next morning with a certain sense of aimlessness. It was 4:30 A.M. I had no appointments, nowhere I had to be, was alone in a strange country spending money at a horrendous rate every day. I longed to be home with Pat and my family, but I couldn't leave. I kept willing myself not to worry. No less an authority than a representative of the U.S. consulate had said I'd be on my way in a few days. From the strength of being back in the United States, I could negotiate. I knew Fazza, and Suliman, and the rest. They wanted to make fifteen million as badly as I did. Once out of Saudi, I could bring them to their senses.

Feeling better, because I had a goal in mind again, I decided to splurge on breakfast. I went to the hotel restaurant. I was just finishing my final cup of hot tea when a voice startled me. I looked around and there was Suliman, smiling. "May I join you?"

I nodded toward a chair, across the table, which he nimbly slipped into.

"You want something?" I've mentioned Suliman's uncanny sense of timing concerning arrivals or departures at mealtimes.

"Why, yes, thank you."

I sat back while he studied the menu, caught the waiter's attention, and ordered the standard, no-changes no-substitutes meal. It came, and I watched while he cleaned his plate. We didn't exchange a single word about business the entire time. Whether or not he appreciated my following his custom of not discussing unpleasant or disagreeable differences of opinion over meals, I don't know.

At last, after slurping down half of his final cup of coffee, we were ready. At least I was. He looked as if there were nothing in the world the matter.

"Mr. John" —his voice was smooth as a rattlesnake's belly— "why don't you come back with me to Fazza's? You can wire for the money, and when it arrives give it to us. We will consider the matter closed, use the cash to develop the site, and when you've paid demurrage on the forms, you can transport them into place and finish the task you came to do. You'll make your money back in no time. Also, there is the matter of my own six thousand dollars in commissions. I could have you put in jail over that."

He did it again. I was left speechless. The ante had upped itself from unloading on site to full-site preparation and the demurrage, which by now was another three thousand or so, in less than a day. He was asking for six more that he owed Jeff, the man who'd introduced us. Judas Priest, at this rate, I'd need half a million if things dragged on. They had switched from using a tack hammer to hitting me with a jack hammer. I decided to play it to him one more time, slowly.

"Why don't you knock it off, Suliman? You know, and I know, and Fazza knows, and Saba knows, and Bidoon knows how the agreement reads. It's clear. We deliver the forms to Saudi Arabia. Then move them to a site your group has prepared. It's not up to us to develop the site. It's your job. Because you didn't have your job done, even though you telexed and said you did, there is now a charge for demurrage. That's your charge, not ours. We had the forms on the dock the day we said they would be there. We were ready to help move them, but no one would tell us where. They can still be moved to the undeveloped site. That way, we'll save more demurrage." I watched him as I spoke, but could see nothing. "All the little details, if you'd like to refresh your mind, are in our agreements. In English as well as Arabic. Including the use of a twenty-ton crane, courtesy of your team, to unload the forms in Jubail." I patted my beat-up brown attaché case and followed his eyes as they locked onto it. "I've got copies of every document here, and naturally the originals in the United States, so if I lose any of these, I can have them replaced."

First emotion. His eyes flickered and I imagined I saw a flash of disappointment. He'd been counting on getting the originals if he could get the case. His comeback was astonishing.

"Oh, Mr. John, you discuss documents and deals. The main point of a deal is the intent of the individuals involved. Our intentions toward you have, as we have demonstrated, been honorable. Yours, on the other hand, due to procrastination, have been questionable. Regardless of what the documents say, the intent of the commitment was for you and your company to build the forms, ship them here, erect them on a site you developed to your liking, and then supervise their use to produce the building units. That much is clear. It included paying for the twenty-ton crane to offload the trucks."

"Bullshit, Suliman. Our agreement says, 'C.I.F.'—Cost, Insurance, Freight. Offloading is always at customer's expense on C.I.F. deals. It's international law. Ask the shipping firm, ask your bank, ask anybody. That's our deal and that's twenty-five hundred you sure as hell won't get from us."

"How childish, Mr. John, for a man in your position to keep referring to an agreement. Experience shows all things in the world change. Change is the only consistent force, aside from Allah and His wisdom, in the universe." He was being very elementary with me. "Your position has changed. The intention of the original agreement was for you to produce forms, was it not?"

I nodded. There was no stopping his irrationality, so I decided to hear him out.

"How could you have imagined you could produce the forms without having a properly cleared erection and pouring area? How did you imagine that we, who know nothing about what you require to produce the forms, which is why we decided to work with you in the first place, could possibly establish a satisfactory site? It is beyond our knowledge. It is past our technical abilities. Therefore, it is clear we would never have gotten into such an arrangement. The implied meaning was simple. It is your task to make the final, poured-concrete forms. You have to be the one responsible for setting up the equipment. Also, it is equipment of your design. Who could be more knowledgeable about the needed requirements of the erection site?"

He looked triumphant and had wound down his convoluted statement to the point where I guessed he'd be ready to listen to my reply. As he talked, I had an inspiration; with it came my answer.

"I agree, Suliman, neither you nor your partners have the necessary technical experience to develop the site."

He looked pleased when I said this. Maybe he was anticipating my general acceptance of his premise. My next words dispelled any thoughts in that direction.

"That's why we sent you this." I reached into my case and

produced a detailed drawing of what the construction site would be like, including grade levels, materials placement, etc. Attached to it was a series of letters. I pointed them out to him.

"Also, your letters asking for specifics, and the last letter giving the dates you'd have the site ready." He was blank-faced again.

"There's something more, Suliman. You say there is no way your group has the technical knowledge to develop the manufacturing site. Right?"

Cautious, he nodded.

"Then you ask me to give your people ten thousand to pay for the site development, which, after I've handed over the money, they will undertake to do. How will they manage that little wonder, pray tell? Will the money give them new knowledge?"

There was a long silence. I'd expected to fluster him, but he looked at me vacantly. Judas Priest, he was cool. Caught like a fox in his own den, he gave no outward sign whatsoever there had been an exchange. He smiled. He actually smiled.

"I can see, Mr. John, there is no appealing to you on the ground of logic, nor of honor. That pains me. It saddens me, too, because this leaves only one course of action. We will have to use all our abilities and influence to make you deliver your part of the deal. Not to mention my six thousand commission, which, if not paid by tomorrow, will be the cause of your being thrown in jail. Even so, Mr. John, do not be afraid. We will not fail our duty. When the project produces income, you shall have your agreed-upon share. It is not our group who are the bandits or the transgressors."

We sat in silence a good two minutes, staring at each other. The breakfast crowd in the restaurant had thinned considerably, so we were alone, the only occupied table on our side of the big room. The waiters had gathered at a large coffeepot in the rear, talking and sipping. The sweating Somali busboys were wiping the black Formica tops of the shaky tables with rags which had seen cleaner, better days.

Suliman didn't speak, I didn't speak. I undid the wrapper from an H. Upmann cigar, bit off the dry end, and struck a match. The steel-blue smoke spiraled upward toward the high ceiling. I looked at my watch. A little after eight. The heat was already building. I looked back at Suliman, who was gazing off somewhere. Suddenly, he smiled. "Mr. John, could you possibly let me have one of your cigars?"

I handed him one. The only time he smoked a cigar was when I did. He may have meant it as an honor. But I doubt it. Sitting quietly, I thought back over his remarks. What he really wanted was his six grand. The rest he was using as a hammer to get me to agree to paying him. That might be my way out.

"Suliman, I'll tell you what. I'll telex my partner George today for your commission. That'll put us in hot water with Jeff, because you know as well as I do you owe him that money. But we'll handle it some way. If I do that, will it square us away? Will you promise me I'll get my passport back and we can put our partnership problems behind us and get on down the road to make some money?"

He brightened like a spit-shined shoe.

"Yes, Mr. John." There was a pause before he added, craftily, "But I need to see a copy of the telex."

I nodded, and together we strolled over to the telex office.

He stayed with me long enough to see me write out the message and pay for its transmission. Then, smiling with satisfaction and puffing on the H. Upmann stoutly, he left, walking in a dignified manner through the large double doors out into the street. I stood staring after him, watching his flowing white robe disappear.

The bald-faced nature of our disagreement, combined with a complete lack of Western ethics, the absence of American logic, and what I saw as disregard for the agreements we'd worked so hard to put together, left me dazed. There had to be justice somewhere in Saudi. There had to be a system to enforce contracts, or the country would fall apart. Even if it were folk law based on the Koran, there was a form of judge and jury. I'd get my day in court. The papers I had with me would prove my position. They'd get their comeuppance, if we could only get before a proper tribunal.

That's what I thought. I didn't know then what I know now, or I might have gone ahead and paid the money. I wasn't dealing with the textbook Saudi Arabia. I'd taken on the part of the country expatriates discussed in hushed voices. The part no Westerner ever sees from back home.

Fortunately for me, there was a possibility of working things out without Suliman's assistance. It would first take the United States' issuing my new passport. Next, I could appear and petition in person to get replaced entry-exit stamps. Sometimes, due to bureaucratic screw-ups, it worked. As soon as my passport came, I'd try. Until then, there was nothing I could do but wait.

On the matter of the broken contract, however, there were a number of possible actions.

I'd spent an hour with a local attorney, recommended by a friend in Houston. According to him, there was the problem of my citizenship, compounded by my religion. I was a non-Saudi, non-(horror of horrors) Moslem. An infidel. It meant I had no effective standing in any hearing. I couldn't be sworn in, so my testimony would be suspect, and the tribunal before which the matter would be heard was religious in nature, not based on a code of civil laws separate from the nation's theology. In other words, the judges, called qadis, would be (1) Saudi and (2) not just Moslems but learned holy men versed in the intricacies of the Word according to Mohammed as put forth in the Koran and interpreted in the strict Shari'a sense. Does that get intricate! Depending on the interpretation, there are so many shades of gray possible, so many nuances to be considered, that the argument of the case could take months, plus more time required to hand down a verdict. Once given, the hearing's decision would be absolute and binding, with no chance for an appeal of any kind. Needless to say, that didn't excite me too much.

A second direction, which would be nonbinding, but could be used in many ways after a decision had been reached, was to submit the case for arbitration before a group formed for the purpose of working out settlements between Saudi and non-Saudi businessmen engaged in business. This action goes under the name of a "Chamber of Commerce of Dammam Arbitration Hearing." There is a single nonreligious referee who will hear the facts from both sides, review all the papers, and give his opinion as to who should do what to settle the matter fairly. Two minor problems: The decision of the judge was far from final. It was not binding on either party to act one way or the other on the judge's findings. Worse, there had been a rumor or two concerning the purchasability of judges. In other words, while the idea was sound the outcome might be surprising. If I could win, the decision would carry a lot of weight. Very few Westerners, though, as history shows, have ever won anything in a Saudi legal action. Some have been lucky enough to curtail their losses, but most find out how well Saudis stick together against a common opponent.

As an alternative, I could, on the day set aside, petition the King of Saudi Arabia for an audience. All I had to do was show up at the palace majlis and wait until I was selected from the petitioners. Might take a while, but sooner or later the King would see me. It's custom. If I didn't want to go as high as the King himself, I could do the same thing at a lower level, by waiting on one of the royal princes who had been assigned the rulership of a province. This was a little faster. Either way, how the prince or King called the deal would be how the deal would be. Period. No more messing around. If I went with a favorable report from the C. of C. of Dammam, it would have some significance, as the practice of turning to these special groups for arbitration was encouraged by the royal family.

The Chamber of Commerce does more in Saudi than in the United States. It has a quasi-official role in business, is used to office tax collectors, and is the place to go to legalize all import-export documents.

While I was debating what to do, the matter was taken out of my hands. Suliman, Fazza, and company held their own meeting, and decided they could handle the outcome of a C. of C. arbitration easier than they could a governmental hearing. The next time I saw Suliman, he broke the news.

"Mr. John, we want to be fair." He was still on a high from the prospect of getting six thousand out of me, so was condescending in a friendly way. "We have decided to place the matter before the Dammam Chamber of Commerce Arbitration Committee, for an unbiased inquiry. Thus you will understand the meaning behind documents signed, after hearing it from a disinterested third party."

I wasn't sure if I should laugh or cry—laugh, because someone else, an outsider, was going to be brought into this mess, and I'd have, I hoped, an honest chance to tell my side; or cry, because I knew them well enough to realize if they suggested something they had an angle. I had no choice, so I went along with the program.

"I've heard of those proceedings. The decisions aren't legally binding, though, as I understand."

"That is correct. On either party. But who is speaking of legalities? We are talking of your need to understand how we do business here."

I had mixed feelings about the arbitration, but it was better than the haggling and lying. Either way, I didn't have all that much to lose. If they did stack the deck, by the time the hearing was over I'd be on my happy way out of the Kingdom, thanks to the efforts of the U.S. consulate. Besides, I was in the right. With the documents I had, it would take some terrific fixing to get a halfway reputable individual to find against me. I decided to take the initiative.

"Let's go over together, first thing in the morning, and make a formal request for a hearing. What say, Suliman?"

There was a pause, he took a breath to speak, let it out, then took another. He nodded his head. "Okay, Mr. John. If that's what you want. You have to promise me one thing. If we do submit to this indignity, and air our private business before a stranger, you must abide by the decision. Agreed?"

"Suliman, my man, of course I agree. Naturally, you and your partners will also accept the decision?"

He nodded, eagerly this time. "Of course, Mr. John. Of course."

We parted in the lobby; me to go back to my room and prepare my presentation, Suliman to talk it over with the others and, as a group, find somebody they could fix. Their way seemed surer than mine, but I was determined to make things hard for whomever they hooked in on their side. The request for the hearing was easy. All we had to do was appear before the president and secretary of the Dammam C. of C. They would listen to both sides and offer an arbitrary solution. It took two days to get an appointment.

I spent the time between my last glimpse of Suliman and taking my place in a chair pulled up to a long table in one of the small meeting rooms going over the case. I was ready, but worried. If the fix were on, it would probably show itself in the first few minutes. I sat on one side; Suliman, flanked by Fazza, his son Fahad, and Sheikh Saba, on the other. I had my briefcase and a pile of papers. They had a small stack of documents and, for all I knew, owned the judge. I could only wait and see. Coffee and tea were quietly served to all.

After we'd been there for a half hour talking softly back and forth, the door opened and a short, dark man with a mustache and black-rimmed glasses came in. He moved swiftly to the head of the table where he took a seat. Apparently comfortable, he placed his hands palm down, then brought them together slowly, interlacing his fingers. I watched him carefully. Suliman seemed startled because the man, who looked aristocratic, was dressed in a conservatively cut, dark, Western-style, three-piece business suit instead of a thauba.

"I am Judge Abdulazine, an attorney from Egypt. We are gathered to arbitrate business differences for the Dammam Chamber. I have been asked to interest myself in this matter."

He spoke with an English-school preciseness which said volumes about his background. His flat features and coarse, receding hair marked him as native Egyptian. His acceptance by the Dammam Chamber of Commerce as an arbitrator defined his legal background. The look of utter surprise on Suliman's face told me he was straight. Whatever fix they'd tried had failed, and old Judge Abdulazine was nobody's bought boy. He was nobody's fool, either. The secretary of the Chamber, a Saudi, volunteered that the judge had over thirty years' experience in legal matters and had been, for the previous decade, a member of the Egyptian Supreme Court.

In two days of meetings he heard my partners' story, listened to my talk of woe, and asked some perceptive, penetrating questions. He went through our documents, making notes occasionally on a large legal pad. His handwriting was tiny and as precise as his diction. He read Arabic with the same facility as English, and wrote in Arabic, using some English letters. Finished with his review, he carefully gave each side back its papers, watched until he was certain we had them in our possession, then returned to his notes.

As he read, the Saudis fumed. They were getting madder and madder. Their attempts at communication with the dapper judge got only a nod or under-the-breath mutter of recognition, not what they were looking for at all.

One at a time, they stood and harangued the man. He remained calmly unflappable.

It wasn't very courtlike, yet the Egyptian conducted himself with the opposing formality of a judge. There was a feeling his decision would be final. Suliman had said his group would abide by the ruling. I had too. I was sure hoping Suliman still felt that way.

"Gentlemen." The judge's voice got my attention. He spoke softly, first in English to me.

"As I read your agreement, it is the duty of your company, Mr. McDonald" —he pronounced the name Mack-Dough-Nald— "to build the equipment, called, I believe" —he referred to his note pad— " 'forms,' deliver them to the port in Jubail, and assist in transporting them to a predeveloped site. Please note the word 'assist.' At the expense of your company, you are to aid in the hiring of a competent crew to move said forms from the port, to complete delivery. Additionally, you are, at this point, submitting invoices in the sum of one hundred eighteen thousand U.S. dollars, which, along with your agreement and the bills of lading indicating the forms are presently on the dock, are substantiated and due to be paid to Heritage Building Systems.

"Next, also according to your agreement and reflected in the international letters of credit, the cost of the cranes for offloading the trucks at the manufacturing site will be, as is usual, the purchasers'. Which are again your four partners." Here, he looked over his glasses at the four agitated but silent men.

"The item of demurrage, which, I might note, continues to grow even as we sit here, clearly hinges to the problem of who shall pay for the offloading of the trucks on the manufacturing site. And since there is disagreement the forms cannot be on-loaded for transport, thus are sitting wharfside, incurring daily charges.

"Finally, it appears your obligation to oversee their use for a limited time in order to train men to operate the equipment and determine that all is working properly."

I was plenty nervous. What he'd just said was a playback of my opening statement and he'd not added anything about setting up the manufacturing site or my paying for the offloading of the trucks. I nodded. Suliman, across the way, fumed. He noted the absence of the reference to the site, too.

The judge had turned away from me, and was repeating his statement in Arabic to my partners. They didn't like it when they heard it.

Judge Abdulazine turned back to me, moving his head slowly.

"Now then. Your partners say their agreement with you included, as an obligation of your firm, the preparation and completion of the site where the forms would be used to produce concrete building modules and for payment of expenses incurred during the offloading of the forms. They are strong in this belief. Are you still certain there was no provision for your company to do this?"

I waved my hand toward the documents. "Not in writing or in any conversation until a couple of days ago. The telexes indicate they said the site was ready, so we should ship the forms. If the site were ready, how could we have been responsible? Besides, these gentlemen are to provide the capital for the venture. Not us."

The judge, for the first time, smiled. "A telling point, sir."

He moved his attention back to the Saudis, speaking again in Arabic. Their faces grew darker and they moved in their chairs. From what I could make of it, the judge was asking a number of polite but pointed questions about their concept of the deal and when it evolved. Suliman did all the answering, staring at the small man with short, sharp looks.

The judge nodded. He made a last note to himself and turned in his chair to face me.

"Mr. McDonald, I am going to address you in English. Mr. Rasi across the table understands English, so he can assure his associates what I say to you, I later say to them, in Arabic. Do you speak Arabic, Mr. McDonald?"

I shook my head. Best to play dumb.

"No? Perhaps you would like the services of a translator, so you will know what I say to them I have said to you?"

"No, sir. I don't believe that will be necessary. I can follow some of what you say." I could also watch the faces of my ex-pals and see the effect of his words. That would be a better indicator than an interpreter.

He nodded. "Very well." There was a long silence as he went over his pad one more time.

"Mr. McDonald, I find the agreement between you and these gentlemen in perfect order." He looked over the top of his glasses at me the way I recall my grandfather doing. But the judge's thick, black bristly eyebrows didn't remind me of my grandfather. They looked more like a girl who had gone wild with mascara.

"There is exactness in the translation of the original Arabic document into English." He stared at me again, as if expecting me to question his statement. When he saw I was not going to respond, he turned to the Saudis and made the same remarks in their language.

I was right. There was no need for an interpreter. With a scream of rage, Sheikh Saba jumped up from the table. Raving in a high-pitched voice, white robe billowing around flapping arms, he took three swift steps to where the judge was seated and began berating him with gutter Arabic, waving his finger under the man's nose. The Egyptian sat stoically through the display, waiting for the emotion to dwindle. Saba began to run down, suddenly shut up, and returned to his seat, glaring. The judge, as if nothing had gone on at all, turned back to me.

"Now, then, Mr. McDonald, in addition to the original

document of agreement, you have also submitted to me a series of letters, telexes, and records of negotiation. In this material, the relative tasks of the two partners are well defined. All expenses incident to your tasks were to be paid by the members of the Saudi partnership."

This time it was Suliman who, screaming like a possessed person, sprang from his seat and was on the judge. He was careful not to touch him, but he came close, shaking his fist and raging in a loud, sharp voice. He was so excited he'd slip into and out of Arabic, French, and English. I could put most of it together. The gist seemed to be a simple question: "What the hell did the poor son of a misbegotten camel who was acting as judge in this matter know about law? Saudi law. The law of honest people. The law of intentions. Not the law of pawky papers and written documents which can never fully describe what is in the heart of a man."

He, too, calmed down after a while. The only notice the judge took was to deliver a short message to the Saudis. Not harsh. As far as I could tell, he told them written documents do carry or can carry the meaning and heart of a man. "Take the Koran, for instance. It is written. It carries the meaning of Allah." As for his own credentials, he gave them. The number of universities attached to his curriculum vitae was most impressive, even in Arabic. Done, the Egyptian, adjusting his heavy glasses, turned back to me.

"This matter is obvious. I do not know why there is any indecision on your part. While I have not seen the forms on the dock, you say they are there. While I have not seen them work, you say they will, and none of these men question that fact. The only points of contention are the responsibility for having the manufacturing site prepared, ready to start operations, and who shall pay for the offloading. From this will also come who is responsible for the demurrage charges." Eyes back to his pad. The Saudis, flaming mad, sat whispering to one another. Suliman translated as the judge spoke, so they knew what had been said.

So far, it didn't sound too bad.

The judge cleared his throat. "At this time, Mr. McDonald, I do not find any indication it is, or ever was, the financial responsibility of you or your company to prepare the manufacturing site for the forms. That task was, and is, the full fiscal responsibility of the joint Saudi Arabian partners. As are the offloading costs. Since they have failed in these areas, they are responsible for the demurrage charges and all costs pertaining to the site and the storage of the forms, added insurance during the holding period, and other matters connected and as a result of their not having completed the site, even though they told you they were ready to receive the forms. Further, if these men are involved in the taking of your passport, they should return it, as not to would be an act of hostility against your country."

The last few words came in a fast rush, running together, to get it all said before the excited, quickly rising voices of the Saudis across the table drowned him out. I heard him say "forms" and then all I heard was the conflicting, confusing jumble of screams and curses pouring from Suliman, Fazza, and Saba. They were all calling on Allah to be their witness, calling the judge names, and calling me an ingrate to have ever brought them here. The Egyptian, perfectly self-contained, as if he were confronted by similar outbursts every day, which, when I thought about it, he must have been as a part of hearing Arab misdeeds, leaned toward me.

"I will make the proper entry into the documents of the hearing. If you will come back tomorrow, the letter, outlining the results, will be drafted and ready for you." He sat back again, looking off into space. The three Saudis, arms waving, continued on, yelling, screaming insults, and indicating their contempt for any man who would claim to have an understanding of the Koran yet could find against their cause.

Suliman jumped to his feet. Spittle rained from his mouth as he spoke. His black hair had fallen over his wild eyes, and he used the sleeve of his robe to wipe it back into place.

"You are a fool, Mr. John, if you expect me to abide by this man's judgment. He clearly is no expert, knows nothing about the finer points of the law, and has, as an Egyptian, no business dealing in our affairs at all." Aroused by the violent noise, the vice-president of the Chamber rushed in. His expression showed he was expecting to find someone being strangled. He helped restore order.

I was smiling blandly as I stuffed my papers back into the brown case. "Suliman, you agreed to abide by the ruling from the arbitration." I looked at him hard.

He looked back, just as intently. "This is only the first round, Mr. John. The matter must be discussed further. It is far from over. You will not soon leave us. We can see to that."

7 And Thus Disdained

December 1977

On the twentieth of December, about noon, I felt like Suliman might be right. I was sitting in a gray-walled cell, twelve by fifteen with a twelve-foot ceiling. It was not a nice place to be.

Neither was the jail in Dammam, where I'd first been taken. But I was better off in Al Khobar, because Abdallah Fazza had less clout there.

As soon as they'd picked me up, they had asked me to write a simple statement concerning my view of the problem over the forms. Sitting in the brigadier general's office in the Dammam Police Station, at a battered desk, I finished it and gave it to the guard. Twenty minutes later, he was back, presenting me with an Arabic document which, he assured me, was an exact translation of what I'd just written. He needed me to sign it.

Suspicious, I balked. Things were just about to get to the physical point when who should stroll by but a uniformed Egyptian from the Saudi civil rights section, and he obliged me with a translation.

The document was a combination confession and concession of six hundred thousand dollars to Abdallah Fazza! That it bore no resemblance to my original statement didn't surprise me. I was shocked, though, by the attitudes of my four partners, who were present, and the police. They all got mad and wanted to lynch the Egyptian passerby, who coolly signed his name, the date, and the time to a page in my notebook so I would have a record of a witness. That man had guts. It didn't do me a lot of good, but at least it was something.

My partners, instead of being ashamed at having been discovered in a blatant lie, screamed at me as if it were my fault they'd been found out.

"Mr. John, either you sign that or you'll end up doing five years in this jail." Suliman waved the paper in my face.

"Go to hell."

"No, it is you who will go to jail," he said, and they stormed out of the office. He was right, but he forgot to say the jail was hell, too.

The lockup in Al Khobar was a grungy-looking, dirt-brown, low building made out of roughly poured concrete and poor-quality cinder blocks given a once-over with paint. It sat on an edge of the downtown shopping district across an overly wide boulevard. There was an empty zone of no-man's land around the front, and it backed up to the blue waters of the bay. A pair of machine-gun toting, brown-uniformed guards stood at the door.

The place was in terrible shape. Garbage was piled ten to fifteen feet high on one side of the building and the rats gamboled through it like squirrels in the oak trees back home. There was no maintenance: broken windows, doors swinging on one hinge, disreputable offices, a beat-up corridor, and a bathroom which had been sorely in need of repair for at least a decade. Dark brown encrustments had built up through the years on the porcelain. Charming accommodations; not exactly the Al Gosaibi Hotel. The walls were rough and porous, the floor tiled with shades of old dirt over the mosaic pattern.

One interior wall of my cell was cinder block. It was obvious that if I wanted to escape I could bust out in a few hours or so. The joints between the blocks were shabby and using my belt buckle I could have torn out enough hunks to make a hole large enough walk through. The floor was another way to freedom. It had grooves in it where someone's weight had broken the tiles, which meant it was laid on sand. Easy way out.

That was it: dirty gray walls, dirty floor, an overhead electric light dangling from a frayed cord about ten feet off the floor, and one barred window, high up in the block wall. Noises came through the slits, as did daylight, in two eye-searing rays. By noon the intensity of the sun was enough to make the constantly burning bulb dim by comparison. Nighttime, the single bulb was so bright as to make sleeping difficult, as I'd found out during the long night before.

Moonbeams also slipped in through the openings, I was told, but I hadn't, as yet, had the privilege of seeing them sparkle on the floor. I'd been locked up there for not quite twenty-four hours.

After the hearing, I'd gone back to my room, packed, and changed my abode to another hotel. I decided a moving target might be harder to hit, so I moved. It would slow up my four partners, because they would have to find me before they could start something else. I knew where to find them if I needed to.

The verdict of the Egyptian judge of the C. of C. sounded pretty good to this New York Yankee turned Texas boy. It was clear, however, it wasn't going to end there.

He was an interesting man, that judge. When he realized his decision would carry no weight, he'd been careful to set up a situation in which the Saudi partners, if they went against his judgment, would be left with only minimal recourse under Islamic law. Minimal turned out to be enough for them.

In less time than most people would take to call an attorney, they arranged for an official hearing before the Ministry of Industry and Commerce. I believe Abdallah Fazza went to the governor of the province, also a relation of the King's, not to mention a close boyhood chum of Fazza's and an Al Khaled tribesman, to get it done. For president of the tribunal, they got Bakr Baghdalli, another kinsman and a top official of the Ministry of Industry and Commerce. This time, they did have friends in high places.

Quick lesson in customs: Fazza greeted the new judge by bumping noses twice and exchanging a kiss on the mouth, then two more kisses, one on each side of the lower neck, the way blood-brother friends greet one another. When I saw their noses touch, I knew there would be trouble. For me.

Those hearings, with more powerful decision implementation, started on the fifth of December and ran until the eleventh of January. We met sometimes twice, sometimes three times each week. I had counsel, but they had clout.

The proceedings were held on the second floor of an obscure, dilapidated building in a back alley near a heavily trafficked part of the city. It was inaccessible and unclearly identified. My attorney, who didn't want any part of the affair, but who had been hired for me through the auspices of an American friend's Saudi contact, was a timid, shy character who started out upset because he had to park six blocks away and walk

He was exasperated because Mohammed Al Qarim, my Saudi friend, who did have strong influence, had personally told him he was to look after my best interests.

If he had been put out before the hearing, it was nothing to his condition when, as an opening remark, the stud duck head judge boomed at me in a loud voice, saying, among other niceties, "Ninety-nine per cent of all Americans are crooks and cheats." My poor attorney was ashen because he realized he not only couldn't win but might be lucky to get out of the hearing without bringing down the wrath of powerful men.

From that point on, for week after week, the three judges went at me with bluster, threats, abusive comments, and bluff. I got tired of fingers being waved in my face and being spit upon by people shouting at me from across a table, but there wasn't a hell of a lot I could do

I was able to bring the consulate into it, for a moment, to protest the treatment I was receiving, but that was all I could do to fight back.

My attorney allowed common sense to override any valor he might have had, and he chickened out after the first day. Which was as soon as he could get outside that room. I managed the services, on and off, of a translator, to prevent the old "get him to sign an Arabic document" trick, and went it alone.

Quick lesson in Saudi law: It all stems from the Koran, and there is little written down. This is because for years only a few people could read. As plaintiff in a case, would you take the word of someone else about what a written law said if you couldn't read it and had no one in your family able to? Not no, but hell no. So, the body of law called Shari'a was developed from the Koran by custom through centuries and is interpreted today by the ulema, a group of leading theologians. It made sense in the nomadic days for a holy man to hand down decisions, because the law came from the teachings of the Koran and who would know it better? It's almost as if, in the West, the Jesuits of the Catholic Church had become the civil-law decision makers for Europe in the fourteen hundreds, basing their findings on how they interpreted the Bible.

Second quick lesson; simple point of law: You and I have a dispute over some goats you sold me. I say you delivered eight, you say ten. We have an impasse. If you like, you can take me into a civil hearing. But what if you're afraid I might take the ten goats you believe I have and slip away into the night? Easy. You go down to the local jail, see the desk sergeant, and ask to have me arrested. When they bring me in, we wait our turn for an audience before the esteemed sergeant, who can have his clerk fill out the proper papers. You put up the amount of the original selling price. I have to also. If I don't, they throw me in jail until you, taking your sweet time, arrange for the case to be heard. If I do, I'm free to go. The money acts as a cash bond. When the matter comes before a tribunal, based on Shari'a, it's winner-take-all. If the holy man–judge decides for me, I get half your money and two goats; if for you, you get my money and my agreement I got ten goats. It's not a bad way to settle things. But it does give an edge to the wealthy, if the practice is not applied with a sense of justice.

In December of '77, I didn't know much about Saudi law. But I'm a quick learner.

I believe I got stiffed every way they could stiff me. Fazza played on his relationship with the King, various tribal rivalries, Bidoon's power, and old friendships, to make things go more to his liking.

After this experience, I can see that I did not give sufficient credence to the factor of tribal relationships in modern Saudi Arabia. They are deeply rooted, constantly changing, and to some extent explain many otherwise obscure actions. Anyone who is contemplating doing business there, or who wants to understand why something is done, had better take a cram course in which tribe has who for a member and who is currently doing what to whom. It's hard to tell about the game without a program.

Early in the proceedings, Abdallah Fazza brought up before the tribunal a claim for thirty-five thousand riyals. He did it so they would ask us each to put up that amount, according to custom. They got mine, but the judge didn't follow through to force Fazza to pay. As far as I know, he never posted his cash.

I had to scramble for the money. I wired George and got him working, called on everyone I knew, and put together what I could.

Adding pressure, Fazza somehow arranged to have the police keep track of me. If he wanted to, as soon as the hearing board okayed the put-up-or-shut-up rule, he could move to have me locked up.

Which, needless to say, he did.

The cops came about noon on the nineteenth. Civil, not unfriendly, they searched my room for contraband, but found nothing: no booze, no proscribed magazines, no pornographic oddities for sale, only my clothes and the legal documents.

It was quite a scene when I guessed part of the reason they'd come was for the papers.

"I'll be glad to show you the contents of these two cases, but the documents are private. I need them."

One, taller then the rest, moved forward and grabbed for the battered brown leather case, but I turned away. He knew physical contact would be dangerous for both of us, so he paused at the last moment when he caught my eyes.

The excitement had improved my Arabic. Before anyone could regain the initiative, I dumped the contents of the satchel onto the bed. Spreading the papers, I began telling them, in halting language, there was nothing illegal. One of the dour-looking men, the only other in civilian robes, stepped forward. He looked through the documents, spreading papers apart with his finger. Satisfied, he straightened up.

The next thing I knew, they were gone. Through the ventilator over the door, I could hear their mumbling and footsteps disappear down the narrow corridor.

Judas Priest. My heart was beating a hundred and fifty times a minute. I wasn't sure what they wanted, but I knew the force of my Saudi partners was behind it.

The visit from the cops frightened me, so I intensified my jumping from hotel to hotel. I'd already moved twice in two weeks, and in an hour, I was packed and off again, this time to the U.S. Firms Guest House, an establishment run by a wild American citizen named Terence James. I'd eaten there several times and rooms were only sixty dollars a day.

Terence was six feet tall, weighed over three hundred pounds, and always dressed immaculately. He looked more like Sydney Greenstreet in *The Maltese Falcon* than Sydney Greenstreet did. Half Italian, half Lebanese, and all avarice, Terence was no stranger to Saudi jails and their ways. He lived one month in Saudi Arabia, then flew to Worcester, Massachusetts, where he would live for a month at home with his wife and eight kids.

He was a great help to me, and a man I felt I could trust, so I moved into his place and told him I thought I'd have more visits from the police. He asked how he might help. We spent hours discussing the law, my need for thirty-five thousand riyals to get me out of a problem with the cops, and how I might raise that sum in the

Kingdom if I needed it quickly. I wired George again, asking him to return-cable me that much, or more, in care of the Guest House, and felt better. Not for long. Terence fed the street gossip to me and it didn't sound good.

Next morning I arose as usual, did my exercises, went out for breakfast, and returned to review my papers one more intolerable time. The hearing was due to start in about two hours. That day's proceeding didn't concern me, since it was to be devoted to a series of swearings by the Saudis as to conversations they'd held with me about the project, but my presence the day before, when the same thing had gone on, seemed to stymie their baser inaccuracies. I hoped it would work again.

I should have expected another police search, because an odd note occurred while I'd been eating. One of Sheikh Saba's sons hustled up to my table and told me I needed to go down to the jail with him. "In a pig's ass," I answered, and thought how crazy he must be to think I'd just follow him out to the jailhouse.

About ten o'clock, I packed my papers, finished dressing by putting on my shirt, which I'd left off because of the heat in the room, and was about to go out the door when it reverberated with the force of someone knocking far harder than needed to get my attention. Before I could answer, it was flung open and my guests of the day before were back, this time with a gleam in their eyes and Sheikh Saba's son at their side.

That gleam meant no good for me. They had the equivalent of a warrant: two machine guns and four sets of strong arms. I would follow them, please.

There wasn't any question. I stalled long enough to pack my gear and grab my case, then we were in the lobby and I was paying my bill. I slipped Terence a quick note, asking him to call the U.S. consulate. He nodded and took charge of my suitcase.

Want to know what helpless feels like? Try sitting in the back seat of a U.S. surplus Jeep with foreign-looking men dressed in robes on each side of you and two more with big submachine guns in the front. No one said a word to me, and the few words they said to each other were in quick, local, guttural Arabic which I couldn't follow.

We were driving at a healthy clip, going Allah knew where, and had to be there only Allah knew when. The thought came to me I might be going for a gangster-type one-way ride. I dismissed it on two counts: one, because thinking about it would do no good; and two, the thought scared me.

Suddenly, with a screech of tires, we pulled up in front of a low, rough-looking building that gave off the aura of an official or governmental operation. Inside, I could see I was right. It was the city jail.

In Saudi, they don't just throw a man into the clink. They herd him into a large room along with all the other miscreants, misbegottens, and misfits, where a desk sergeant hears his problem, he gets the opportunity to answer, and then, according to the terms of the Shari'a, they throw him into the clink. There's a number of interesting offshoots to this, though.

The place was bedlam. Saudis, foreigners, accused, and the accusers were milling around. All were talking frantically at the top of their voices, shouting oaths, pledges of eternal gratitude if they might only be allowed to use the telephone, or anything else they thought could help their cases. Through it all, a tea servant calmly moved about serving his beverage to anyone who stopped him.

I was taken to the desk sergeant, a short, heavy man with a goatee and glasses as thick as the bottom of a Coke bottle. Standing coolly, waiting, were Suliman, Fazza, and the other two partners. They had gotten me brought in over the thirty-five thousand riyals as ordered by the hearing.

By this time, I was madder than hell. Scared, but mad, too. Like anyone who had never in his adult life come into contact with reality of prison, I was frightened by it. But I knew who to blame and focused on them.

I started in on the sergeant, demanding to use his phone. Not too wise an action. He ignored me, so I forced my temper under control.

The scene around me was past believing. Men were talking to each other, being interrupted by a third person, starting conversations with that one, then being interrupted by the man they were talking to in the first place. No one could possibly be achieving anything.

Except for Suliman, who, because I'd made the sergeant mad, had the man's full attention and was using it to describe precisely what the angry American was trying to do to the four nice Saudi gentlemen, including a brother-in-law of the King himself. The situation was not going well for me. I used the telephone. It took about fifteen tries to get the Guest House so I could tell Terence where I was.

I figured I was into the put-up-or-be-locked-up deal and that meant trouble. For me. My money hadn't arrived.

My second phone call was to one of two men I knew who might be able to help me. Mohammed Al Qarim, the friend of my friend from Houston and a man I knew to have influence, said he would come down. Al Qarim was a well-placed executive. He showed up in ten minutes with his manager, and they buttonholed the desk sergeant.

It was clear from his expression that Suliman had already explained their situation. Real creative pleading of his case.

The four partners, seeing Al Qarim speak to me, came over, and we six got into a fracas, making more noise than other groups in the crowded, large room. I could understand they'd scored a big point with Al Qarim when his face fell.

He later told me they'd brought the King into the argument. Al Qarim was a loyal member of a faction of the Al Khaled tribe, and therefore a staunch supporter of the King, as well as bound by certain oaths of loyalty. Since fat Fazza was the King's brother-in-law, he was hog-tied.

Al Qarim, eyes downcast, quietly said something I can still hear late at night, this many years later. "Mr. John"—he almost had tears in his eyes,— "there is nothing I can do. They will never let you go from Saudi Arabia."

Not "for six months," or "until you settle with them," or "until you pay up," just "never." A very final word.

No one was in any hurry to act. They were letting me stew, and believe me, as I watched Al Qarim walk out of the cop shop, I was on the boil. Anger helped keep back the fear I felt. I'd heard stories about what would happen once I was inside a cell. In this bisexual country I could imagine almost anything.

Twenty minutes passed. Fazza and Suliman left, the other two staying to keep an eye on me. The confusion was so intense it was impossible to decide what was going on, but I guess there was some order because we were obviously all waiting for our cases to come officially before the honorable farsighted sergeant in the dirty white robe.

Then came shock number two. I heard my name being called, looked up, and spotted an Arab, Hussein, whom I'd met at

Abdallah Fazza's. He had burst into the room and hurried across to me, calling my name.

"Mr. John, Mr. John! What in the world is happening here?" He kept his Arabic simple.

"I wish to hell I knew." Hussein was a new and used horse dealer by trade. Most people insisted he was also a horse thief early in his career. That need not have been true. Horse traders in Saudi, along with camel traders, have the same reputation as used-car salesmen in the United States.

Hussein was a man of medium height, not fat by the standards of the country, with a sly smile.

"I just heard of your plight, and have come to assist you." He spoke a combination of Arabic with a few words of English.

By Allah, he swore, he'd have me out of that damnable jailhouse in fifteen minutes flat. He cheered me greatly. But there was one small thing he needed to know. What was the exact cost of installing the forms?

The fact that he was one of the conspirators shouldn't have surprised me, but my situation at the time, and the unending confusion of the jail reception room, kept me off balance. Thank God he was so naïve as to have been direct. Fazza had been after me for days to come up with that figure so they could show the tribunal they knew what they were doing.

The cost would also, I guessed, be used to back up their appeal to the desk sergeant as to the correct amount at question in our deal.

Hussein explained that he needed to know so he could personally go and get the cash for my bond. He'd be back in thirty minutes, bringing whatever money it took.

I hoped I might buy more time, so I selected a sum small enough for me to be able to post as my bond and told him, "Five thousand U.S. dollars." I could see the wheels turning in his head as he did the conversion calculation, then, without a good-bye, he rushed through the mass of men, heading for the door. I decided not to hold my breath until he returned with my bail money, as he was clearly off to tell the Saudis how cunningly he'd tricked "Mr. John" into giving him the heretofore unavailable figure. Big deal.

In a few minutes the missing two partners came back, and the four, together, surrounded the desk sergeant. They talked intensely for a few minutes. What they said, or offered, aside from

Fazza's relationship with the King, I don't know, but within seconds of their breaking up the huddle of robes, the sergeant said something and pointed at me.

I stormed over. The mixture of languages made an awful racket, especially when the sergeant decided to make me understand by shouting louder. Ten minutes later I was left alone again in the middle of more screaming people.

Whew! It was some place. I looked at my watch and that was when I realized their game. It was after four. The desk sergeant, like every other official in the Kingdom, was going to close up shop at four-thirty. I imagined those who had the misfortune not to have had their cases decided before then would be asked to stay for the night. And I didn't think they'd let me sleep on the hearing-room floor.

Was I ever right. I was able to use the telephone one last time, but it was a lost cause. In Saudi, after about seven in the morning, the instrument is practically useless. It takes ten to twenty tries to get a ring, and even then the odds are strong for a wrong number.

I tried the U.S. consulate, the few Americans I knew, my attorney, the sheikh of the long-ago drinking party and trip to Houston, who might help, and finally, a man named Lorenzo di Fino, whom I'd known in the old days back in New York. Luckily, I got through to him. Screaming to be heard over the noise, I yelled out my problem. Before he could answer, the sergeant hollered something and two guys with submachine guns stepped up to me, took the phone away, and pointed me toward the lockup.

The jails in Saudi are like those in Mexico and many other countries in one respect. If a case is in progress when the office closes, or comes up after closing time but before the office opens in the morning, all concerned go into the cell. And stay until opening time the next day. I figured I might be "forgotten" and have to wait a little longer. It worried me, but what the hell?

The two guards with submachine guns moved in close and the sergeant watched me warily. He was wondering if I was going to make trouble. Apparently the few Americans they'd held were bad guests.

The sergeant said he'd see me in the morning, I nodded to Suliman and Abdallah Fazza, who were standing by to see me locked up, and away we marched. I called the blind bastard a "fat-assed cocksucker" as I passed, and even though the guards couldn't understand English they knew it was a bad name and snickered.

They tightened their grips on the submachine guns and we were out of the guardroom into a narrow corridor. We turned a corner and there was the one and only cell, closed by an iron door painted scratched gray. It had several small steel bars which formed a hole to look in or out, and a medieval lock.

I'd seen the inside of a jail before, once, on a tour with my two teenaged sons back in Houston. The purpose of the visit was to show them what happened to someone who didn't handle his business very well. I guess I wasn't doing mine right now, because I was on the inside, but not on tour.

Without stopping to pass go, I was tossed in; no booking, no photos, no fingerprinting, no conversation, no nothing. Out of hotel and into the worst pigsty of a cell you can imagine.

There were ten men in the room, which smelled of old shit, unwashed feet, and bad cases of ringworm. The prisoners sat on prayer mats in groups of two or three, talking. They looked up when the door slammed open and the guards marched me inside, then, seemingly uninterested, they went back to their endless conversations.

I was emotionally shell-shocked. I found a place in the corner of the filthy room and hunkered down on the floor, staring across the cell. The flies were everywhere, thick enough in the air to form a living black cloud. The heat was so intense I sweated through my shirt in a matter of minutes. The buzz-drone of the flies and the murmur of voices was set apart from the sound of a radio down the corridor turned up too loud, playing what passed for popular music. Occasionally an iron door would clang-slam, causing everyone to look up. From the doorway across the room there was a strong smell of human excretion. It wasn't a constant odor. It came in jolts through the air and bit my nose sharply.

For the first half hour, I didn't do anything but sit. I can honestly say I don't recall much of what went on or what I thought. Looking back, I realize I'd fallen into instant despair. I had no idea what my position was, no idea how to get word outside to what few friends I had in Saudi Arabia, much less to my wife and partner, no idea how long I'd be held, no idea if I had been charged with something and would have to face Islamic justice, and no idea what my being there was going to do to my chances at the hearing. Really neat.

The thing that bothered me most was not knowing how long I was going to be a prisoner. From the look of the cell, several of the men had been inside for months. From the look of the men, several of them expected to be there months more. Was I in for a week, a month, a year? I had no notion, and this upset me badly.

There was absolutely no furniture in the room. Along one wall were pads, but no sign of blankets. The guards would come once in a while to count the bodies. Quaint but effective custom: if a prisoner got away, the responsible guard took his place until the escapee returned. The same guards, or at least I think they were the same men, would walk down the corridor twice a day collecting money from the prisoners to buy their food. Hours later, they'd come back with flat, round loaves of unleavened bread and a white, cheesy-dairy, runny mess. If I anted up a few more riyals once a day, they'd bring me a couple of Pepsis and some stale English cookies.

It wasn't a bribe. I paid the guard and he performed the necessary additional work to get me a desired amenity. Food was not a part of the accommodations, since all prisoners hosted by the Saudis are paid a monthly subsistence allowance of about $24 dollars by the government. I had my wallet and a considerable amount of cash, but I didn't know the ropes well enough to figure out how to use it. There was no instruction book. Besides, I wanted loose, not just to get along.

After three hours of sitting, my butt was sore, so I stood up and stretched. The other men watched me carefully.

All my life I've heard stories about being in jail: the kangaroo courts which seasoned inmates hold to take the possessions of newcomers and the homosexual rapes used to initiate a new guy into the system. Those stories came back in a flood as I watched the men watching me. Judas Priest, did they ever look like a sinister bunch: short, dark, robes torn and dirt-caked, barefoot, bristly black mustaches, and a way of sitting on their heels for hours without moving.

I decided that if I were attacked, I was going to fight with everything I had. They might take me, and in fact probably would, but I was going to leave a few of them in bad condition, so they'd think twice about messing with me again.

I needn't have worried. What may be true about American jails was not true of this one, or not for me in the cell where I was tossed. The men were not overly friendly but they also weren't violent. It may have been my foreign appearance or the fact the guards came by on an irregular schedule to peer in at me, but I was left alone. A prisoner spoke a word or two now and then, but from what I could gather from their talk, they didn't think I could understand Arabic. I couldn't at first, because of the accents, but in time I got a lot better at it from having nothing else to do. I also learned by using my eyes.

I'd been locked up for about four hours when one of the guards came to the door, knocked on the small bars with his rifle barrel, and crooked his finger at me. I went over, and there was Lorenzo, the man I'd called. He quickly stuffed a blanket through the foot-square grillwork and gave me a reassuring smile. He knew things were serious and whispered a message before the guard moved him along.

"I've called the U.S. consulate, John, and told them what happened."

"Thanks."

"Keep your spirit up. When you get out of there, then you can deal with the fuckers."

"Yeah."

I was feeling mighty low, but the blanket and the fact that someone I could trust, another American, knew and cared about my situation, helped.

I settled into prison life by praying for constipation. That may seem an odd start, but under the circumstances, it was realistic. The area used for a rest room was through a narrow, battered green-painted iron door. Every time one of my fellow inmates would get up to use the facilities, he would take a deep breath before opening it. An unspeakably fetid odor emanated from behind that door. A big St. Bernard dog fed on fish and allowed to fart in a closed car on a hot summer day can't even come close. I hoped I'd be out before I was forced to pay a personal visit to the men's room. I didn't make it, but that comes later.

Once I calmed down, I started looking for a way to get loose. People had busted free from Saudi jails before, and although I hoped I was only there for a few hours, it was always possible someone could be persuaded to "lose" my name. Besides, it was a way to pass the time.

The movement of the guards bothered me. They marched about on an irregular schedule, and if I didn't know when they were coming, they would be able to catch me in the act of making my break. So I considered the problem of getting advance warning.

One of the prisoners had a bag of pistachio nuts and was eating them morosely, cracking them open with his stained teeth and spitting the hulls on the floor. I gathered up a couple of handfuls of the drier shells, and by sticking my arm through the bars on the door, tossed them both directions down the hallway. The husks fell among the garbage already down on the checkered tile and blended right in.

I sat back to wait, and sure enough, in about twenty minutes there came a crunch, crunch, crunch, and the guard peered in. Problem number one solved, and as it looked like they hadn't swept the floor in years, it should stay solved for some time. The trick helped my morale, not to mention my status with the other inmates. They had watched with interest and when they heard the crunch, crunch sound and saw the guard, they realized what I had done. I took their smiles for sincere approbation.

Later it was crunchy, crunch again, but this time there was the sound of a key in the lock and the door swung open. For me. Hail Columbia, it was Jack Butell, the U.S. vice-consul and his trusty interpreter Bushay. I learned then, that no matter how strong the desire of the consulate official to see you free, or how much he might wish to protect a fellow American, there is little or nothing he can do. Jack is a good State Department career man, but like me was powerless. He had encouraging words, wanted to know if I needed anything, and said he would do all he could to spring me. It was good to know my government knew where I was. Better still to see the pain openly expressed in his face over my predicament.

I had a note, written to Terence, telling him what had happened and asking if the money from George had arrived. I needed that extra shot of funds to fall back on in case I got the opportunity to post bond in the Saudi fashion. I was going to pass it to Jack, but a guard saw me and motioned for it. I shook my head and slipped it back into my pocket. There was no sense getting Terence's name into my mess. The guard, unconcerned, walked away.

Jack and I exchanged a few more platitudes; I asked him to be sure and check on me every day, so I wouldn't linger here forever. He agreed and, looking concerned, left.

The visit from the U.S. vice-consul caused a stir among my fraternity brothers. After a lengthy conversation, one came over to me, and in street Arabic said, "You know this man?"

He handed me a card. It was a business card from a competitor with a Houston company. The prisoner told me a complex story which I discounted, but later heard was true. It seems the poor American arrived at the airport on his first trip into Saudi and was taken directly from the plane to the jailhouse. A former agent of his firm had a disagreement with his boss, and arranged a special welcome. After a week in jail, a million dollars was raised, and he got out. At the time the sum made my money disagreement seem like small pickings.

Nighttime in the jail, Saudi style: Each of the prisoners paired up with another and slipped under a single blanket. From the sounds they made, I could tell they weren't sleeping. I was happy there was an odd number of people in the cell, and I was odd man out. Or, maybe it's straight man out. Depends on geography and upbringing, I guess. They all thought it was the most natural thing in the world and their grunts and sighs exhibited enjoyment. I drifted off after the others quieted down. Not comfortable, but alive. And secure in one thing. If I had to, I could break out.

During the night, the guards brought in a young Saudi gentleman. He was drunk and his comments revealed he had run his Mercedes into a truck with two Pakistanis aboard. Both were dead. The man's dress, white robe, standard upper-class gold threads, announced he was a wealthy sheikh or possibly even a prince. He spoke perfect Middle American English.

"Hey, man." He spotted me through the grillwork. Smiling, he gripped the bars. In the dim light, I could make out a college ring. Michigan State. "This Saudi Arabia is the shits."

A simple declaration, but at the moment, I couldn't have put it better.

They hauled him away, to private quarters, so he could await the coming of his father. If the two Pakistanis had killed him in the wreck, they would have been tied down and members of the young man's family allowed to drive over them a few times for revenge. Tough laws when you're on the other side.

Most of the younger Saudis who get the opportunity to spend a few years in the United States discover a better way of life. It's hard, like the old World War I song, to "keep 'em down on the farm" after they've seen Nirvana West.

Six o'clock. Dawn, with a thin beam of sunshine. Promise of another hot, wet day. I had the need to heed the call of nature. I stepped over a few of my new comrades and opened the door, telling myself it wasn't as bad as I knew it would be. It wasn't. It was worse. A hell of a lot worse.

There were two rooms. The first, about a ten-by-ten finished in natural concrete block, was a washroom. A few fixtures were still brokenly stuck in place. Several years earlier some Moslem had climbed up on the single porcelain sink to run water over his butt after defecating and had broken the facility from the wall. The jailers cut the water off after that. There was a shower pan on the floor in one corner, occupied by a rat the size of a French poodle. Resenting my company, he slunk through the door to the second room. I followed him.

What I found was a dimly lit ten-by-eight Mideastern toilet. In roughly the middle was a water closet, without the closet or the water. It was a hole which supposedly led down to a sewer line. The user squats over the opening, lets her rip, then hoses down the slanting floor to clear up remains and near-misses. Water and fingers are used in lieu of toilet paper. In the recent past, either the misses became not so near or the water supply failed. The fly-covered pile of poop formed a ring about three feet in diameter and a foot high. The bugs were everywhere, buzzing. Once the original dung heap became unmanageable, other visitors decided to leave their calling cards in odd corners, until finally there were no more odd corners. The floor was covered with squishy little piles. All a user could do was forget fancy footwork, walk to the clearest area, and get it over with. This feature also explained why everyone in the cell was barefoot. They'd all left their shit-covered sandals just inside the door.

The Arabic name for the relief room is hammam. I don't think even they would have used that term for this mess. To make it worse, the light wasn't any too good, and that big rat could turn out to be an enemy. I don't know what that poor beast did to have been assigned this particular franchise territory, but whatever it was, I had little desire to run him off. He was welcome to it, as long as I could make an occasional visit.

I checked out the small, high, barred window, and found it was more secure than the one in the main room where we slept. Thank God or Allah for that, I thought. It would have to have been a hell of a lot easier than the other one to keep me in there to work on it.

The sight of those hundreds of flies upset me. The state of this place was unpardonable and I resolved to do something about it as soon as I could.

Middle Easterners are shy about their bathroom habits, demanding privacy for defecation. You'd never find two of them in there together. But I was going to organize a team, get some cleaning stuff from the guards, and straighten the filthy room out. I did my business, left my shoes, and went back into the cell where I sat down and composed a list: shovels, brooms, disinfectants, detergents, light bulbs, wiring, the works. I wrote it most respectfully, addressing the captain. The next opportunity I had, I was going to try and get my request to him.

One other incident from the previous night: before going to bed, I stripped off and rinsed myself down with a bottle of nonalcoholic aftershave. Didn't smell too great, but it felt better. The others were fascinated by my white skin, but I later found there was some anxious discussion as to whether or not I had leprosy. I'd been hesitant to get naked because the sight of my body might entice someone to rape me, but I smelled so rank it was worth it. Besides, by this time, I'd sized up my roomies and there wasn't one who looked tough enough to do it. Bad-looking, yes, with missing teeth and eyes, but tough enough to screw me, no.

I was locked in what would correspond to a central city jail in this country. Unlike the county facility we have, the Saudis only have three tiers: a holding tank, like mine, a larger place serving what would correspond to our state prison, and a couple of federal units. The next two higher levels were hard places. The one I was in, while no site for a Girl Scout picnic, wasn't totally horrible. Book a room there on a visit I wouldn't, but as rough as an Arabian jail can be, no. In the others, they kept you in wrist or leg shackles all the time.

Prison life sharpens the senses, or it did mine. In spite of the nagging fear and doubts as to how long I might remain, I established a routine around me in the first six hours. I made contact with the guards, using my faltering Arabic, got something better to eat, a jar of tea, and laid claim to a sleeping mat. I needed it, because I spent two very long fly-buzzing, rat-gnawing, fetid-smelling, mosquito-bitten, insect-ridden nights there.

I even concocted a surefire escape plan. The one wall, as I've mentioned, was laid down with Saudi standard-quality mortar.

Using my belt buckle and fingers, I amazed the others by easily scratching an inch-deep hole through it. I had no definite time set, but if I was going to be held much longer, I decided to dig away the material from between three or four blocks, get out into the corridor, and go over to where a huge pile of prisoners' belongings was stacked. I'd find a kafiya headpiece, a thauba robe, some sunglasses, and wait my chance to mingle with the continual early-morning crowd visiting the jail. I believe it would have worked, and it's an interesting insight into the different psychology of Americans and mideasterns. To them, the wall was solid. To me it was almost falling apart.

Late on the afternoon of my second day, a guard came, rattled my cage door, and pointed to me. I slipped into my smelly shoes and followed him down the now-familiar corridor into a large, open room. He gestured casually toward a door. I shook my head, expressing my lack of understanding, and he nuzzled me with his machine gun, not gently, but not rudely, and guided me to the room with the sergeant.

The policeman indicated I should be seated, staring at me through his thick glasses. He ordered a Pakistani to bring us both tea. Using a careful Arabic, with little or no local accent, he asked me how the jail was. Knowing better, I decided to break Moslem custom, and heatedly, I told him, using Arabic, English, and body motions to get my point across. Judas Priest, I thought, you get a break, then you go and get yourself thrown back inside. Really diplomatic, McDonald.

The sergeant looked at me sternly when I started to talk, but after the first few hundred words, he smiled, then laughed out loud. The others in the room, fifteen or so disputants and the rest of the guards, had watched my bad-tempered outburst narrowly, not stopping their own pleas. When the sergeant laughed, they all laughed, and the room sounded like a madhouse.

Still smiling, he went through the papers which dealt with my case, a puzzled expression on his face. He spoke with his administrative clerk, then looked through the documents again, slowly and seriously. He handed the file to the clerk with a few soft, intense words. The man immediately disappeared into another room, and we sat, silently, sipping our tea. I didn't know what to make of it.

In five minutes the clerk was back, whispering to my host, who got up and went out with him. He was back shortly, calling me to follow him.

The office was as plain as the outer room; smaller, but better furnished. There was a rug on the floor and real chairs. The man seated behind the gunmetal-gray desk was taller than the sergeant, and from his insignia I guessed he was the head honcho of the station.

He looked up from my file and spoke to me slowly. "Can you post the necessary thirty-five-thousand-riyal bond, Mr. John?"

I nodded. Then said, "Yes, sir, I can. I could have two days ago, too. But no one would let me." I was bluffing, based on a hope my cable had come.

He went over this gem of information twice more, asking the same questions in different ways. Then the capitano blew a gasket. His jail was not, repeat not, being run the way he wanted it run. Or the way it should be run. He was not, repeat not, going to stand for it. For a man to be held two days without opportunity to post bond was an outrage. He was sorry.

Before storming out, he asked me to please make myself comfortable behind his very own desk, feel free to use the telephone, and the guards would care for any of my needs. In a huff, he was gone. Where, I never learned. The governor's palace or to his boss, I guess.

I made myself at home, not knowing if it was going to be another day or an hour. The Salvation Army level of room furnishings was sparse, but a hell of a lot better than the cell I'd been in and might be going back to.

I decided to try to call Sheikh Mohammed Abdullah. After twenty tries, I got him.

"You're what? Where, Mr. John?" His voice was full of disbelief. I could hear him shout to someone off the phone, "Quickly, you idiot. They have Mr. John McDonald in jail. Find my brother-in-law, tell him to drop everything, and get him out. Right away."

I was astounded by his reaction. I'd expected him to be friendly, but nothing like that. Relief overwhelmed me. At last, I had a friend with power.

Enter Fazza, Suliman, et al. Good-bye relief, hello trouble.

The four came into the guardroom, looked around for me, asked a few people, learned where I was, then descended on the sergeant like a pack of wolves. Abdallah Fazza demonstrated he had balls as well as clout by yelling, and I mean yelling, at the sergeant. The other people in the room, who usually didn't pay attention to anything, all shut up to listen. Whatever he said must have been stout, because the sergeant, after taking several minutes of the loud abuse, started talking back. Boy, that tore it. When he told Fazza his capitano had taken a personal interest in the situation and stormed out, the brawl started. I thought Fazza had been shouting before. Maybe. I don't know what to call the volume he reached after he heard about the captain's interference with his plans. Some of it I could understand. He wanted me back in that damned cell now, right now, not later, now.

The sergeant, secure in the knowledge his captain would back him, merely shook his head.

I waited not knowing what would happen. Just when I was getting nervous, the door opened. It was the sergeant of the thick-lensed glasses, and he was smiling broadly.

"You may go, sir. This gentleman is standing good for you."

He moved aside to reveal an aristocratic-looking Saudi. Tall, thin, with sharply chiseled features, black, piercing eyes, and a firm, white-toothed smile. Obviously someone of character with influence. He came forward, hand extended, speaking top-grade English, not American, but university English.

"Mr. John, I sincerely hope you remember me. I am Sheikh Mohammed Abdullah's brother-in-law.

I remembered him vaguely as one of several distinguished men Sheikh Mohammed had around him during one of our dinners. I shook hands, smiling, too.

"Yes, of course."

"I have signed an agreement with the desk sergeant to the effect that I will personally guarantee your appearance at any hearing or other legal proceeding where it is required. Mohammed is concerned and anxious for your safety and does not want you to worry."

I nodded. "There is no way I can thank you or the sheikh enough for your help."

"Do not worry about it, Mr. John. You have been wronged. Now, quickly, before those low men who are regrettably your partners come in, let us·go "

I said good-bye and thanks to the desk sergeant, who looked at me owlishly through his glasses, and hit the street.

I didn't worry about what had transpired, chalking my release up to one of the complex intertribal feuds always in progress. The captain and the good sergeant were both from Mohammed's tribe in Hofuf, a hundred miles west, which was allied with the Al Khaled tribe. The jail was in Al Khaled territory, so Mohammed's team could ask for and receive cooperation.

Even the sunlight on the outside seemed brighter.

Talk about an adjustment shock. That morning I'd been sitting in my cell, trying to figure a way to get loose, and now I was out. No more dry shaving or washing toothpaste out of my mouth with old tea. It told me one thing. My Saudi partners could mess with me a lot worse than I could screw with them. I had to be careful.

That late afternoon, right there, riding through the busy street with the sheikh's brother-in-law toward the Al Gosaibi, after having been psychologically jerked around, I began to form a new attitude and awareness of the Saudi situation in which I found myself entangled. None of the accustomed routines of America, none of the ideas of fair play, none of the moral concepts I'd been a lifetime developing, were going to do me any good at all. It was a different place, might as well have been a different time, and I was in it. From that second on, I changed my ways. I'd already studied the Saudis, but now I began to make a religion out of watching them. I decided the only way to overcome them was to use their own system and culture against them, a thing I was ready to do.

I started with my Arabic. The part of the language I knew well dealt with construction and engineering matters, a little polite conversation suited to the majlis of the wealthy, how to order in a restaurant, and other situation phrases I'd had need for and therefore practiced. In jail, the street Arabic was strange, but not so strange I couldn't comprehend it if I worked on every word. Low-class Saudis from one tribe have a hard time understanding low-class Saudis from another. The difference was pronounciation. I began to listen.

Day by day my knowledge of the language increased. A good thing, too. I was going to need every possible factor in my favor before this mess was over. It was a long, long way from being done.

8 *Season's Greetings*

December 1977

I was really surprised. The sound of the dry, soft, lonesome sob that hung in the still air of my room had come from me. Merry fucking Christmas.

To an American, or any Westerner for that matter, Christmas in Saudi Arabia is an especially bleak time. All decorations, trees, carols, anything openly signifying the holiday, are forbidden. Break the rule and you run the risk of arrest by the religious police.

The morning of the twenty-fourth I got out of bed and faced a new day of hearings. I had to leave early, because the trip to Dammam would take a series of transfers from one Toyota jitney taxi to another.

The jitneys don't cruise looking for passengers. They have a deeply rutted, bare-earth football-field-sized lot which is like an open-air bus station. None of the cars are marked, and there are no signs. You figure out where one is going by memory or meandering about. The sixty or so cabs all have different routes and the drivers are constantly blowing their horns and shouting babbled, vague pronouncements of their eventual destination. Once one of these Toyotas successfully captures five unwashed passengers, who jam themselves inside, it rips off at a deadly rate.

Crushed in, you know what your neighbor had for breakfast or dinner. Radio blaring, people talking all at once at the top of their voices, you sally forth, certain of your, or at least I was always certain of my, impending death or dismemberment. I never rode without, at some time, deciding this was the trip that would kill me.

Two other neat tricks. After they've loaded up, the driver

164

always stops for pear nectar or coffee. You can't expect him to face the open road without a bracer. Second, there is never again a complete stop until all passengers are off. You jump free of the vehicle while it is still rolling. A matter of style.

Again, remember, unlike most other countries, it's all men. No women. They might be allowed, with proper escort, to walk a few blocks, but never, ever, ride the jitneys.

Early risers in Saudi are definitely nonstatus. The time a man arises is directly linked to his success in life. No person of stature ever rolls out of bed before 9 A.M., and eleven is more common. A boss would never be seen in the office or on the job before his assistant. It's a nationwide pecking order. Made me feel even better. I was out in the streets with the lowest level of laborers.

I arrived at the ministry offices after passing through the narrow, hot, humid streets, had my usual brush with death by impalement on the hood ornament of a Mercedes Benz sedan, and went through more hours of total bullshit in which I was again told I was responsible for paying all demurrage costs no matter what the original contract said. One more time I was reminded of other dire consequences to my person if I didn't sign the recently prepared agreement.

I'd had it. My long-pent-up anger, buoyed by my Christmas depression, welled to the surface, and in addition to telling them where to stuff their papers, I suggested, as a parting sally, that they perform an anatomically impossible feat with their genitals.

I started back for the hotel, where I could sit in one of the public areas and see what was new on *I Love Lucy* and *Sea Hunt*. Both these shows, running without commercial breaks, were about twenty-minute productions. Just an all-around great Christmas Eve.

The one high point I had to look forward to was calling Pat. I was going to wait until about seven, Saudi time, on Christmas Day, then go to the telephone company building, where I guessed I could get an overseas line by waiting a few hours.

There were four trunk lines out of Dhahran, and twenty operators to man them. Why they needed that many, I'm not sure, but the job had to be a soft touch.

A dark-skinned porter, stationed in a huge hallway, ushered callers into one of four beat-up closets, which served as telephone booths, to pick up the receiver for their calls. An old-time oil rig tool pusher must have gotten hold of the man and taught him his stock of

English, because his sole words were, "Move your fuckin' legs, move your fuckin' legs." He said it to every caller with lots of goodwill.

I started talking to the operator in Arabic, and he took it as an opening to tell me his problems. Not all of which I could understand. I translated that he had a dilemma because of a religious holiday. According to the tenets of Islam, he was not allowed to make love to his wife for that day and the next. He made a suggestion to me about how I might alleviate his difficulty, but I declined. There was a constant problem in speaking Arabic too freely. Some wild man or another was always propositioning me. I could do without that phase of Saudi life.

Between then and seven the next evening I had a lot to do. I started with staring at the walls. I'd spent so many hours in the past two weeks staring at those walls I'd left my eyeprints on them. So I went for a walk. My usual brisk six to eight miles.

People everywhere, dressed like the characters in the manger scene every year at the little church back home. But none of these men had ever heard of the manger, or Christmas. Atonal music from a few open buildings, the instruments keeping a strange rhythm with each other. No carols or "White Christmas" or excited kids or a tree or any sense of belonging or anything I'd ever before associated with the big holiday.

I'd been alone at Christmas before. When I say alone, I mean away from the family. George had been with me last year, and he's a friend. This was my first time alone, alone. No Army buddies, absolutely no one to talk to, and the people on the street unaware of the special nature of the night or the coming day. I've read about Christmas depression and how it affects somebody, but Judas Priest, the state I reached was almost catatonic. I'd been thrown into a hellhole of a jail, gone through days of so-called hearings in which the men who were sitting in judgment seemed to hear only what they wanted, was pretty sure I was facing jail again, had a $4500 hotel bill, and knew the final results of the forced negotiations would cost me another hundred grand when all was said and done. Lovely little Christmas present, that last hundred.

Somehow, though, even as dispirited as I was, I still believed in the deal. If I could manage through this one rough spot, get the forms up on the site, and start using them to build the modules, the big money would come. It was still a viable deal. I just had to control the situation, keep everybody in the action, and not let them steal every nickel I could raise in the meantime.

A happy happening on that Christmas Eve was being paged to the telephone to speak with a man who must remain nameless. I'll call him Norman. He was one of the few Americans I'd met while in the Kingdom. He worked for Aramco, was an old hand, having lived in Saudi for more than ten years, and had a job high enough up in the company to have been given the maximum luxury of a three-bedroom house in the compound.

Compound is a crude word, depicting a fenced-off area where people are kept segregated under lock and key. To that extent, it fits the Aramco settlement, because the Americans there are being segregated, away from the run-of-the-mill Saudis. The ostensible reason centers on religion and way of life, but the level of life-style also plays a big part in the decision.

The Aramco compound is an oasis of America in the middle of the desert. It's like an Army post or an Air Force base without runways. Completely self-contained, it offers an extra large convenience store, restaurants, a movie, library, swimming pool, recreational facilities including a bowling alley, schools, offices, houses, and everything else that goes to make up a pleasant town of several thousand. It's all there, with pale green-brown grass, street signs in English and Arabic, fireplugs, dogs, parties, bacon in the meat counters (even though it's marked "Breakfast Beef"), and a still in many households to run off a batch of white lightning.

Aramco personnel are protective about their stills. When an old-timer leaves he wills his equipment to someone else and it's considered a gift of high value. Arriving newcomers get a recipe for "scotch" and "gin." It's possible to make a potable, potent, 180-proof product.

Aramco puts up Christmas decorations in the compound, but not where they can be viewed from the outside.

Norman's call was a complete surprise. I was in the hotel lobby when I heard a bellboy shouting my name. Thinking it was more trouble, I almost didn't respond. The break from boredom was too tempting, so I answered, and in a minute found myself invited to spend a part of Christmas Day having a traditional holiday meal with Norman and his family inside the gates of Little America. It vas something to look forward to.

Another person was nice to me that evening. I'll call him Paul because still lives in Saudi Arabia, so he could come into hard times if certain people knew he'd helped me. It's one thing to be clear and away, with no intention of ever going back, another to be there and dependent upon the whimsical goodwill of the government.

Paul had purchased a six-pack of beer from a ship captain for a holiday celebration. It had cost him $180. Now thirty dollars for a can of Bavarian brew might seem a bit pricey, but not in Saudi. Case rates for beer were the same as for scotch. It was the size of the box which dictated storage space needed to smuggle it in, not the alcoholic content. To religious enforcers of the law, a little alcohol was just as bad as a lot. Alcohol is prohibited, period. Thirty days was the Saudi sentence for the first offense, two years for the second.

No matter the price, and no matter from whom he'd received it, Paul had a six-pack of beer. He invited me to split it with him, inside the sanctity of my room, as a Christmas Eve festivity. Any other time I might have said "Whoopie" to the thought of a celebration centering around three cans of beer and an hour or so of quiet, reflective conversation between two guys far, far from home, but that night, in that place, it was a hell of a nice thing for him to have done.

We sat, sipping the bubbly, tepid drink from the cans, reminiscing about better years in better places. Paul left and I went to bed.

I lay a long while, thinking. There had to be a way out of this mess. We had to make the deal work. There was enough profit for everyone. If only I could make the greedy bastards see that all they were doing by screwing with my head over a few grand was delaying the final payoff time. I swore I'd try. I'd really try. For the money, sure, but also because they could use the buildings we'd construct. Homes for families. Besides, getting the job done is a tradition with me.

I wished I were with my family. It was going to be a lonesome Christmas. A Christmas of lonesomeness. A lonely time in a strange and threatening land.

9 My New Year's Resolution

Into January 1978

I have discussed rats and how they have their freedom in Saudi Arabia to run as they please. What I haven't made a point of is their size (about as big as a small dog) and their habit of climbing into my bed, which I assure you causes wild leaps from sound sleeps, usually accompanied by shouts of "Goddamn!" or other such oaths.

I had seen champion wharf rats in Kuwait and Cairo, and the New York City variety is more fiercely aggressive, but the ones in Saudi are pervasive. They are everywhere. There are distinct types, with differences in behavior. The gray ones, for example, are outside rats and run over roofs, like squirrels. They play in the streets like squirrels, too. The black robber is a house rat; he runs where he likes. Anyone who stays in Saudi learns to get along with the rats.

The reason for this discourse on rats is it was with them I spent several days, not long after Christmas, because again I refused to fork over more cash, as demanded. I was back in the Al Khobar hoosegow, which is a Texas way of saying jail, and one of my few pastimes, aside from writing, was watching the rats play on the window ledge. I mentioned the flies in my last recounting of jail, but only one rat. More were there, I just didn't say they were. Very hard to become affectionate toward a rat. I guess they'd make a good pet if you could ever housebreak them, but there is little satisfaction in one because no endearing names come to mind to fit their species.

I was back in jail after a dramatic series of events. The hearings before the ministry on the contract continued for some time after Christmas, through January 11 to be exact. A few things went for me, most against me. My partner had scuffled around Houston to

169

raise the necessary money to pay off the demurrage, which had been found to be our expense, though only Allah knows why, and I was maneuvering to get a written settlement statement from the Ministry of Industry and Commerce board hearings.

The way it came out, I was going to be charged about thirty thousand dollars' worth of costs not included in the original agreement, plus demurrage. Fazza and company were to stop bothering me and prepare the site, leveling it and putting in the concrete bases to support the forms, which was in the original agreement. So they were coming out many thousands of dollars better than they had gone in. All this is silly, because none of it would have happened if Fazza hadn't been so shortsighted. He was a nice guy, but when it came to money he was a son of a bitch in spades, as I should have guessed months before when I heard him go into fits of emotion over the payroll for his tile business. I've never seen anyone like him before or since. A real original.

Once, while driving, he got a hankering for dates. Dates in Saudi Arabia are like unto our chewing gum. They have that, too, but the date has special significance. It is a sweet, it is chewy when dried, and it's a traditional treat for the people of the desert because it grows only near water. Which means a place of peace and celebration.

Fazza told Fahad, who was at the wheel, that he wanted to buy some of the long, golden-brown kind. The way he said it set the kid's mouth watering, so he stomped on the accelerator, and down the road we fled, looking for a date stand.

One came up, on the other side of the road. No problem. Just a quick U-turn, with ten dozen buses, Mercedes trucks, and assorted cars coming at us, horns blowing. Not to worry. Fahad jumped out and asked the price. He came back to the front window and whispered the magic number to Fazza, who grunted negatively. The boy got back behind the wheel. He'd never even stopped the engine.

Back into traffic, more horns, more near-misses, more curses, more panic on my part than I'd care to admit, and we were off again, the way we'd originally been headed. Looking for the next date seller.

Same result. And so on. We must have stopped at ten before Fazza bought. At a price only a couple of cents different from the first stand.

It wasn't the price. And Fazza wanted the dates. He just had to be sure he was paying the going rate, and the only way to find out was to shop around. Even if it meant spending an hour for a fifty-cent purchase. No one was going to get the better of him, no sir.

Or, take the matter of Fazza versus Behring International, Freight Forwarders. A freight forwarder is an organization which does exactly what its name implies. It moves freight forward, first from one set of docks or the loading ramps of an airport, through customs, then across country to wherever it's supposed to go.

We shipped our forms with Behring as the freight forwarders. When our cargo arrived, the Behring district manager, a tall, nice-looking guy named Bob Hall, became responsible for the consignment. He had an army of clerks and trained people to get an unbelievable amount of paperwork done. He needed every one of them, because each document had to be carried in person to various officials. Worse, when copies were needed, they were made by hand. Duplicating equipment, when it could be found, was very expensive, with copies costing almost a dollar each.

Everything starts with a notice-of-arrival form. We got ours and went down to see the goods. From there on, nothing went according to the system. As I mentioned earlier, Fazza refused to pay the duty. He had apoplexy over the amount. Without duty payment, Behring couldn't get the forms off the dock, so it was a stalemate. Which, true to Fazza fashion, finally, days later, ended up in more hearings. In what passed for a Saudi court, yet, over money owed to the government as duty, and everyone knew Fazza should pay. Money Fazza intended to pay, but not before exercising every nefarious gambit in his portfolio to keep even a dime a day longer.

Fortunately for Bob Hall, but not for me, Behring's Arab sponsor in the Kingdom had stroke, and the matter was settled. It cost the company, though, and Behring passed down word that they were closing their books on my cargo. It was now my problem to find a way to get through the red tape of moving the forms into Saudi Arabia. All because Fazza insisted he make the duty payment by cashier's check.

Cash is the accepted method of payment in the Kingdom. Certified checks or personal checks are never, repeat never, considered neat. Too many things to go wrong, even if the check is good. Every Saudi businessman is hung up on exchange rates. They play them to a thousandth of a decimal point, taking pride and glee in making a trade which nets them ten cents more than the originally proposed amount and causes the other party to lose ten cents. It's not the thin dime, it's their thick desire to be quick and grasp any advantage.

It took nearly three weeks for the issue over that damn check to clear. Naturally, the wasted time added to the demurrage on the forms. I fumed, which is what Fazza wanted. I also sat around my hotel room trying to figure out the best way to move the forms off the dock, out to the site, and get a crew to erect them in place. It was too large a task for me alone, and there would be no assistance from Fazza.

A quick review of our business situation: We were out $118,000, which, although promised, had never been repaid. This was the money we'd spent after our collection of the letter of credit, for air fares, bringing over the doctor and the nurse on the hospital project, drawings, engineering, and other minor matters. The hard cost of the forms had been covered by the letter of credit from the partners. I hoped. Irving Trust in New York and Texas Commerce Bank in Houston were telexed for confirmation that the forms had been shipped C.I.F., which meant with payment guaranteed by us to cover their cost, the insurance, and the freight. George was doing what he could to get a response, but the bankers told him they didn't want to get involved. It wasn't their battle. The C.I.F. point was important, because with the C.I.F. clause, there was no question about the limits of our responsibilities. The cost of moving the forms from the trucks to the ground, on site, which was to have been an expense of the Saudi partnership, was now ours. Check off another thirty to fifty big beans. We were reaching a point where this deal had to work. We were out too much, without including the work and sweat George and I had put into it.

I was, however, getting deeper into trouble. The Ministry insisted I turn up with, at the very least, a major part of the fifty grand which had been deemed, by them, to be our responsibility, and I knew that if I didn't they'd jail me to show good intent.

Which is exactly how I landed back in the Al Khobar slammer. This time I knew my way around a little better. It didn't do much good, but even sitting in jail has a bright side. I was in the same lovely cell and nothing had changed. The personal ablution room was as homey as ever, the prisoners as laconic, the guards as efficient. It wasn't quite as bad this go-round, because I knew as soon as George raised the dough I'd be out where I could keep things moving. Before, I had no idea how long I'd be locked up, a highly demoralizing position.

The money necessary to get the forms onto the site finally reached me around the fifth of January, and I was forced to make the necessary arrangements for the transportation from their resting place on the dock out to Jubail and the site, which was now, at long last, supposed to be ready. The partners were still hassling me over the costs, so I knew I'd not heard the last of it. But it seemed better to move things along, get our forms out where they could be used, stop the ever-increasing demurrage charges, and set up shop to earn back our investment. I began making arrangements.

First I tried Behring. They'd had enough. Bob Hall was able to offer advice on how to go about clearing a cargo through customs and the port, but he couldn't do it for me. His Saudi sponsor wanted to avoid taking sides in my mess. Nor could he find and hire the necessary heavy duty trucks I needed to move the 350,000-pound forms fifty miles overland to our site. I was, as they say, on my own.

I found out in the first five hours I was faced with an enormous task. There were, apparently, no trucks. Or, rather, there were trucks, but no central source from which to hire them, other than a couple of small companies with less than enough equipment to do the job.

Then there was the matter of clearing the forms through customs, through the costs of the dock system, and the physical act of lifting them up onto the flatbeds of the trucks I couldn't find anyway.

After a little field work, I realized the paper trail was going to have to be executed with the precision of sidereal movement. The rest, including the actual loading, would be damned hard, because it had to be completed during the same twenty-four-hour period the final release document was signed by the port master. Getting down to that final document, however, would be the real trick.

I started by calling on an old friendship. Pat Loughnane, who had been active in the oil patch for years and was well connected in Saudi, lived around the corner in our neighborhood back home. Through a mutual friend, my bridge partner, he had learned of my trouble. As top officer of a major company based in Houston, he couldn't get involved personally, but he made a local contact for me, with a gentleman who seemed sympathetic and reliable. Mohammed Qarim, whom I mentioned earlier, looked me up at Pat's suggestion. He expressed his desire to help, offering me a place to stay and some inside advice. He wasn't sure how strong the fix was on, or how powerfully I was being hindered, but he would try to arrange for the trucks. What day? I calculated quickly, deciding how long it was going to take me to get the release signed, then took a chance and told him January 14. I didn't have the slightest idea if I could make that date, but I knew if there was a way, I was going to find it.

So, trucks in my back pocket and a better feeling toward my Saudi friend, I started an endless series of office visits. I was going to have to see each official if there was to be anything to load onto the expensive trucks in a few days.

It was a difficult task to get those papers filled out and approved. Naturally, all writing was in Arabic. No end of problems for me from that. Then, there was the widespread location of offices. I would traipse down garbage-strewn alleys, following a sandal-footed messenger or clerk, cross railroad tracks, go through side roads, up back stairs, past two or three unrelated offices, to my destination. Each stop would be twenty minutes of conversation with the guy in charge, including glasses of tea, only to discover I was in the wrong place. Back out, down more garbage ways to somewhere else, where two more teas let me know I was in the right spot.

There were rows and rows of tied bundles with thousands of loose pages and no manner of consecutive filing. They had to find my cargo papers, so they looked through every damn bundle on every damn shelf, and that took a day or two.

God help me, they found a discrepancy in the forms. On one document, the weight was given as 350,000 pounds. On another, it was 350,000 kilos, a difference of over 400,000 pounds. During all this mess, I had to remain stable, calm and diplomatic, lest someone become recalcitrant and stop everything for months. It was possible my cargo might have to sit until Allah knew when or Mohammed returned. We got it resolved, more through bullshit than through logic, but nonetheless settled.

At times, during the chasing of the paper, I was ready to scream. No one would take anything at face value. One computation, changing dollars into riyals, was made, I know, fifteen times, which doesn't sound too bad, until you understand that in Saudi, the calculation was done with deliberation. First the amount got run into a Japanese calculator. Then the last known and generally accepted exchange rate was slipped in, and the revision computed. A call to the bank was mandatory. The same man might have called the bank only a half hour before, and the bank was not equipped with up-to-the-second international-rate telexes, but nevertheless, the bank was called, and the latest rate carefully discussed one more time. Along with all its possible permutations. It was likely to go up, down, stay, or what.

It took me an entire day and half the next one plus all the cuss words I knew or could make up, muttered to myself, to get my documents set, every *i* dotted, every *t* crossed, only to find out the complete set of papers was good for a twenty-four-hour period. More muttered curses. At the close of the work day on which I got my stamp, I had to have my materials clear of the wharf area or the approvals would become invalid, causing me to start all over again.

I started again. This time my target was the morning of the fourteenth, the date I'd set with Al Qarim to have the thirteen forty-foot flatbed trailers line up outside the gates. "Thump-bump" went the last rubber stamp onto my pass papers, "scratch-scratch" went the nib of the solid-gold fountain pen as the wharfmaster signed my release, and "pitter-pat" went my little feet to the front gate, to bring in my convoy so loading could commence.

We were on our way at last. Except there was no convoy. Not then at five-thirty, nor at six, and by seven I was desperate. I had my pass. I had to start loading or go back through it all over again. And pay even more dock charges. There I stood, looking both ways up and down the wharf road, traffic passing to and fro, and not a goddamned convoy in sight. I called Al Qarim and got nowhere. Looking back, I think he didn't want to get more deeply involved, and so did nothing except try to balance losing face with me against losing out to my Saudi partners.

That was the moment I believe I became a good hand in the Middle East. Cussing like a trooper, I hitched a ride with a Palestinian seven miles to a small truck park where, one at a time, I rounded up drivers. We talked. I promised a premium if we could get a dozen or more trucks together. The Saudi drivers talked while I fumed, but they agreed. They'd make the haul. I knew that meant the loads they were supposed to carry would go wanting, but I didn't give a damn. I needed those trucks to move my freight, and by God, I was going to have them. I got thirteen vehicles. Lucky me.

It was a motley assortment: all new Mercedes, with the three-pointed star emblems on the radiator, bought with government-backed loans. Each was individually painted to the specifications of its driver-owner. Some were colorful, done in azure blue and orange with Arabic lettering, others appeared as if they were a part of a larger freight line. One by one the chauffeurs fired their diesel engines, racing them for a moment, holding them at a loud drumming fast idle, sending back oily smoke into the morning air. With some clashing, crashing of gears, they rumbled into life and, formed into a line. I rode on the running board of the lead vehicle, encouraging all and showing them the way with wide sweeping motions of my arm.

People along our route stopped to stare as our convoy spurted by. Building speed, we passed the first port checkpoint along the waterfront and thundered up to the gates of the pier. The guards, taken aback by the style of our entrance, waved us along, and we screeched to a halt, nose to tail, in the loading area of the dock where my forms were stored.

The shipment was scattered and a Pakistani family had decided to establish a housekeeping homesite. I didn't mind, except the six of them left several weeks' excrement on the last row of forms rather than walk a little way farther to the water.

The Pakistani crane operator I'd arranged for was standing by, so it only took a minute to start the boom swinging over to the first of the huge steel fabrications. That's when I learned something else about Saudi truck drivers. They drove. Period. They didn't load or help load or unload. They drove. Whatever load the person who hired them got onto their beds. Since I was the one who'd signed them up, it was my job to get their cargo into place and secured for the journey.

There I was, me, alone, jeans, a blue work shirt, and brown leather gloves, on the back of a forty-foot float, guiding down eight tons of worked steel. I had less than six hours to load and boomer down 350,000 pounds.

I've had some bum jobs, worked on some hard projects, but that day, in the sun and humidity at the port, I busted my ass. Everytime I'd get my temper settled down, I'd look over to where the Saudi truck drivers were sitting in the shade, sipping tea, dozing, and idly talking. I knew it wasn't their job, but if any one of them had offered to help, I'd have been so grateful there's no telling what my reaction might have been. One man, whom I'll never forget, at least tried to convince me not to stand under a swinging load. He was right, but alone, I had no choice. I'd as soon have been dead as not get them loaded that day.

The banging and clanging, as the crane dropped the steel forms a last two inches onto the trucks, coupled with the roar of the truck engines and the squeak of their chassis as they took the load, numbed my head. We didn't stop for lunch. I was racing a 3 P.M. deadline. That was when work officially stopped along the wharves, and I had to be done by then or start all over. I'd have thirteen trucks, I was sure, in convoy to Jubail, with only ten loaded. Instead of being there to direct the unloading, I'd be running papers through the routine again. By the time I got all the forms to the site, I'd have to pay truckers for at least four days. It was a grand incentive to keep me moving.

About one-thirty, when it looked like I was going to make it, because we were down to only one and a half truckloads left on the wharf, the crane operator climbed down from his control chair to speak with me. He was succinct.

"It's time for tea and we have worked hard. We go home now."

"Only this bit left, and we'll be done."

"Ah, yes, but I've had to work through my lunch hour."

"I'll pay you extra for that." I was glad for the short break, because I'd been climbing up onto and down off the four-foot-high truck beds for hours, using full body exertions to force the heavy forms to settle down just right into the cargo spaces. I was sweaty, smelly, thirsty, hotter than hell, and bushed. The crane operator smiled. He had a space between his two front teeth and a scraggly black mustache. I tried to explain my problem and offered a bonus, but it did no good. He was going to quit for the day. It didn't make any sense to me. The baksheesh for labor always worked unless ... I had it. He was a Pakistani and we'd just moved six of his Paki buddies, the careless shitters, out of their newfound home.

"There's nothing I can do to get you to lift those last forms?" I pointed to where his countrymen had taken up squatters' residence.

"It has been a full day. I must catch the crew bus back to town."

With that, he nodded, a pleasant expression on his face, and walked away up the pier toward an open-front stand selling tea and light snacks. Armed with a cooling plastic cup full of ice, he strolled back, climbed up onto the crane, and used the hydraulic control to retract the outrigger stabilizers. I crossed my fingers. If he left the machine, I could hot-wire it and finish. No such luck. He started the engine and drove away, up the dock road to the guarded gate of the equipment compound. I checked the fronts of trucks, but none of them had a winch. I was out.

For something to do, I went over the loads. I'd had trouble with the cheap cast-link tie-down chain. It had broken a dozen times, dumping a lot of clanging steel like jackstraws. I pulled the end boomer down on the last-filled truck and straightened my weary back, sizing up the remaining forms. One more load. I was one load away from completing the job. One damn load. I was also close to tears of frustration.

I looked around the pier. About a hundred yards away, two European-looking men were directing the unloading of a freighter with a huge 35-ton crane. From the way they were going about it, it was clear they knew their business, so I guessed they were a part of the English contract group hired to clean up the bottlenecks in the wharf area.

Six months earlier, before the English teams arrived on site, ships had to wait many weeks to dump their cargoes. The average stop was over a hundred days. Imagine having to tie up a vessel by having it sit at anchor, awaiting space to off-ship a cargo? Talk about expensive. There was discussion about inadequate dock space, but the English company offered the services of several handpicked crews. They knew their business because in less than three months they'd reduced the average turnaround time to two days. Forty-eight hours to accomplish what couldn't have been done in three thousand. That's efficiency. They did it by hard work, careful direction, and being smart as hell about wharf operations.

Wharf operations. Those were the words that flashed into my mind and solved my dilemma. Smiling, I wiped the sweat out of my eyes and strolled over to where the two men were standing. I had one chance left, but it was too delicate a situation to ask and depend on someone's decision to help. I needed a crane, and needed it then.

From about twenty yards away, I cupped my hands and called, "Say, you guys with the English dock management team?"

One of them stepped forward, leaving the other looking at his clipboard.

"What's that?" His accent showed me I had the English part right.

"The English wharf or dock or whatever you call it management people. You part of that group?"

He was light-haired, suntanned from hours of exposure, wearing a worn khaki safari jacket.

"Right. What's on?"

"Guy came over to me by mistake. Said the dock manager called. Needs both of you for a meeting. Right away."

"Dock manager?"

"Port captain, he said. In the port captain's office, as soon as you can get over there."

"I see." In even those two words, his accent was Liverpool dockside. It was all I could do to understand him. He turned and called to his partner.

"Bill, we're needed at the port captain's office." A puzzled look came over the other, shorter, stockier man's face, but he nodded and started walking toward an open, olive-drab Mini Moke, a jeeplike front-wheel-drive car with no top.

"Thanks."

"Oh, that's okay." I smiled my Sunday best. "Just wanted to be sure you got the message. Some of the Arabs around here aren't too reliable."

"You tell 'em." He left me standing as he went to join his friend. In a moment there was the reverberation of a starter, the small engine roared, and they drove up the road toward the harbor offices, seven miles away along the gigantic quay.

I didn't waste any time, figuring it would take them fifteen minutes to get there, ten more to be assured there was no meeting, and ten to get back. If I was lucky, I grabbed a half to three quarters of an hour. I had to make it count.

Their Indian crane operator was just climbing down from his perch as I came alongside the gigantic machine.

"Your boss told me to get you to help finish the load over there while they're gone."

He nodded, and without a word, we started walking toward the crane.

"Only got a couple more forms, and I want to get 'em up and out before the end of the work day. Can do?"

He studied the remaining three stacks of steel, shrugged, and climbed into the operator's seat. The outriggers came up with a chugging of the engine, and he trundled his unit into position. He lowered the outriggers to prevent being tipped over by the lift-weight, and let out the hook and cable.

I was smiling as he picked up the first of the remaining units and laughing out loud as he lowered it gently onto the flatbed. In a half hour, the job was done, and I was just linking the last of the hold-down boomer chains when the Mini Moke skidded to a stop. Two angry Englishmen climbed out, and one of them came straight for me. From the expression on his face, I recognized rage. I didn't want to fight him, but if I had to, it was worth it. The whole cargo was loaded.

The big man stopped a couple of feet away, breathing hard. "What's with it, mate?"

I played innocent. "With what?"

"The phony message about the meeting. There was no bloody meeting."

I had a choice. I could tell him my troubles and take my chances, or act dumb, insisting an Arab had come to see me and the story was like I'd said. I was bone-tired. I'd sweated off several pounds of water, so was in no condition for any athletic contest, and had the most wonderful, relaxed feeling because my trucks were ready to roll. He seemed like a good guy. Besides, I had a lot of respect for all they'd helped accomplish. I told him the truth.

At first he was belligerent, but as I talked on, and he could see how much work I'd gotten done in six hours, he relented. The two of them turned out to be damned nice. We had a cup of tea together on the dock in an empty packing crate they used as an office, while I patched things up. When we parted, they were actually laughing at my audacity. The big fellow was from Liverpool, by the way. No one else in the world has an accent anything like that one.

My truckers had all watched the little show, and they were enthusiastic supporters for me. Realizing what was going on because of their familiarity with the crane operators' ways along the dockside, they'd waited to see how I'd handle the situation. My unorthodox solution appealed to them.

We agreed to meet at six o'clock the next morning. I knew I couldn't expect to hold the convoy together for the entire distance, so I still had some work to do. None of the drivers knew the turnoff or spoke a word of English. I'd have to get there first to show them where to leave the main road after they passed through the little town.

I don't know what I had for dinner that night. I do know I was excited because I'd done a week's work in a day, and I fell asleep after a quick shower while it was still light outside.

The next morning at three-thirty I was up, and by five o'clock at the large open sand lot where we'd agreed to meet. You can imagine my relief when I saw all thirteen of the huge Mercedes trucks sitting like a covered-wagon train drawn up in a circle. A driver had a fire going using diesel oil and newspapers. It was smoky, but welcome in the still cool of the morning. The men were making tea in a beat-up pot layered with soot. I joined them for a cup.

When I say it was cool, that's a relative observation. The temperature was about 75, the humidity near 100. By noon, the total of the temperature and humidity figures would add up to at least 180, so the morning was, by comparison, coolly fresh.

We were half done. I had thirteen maniac drivers with 350,000 pounds of steel, and fifty miles of the most dangerous road in Saudi Arabia. Which is, by any standard, world-record dangerous. If any of them had a smashup before we were through, I was the one who would go to jail until the issues were settled. That was the law. I've often wondered if I'd have risked it if I hadn't been in a Saudi jail already. I'm not sure.

The drivers were all business. I called them together and explained where I wanted the loads to go, using landmarks to help my description. This never would have been possible in the United States. We have road maps and street signs. But these guys were used to turning off the two-lane blacktop at some half-washed-out trail and moving their big sixteen-wheelers cross-country into the desolation of the desert.

When I was as sure as I could be, using my limited but improving Arabic, which they all admired, that everyone had some vestige of an idea as to our destination, I jumped into a borrowed Toyota and took off. The early morning was rent by the ripping sound of their exhaust, and one after another, the big trucks, like prehistoric snorting beasts, followed me in the general direction of the main highway north to Jubail. I sat behind the wheel, smiling, puffing on an H. Upmann.

Arrangements were going too smoothly for Saudi, though, because when I arrived at the place I'd selected to have the semis unloaded, there was no unloader. I'd made a deal, three days before, for a thirty-five-ton crane on a truck and an operator to be on site, ready for business, by 6:30 A.M.. I'd said six-thirty because I expected to be there by seven, and anticipated the first truck pulling in at eight. By allowing an hour for tardiness, I thought I'd still have a half hour in the plus column. No way.

The site wasn't much to see. A couple of acres of natural desert sand dunes. Nothing else. This was the place, I'd been assured by Allah, the Islamic court, and Abdallah, that had been fully compacted with concrete foundations poured in place. Everything, they all said, was ready. The only thing I could see it was ready for was to bog down a vehicle and break an axle in the loose sand. I walked out a few feet from the rough trail we pretended was a road, and the grit was ankle-deep. I had no choice, so I decided to unload on the edge of the road.

My system was going to be simple. I had two men to help. A truck would pull into a marked position, the portable crane would lift off one of the form parts, then lower it, being guided by the two men, one at each end, so that it rested on the uneven shoulder of the narrow track. Easy to do with a small crane. Impossible by hand.

Another bad fix. Thirteen trucks, laden with steel, out in the middle of the desert, and it looked like I'd have to keep everyone on site an extra day. I got mad again. Maybe adrenaline flow gets my brain to going. I said to hell with the crane I'd hired, told one of the workers on the site to show the first trucks where to park, and crawled into my Japanese pickup. I was stiff from asshole to Adam's apple from the work I'd done the day before, and not moving too spryly.

I didn't know where in the hell I was going, but I figured if I drove into the area where there was building, over toward the port, I'd be able to spot a crane. Once I found one, I'd have to see if I could make a deal.

Six miles later I almost ran over another Englishman. A redhead of Scotch descent named Campbell. He was the manager of an operation constructing prefabricated houses for the government. Not a bad product, but nothing compared to the simplicity and durability of ours. Allah be praised, his job was down for the day, awaiting supplies, and he had a small, eighteen-ton portable crane.

The Saudis never could understand how Westerners work together. Had they been in our shoes, there would have been three days of polite conversation, two more of dickering, and the man with the crane would have pointed out that he couldn't possibly rent it out or loan it because the supplies they'd been waiting for had come and they needed it on their own job. As it was, Mr. Campbell and I struck a deal in ten minutes. An hour later, when the first of the big trucks rolled in, the crane, complete with an operator and a field foreman Campbell had thrown into the package, was ready to go. By late afternoon the first of the trucks had started their jolting, banging journey back toward the highway and we were lowering the last of the cargo. The drivers, caught up by the spirit of the obviously crazy American, had done what they could to help. We all felt triumphant, and parted, after payment, the best of friends.

The forms were there, where the court said they ought to be. It was finished. Everything we'd promised, or been forced to do, was done. Each of those great metal honeys could start squeezing out gold as soon as somebody set up the site.

I was sad, then glad. What I'd come to do, I'd accomplished. It was a feeling of triumph. Albeit short-lived.

10 *Alternatives*

March 1978

I woke up on the morning of March 15, 1978, and lay still. After all those months, I had yet to get used to waking to view a room from a corner on the floor. Changed my entire perspective. My watch showed four-thirty. The sun was already up, the sky colored a dirt-umber-orange from high-altitude dust, and I was madder than hell.

Since December, I'd been in and out and in and out and in and out of jails, paid off the very people who were causing me such grief, only to have them cause more; worked my ass off to fulfill the demands of the Saudi judges, only to have my partners smile at my stupidity as they made new demands; been hassled by the U.S. consulate because I was an embarrassment to them; treated damned poorly by the various governmental ministries; ignored by the King and his people during several claims for justice in the majlis; and finally, financially broke.

Across the street, a rooster crowed. Down the block, an unmuffled engine started with a bang, then roared away. I just lay still, on my little pad on the floor, looking up.

A lot had happened since January. None of it good. When I'd delivered the forms to the site, I'd thought my fortunes would pick up. After all, there were millions of dollars in potential profit and only a few hundred man-hours separating us from it. But I swear, if Abdallah Fazza had the choice between making a dollar by working or holding me up for a dime, he'd hold me up. Put another way: If he had the choice between a free dollar, no strings attached, I just hand it to him, he'd still take holding me up for the dime. It was a part of his nature.

The only thing I got from the backbreaking work and the money spent to move the forms was another stay in jail and another decision by the Ministry tribunal that I should pay over another bond amount, even though Abdallah Fazza didn't have to.

I tried everything I could think of to get along with that group before the truth hit me. When I faced it, I almost got sick. The fact was, if I did everything they wanted, completed the site, got the rock crusher working, mixed the concrete, poured the forms, and delivered them to building sites, the partners were still going to hound me, and I was never going to get a whiff of the money.

The time had come, I thought, to take some action. It was time to buckle up and get out. It was time to be back home. Thinking about home started me off on a chain of thought about Pat. She sure as hell hadn't been idle. Some of what she'd done had the effect of irritating the Saudis. Not much, perhaps, but still more than I'd been able to do.

Pat had sent letters and telegrams to every congressman and senator from the state of Texas, to the State Department, and to the President. The response was disappointing. She got only one or two answers, and those were form replies. I had the same luck on the telexes I sent to the FBI and various officials. What this said was that whatever fix I was in, I was in it alone. And would have to get out of it, the same way.

The biggest hit I'd made was by having Pat take out an ad in *The Washington Post*, telling my story. It made the Saudis madder than hell, but it did nothing to relieve my problem.

My situation had a zany side, too. Pat's family found an over-enthusiastic private detective who volunteered to get a passport, with an entry stamp and all authorizations, and smuggle it in to me. The closer her family got into that deal, the less they liked how it looked. There was to be a fee of ten thousand dollars, plus a bonus, to be determined, if the detective was successful. I'm glad, now, the man never got the opportunity to try. Or had the good sense to back out. Or whatever happened. Anyway, I'm happy today he didn't attempt to get to me with a falsified passport, because by the time he would have made the try, I was being watched. All my moving around to confuse the partners and make myself less susceptible to jail time had resulted in their arranging a tail for me. More foreign fun.

George had an idea that probably would have worked. It appealed to me because I wanted to strike back at my tormentors, and it was an aggressive way to get even.

George learned there was the son of a top man in one of the Saudi ministries studying at the University of Houston. More, the boy, who was about twenty, had a bunch of money and was wont to stop in at one of George's girly clubs of an evening, sip a little scotch, and stare at the girl's bazooms. He was a quiet, shy type. Never made any direct advances, even though, from time to time, George got in a lady who would play for pay. No matter how careful he was, and he tried to be extremely careful, one or two babes with money on their minds would slip into the crowd of working girls and knock on a regular customer. It made for bad business as well as bad will and liquor-license trouble, so as soon as George discovered the action, he'd move her out.

One night, George came up with the great idea of kidnapping the kid and holding that young Saudi for ransom. Me. The plan would have worked like a charm. The boy was nuts over a lithe blonde lady who served tables. She was willing to tell him about a party, lure him out to a duck blind near a hunting cabin George owned deep in a backwater marsh, feed him knockout drops in his Chevas Regal, and, with the help of one of the club managers, tie him up.

George was going to contact the boy's father and offer to swap. Additionally, there were to be photos taken of the boy drinking whiskey, playing with one or two of the girls, and lying drunkenly unconscious. That was George's insurance, because pics like that generously distributed among Saudi ministers would have caused the kid serious trouble later in his life.

I didn't know anything about the plan and am glad, now, George didn't do it. The only thing that stopped him was the fact the student switched schools, reportedly to follow a blonde he'd met during semester break. When George was set, no one could locate the target.

I wasn't desperate by this time. I was through all that. I'd been desperate the month before when I'd thought up a scheme to lure all four of the partners out to the erection site, kill them, put them back into their car, drive it off to a lonely part of the road, and set it afire. No one would have thought anything about it. Wrecked cars blazing by the roadside were a familiar scene. In 1977, the death tally from auto accidents exceeded the birth rate. A burning car didn't even cause many Saudis to slow down as they passed. Hulks and remains lined the roads.

I was stopped by a feeling that no matter what had happened so far, I was still in the right. Plus the fact that I'm no coldblooded killer. Taking a life is a lousy solution to most any problem. Few things are sufficiently serious.

Instead, I'd mailed petition after petition, had meeting after meeting with the U.S. consulate, talked to anyone who would listen, had a run at seeing King Khaled himself, which failed abysmally, sent a telegram to the FBI, and anything else nice, legal, and through channels I could think of. What it got me was zilch, zero, nothing. I was still in Saudi, still being hassled, still without an exit visa, and still had no forseeable means of leaving the country.

As I lay there, mad and getting madder, I could see the time had come to do something besides go to hearings, talk to our consulate, and keep a low profile. I decided to go home. It's said, "When a Texan reckons to take his chances, chances will be taken." I was going to take a chance. The only question was which one.

11 Allah Helps Him Who Helps Himself

The Early Part of April 1978

There were four ways out of the country, and two subroutes which fit one of the escape channels. I tried a direct bribe for the proper entrance-exit stamp. It was hastily refused.

The next was to leave by sea, aboard a boat, obviously, as a stowaway, a crewman, or cargo. There was no way I could get a visa to go as a tourist. I'd had some experience on the docks, and the first thing I did was go down to visit Bob Hall, the Behring man. I didn't let on what I was planning, but talked instead of a shipment I might have. We discussed routes, wharf procedures, and other useful points of information. I was able to develop a good understanding of the way ships were cleared. What I learned was disheartening.

Posing as a crewman was out. There were checks and rechecks on all members of every ship's complement. It would be even harder because I'd need the support of each one of the crew. Sneaking aboard and stowing away was out, too. Stowaways are a part of popular fiction, and possibly, some years ago, such a thing was possible. I doubt it, now, at least on the ships docked in Saudi. They were the new, minimum-staff, minimum-waste-area designs. Even if I got through the hordes of Arabs all around the vessel and made my way on board, I'd still have to find a hideout to sustain me through twenty days on the open sea. The first time I came out for food or water, I'd be caught. What would happen then, I can't say, but I did know I'd rather not get caught.

The other alternative would be to pack myself in one of the ten-by-twenty containers, marked as cargo, and live in that box for almost the month it would take to get somewhere. Twenty-five days in a packing crate, afraid to fart because someone might hear you, isn't my idea of a fine sea voyage. It could be done, but the doer would be plenty damned glad when the trip was over. No thanks. So much for the international high seas.

The dhow is a single-sail, lateen-rigged boat of classic proportions. Lateen-rigged, I found out by spending a few days on the quay and hours at the library, means the sail is supported by a single mast with a crosspiece instead of a boom. Its sailcloth is more like an equilateral triangle. Dhows have been built under different names along the Red Sea coast and the Nile River with few changes since the time of Jesus Christ. The boat is rugged, reliable, and, for the most part, safe. Some are lost each year, but accounting for them is hard. Only their home ports miss them, as they come and go carrying cargo and passengers on an irregular schedule. Which makes them the perfect boat for smugglers and ideal prey for the dense, erratically timed powerboat patrols run by Saudi Arabia and her neighbors. Lots of fun to be on one when stopped miles from land. If my papers didn't seem right, I'd hate to think what might happen. Strike two against the sea routes.

Strike three was the fact that I get damned seasick. There is no such thing as a little seasick, and none of these alternatives had much attraction for me. Don't misunderstand, I'd have gone in a minute if one of them had seemed feasible. An ocean escape was preferred to an overland route.

Overland means traveling off the road, across light years of scorching hot desert, by camel or Honda motorcycle. Which in turn means an eternity in hell. Worse than the ocean but still worth investigation. How does one cross the trackless wasteland between Saudi and Jordan or Kuwait? Like two porcupines making love. Carefully. Very carefully.

I bought some slightly used Arab clothing and on the second day of April went to the border for a look-see. I didn't like it at all. Two choices again. Go it alone, or stow away in a truck. Either way, if I followed the road and the rest of my party weren't loyal, the frequent, moveable, irregularly spaced checkpoints would be sure to pick me off. The soldiers didn't just search, they used the latest equipment, including heat sensors and metal detectors. No chance.

Cross-country? Wow! Not after seeing the country I'd have to cross. A mile from the road, equipped with a compass and a map, I'd be on my own through scattered minefields, sudden borderline outcrops of patrol posts, and occasional stretches of fence. Cross-country would be a difficult, if not impossible, journey for a Westerner, and when I got to the other side, I'd still be in an Arabic state more or less friendly to the Saudis. If they picked me up and inquired back, my partners had already shown enough influence to have me returned to the Kingdom. There was also the problem of wandering nomadic caravans. If they came across me, my watch, my wallet, and the gold in my teeth would be all that was left after they buried my body in a shallow, sandy grave, and left me to die a slow death.

Back to the dhow. Since most of the interceptions were made by radar contacts from hydrofoils and other patrol vessels, it would be possible to jam the electronics, as had been done in World War II, by using metal foil strips called "chaff." A little study. Damn. Do you know how far radar technology has come since World War II? An awful long way. The Saudis could afford to outfit their patrols with the best equipment. Good-bye bright idea.

Only three ways to travel: across the land, across the water, or through the air. Land and water were out. Air needed a close look. On April 6 I started looking. The Dhahran Air Base is a hodgepodge of a place, serving both military and commercial traffic. It might be able to serve my needs, too.

Alternatives came to me after several hours of walking about and passing out ball-point pens to make people talk. My Arabic had improved to the point where I was able to ask questions as well as poke my nose around. First, if I could knock off a hand-tailored uniform like, or nearly like, those worn by air crew personnel, I could board a passenger plane, be hidden in the rest room during the final check, and then fly away to freedom. This would require: (1) the uniform, and (2) assistance from one or possibly more of the flight crew. Hard to come by. Both things. The uniform could be done up well enough to pass, because Arabs, except for the Royal Battalion Army and police, wore robes. A man could be cognizant of nuances in the design of the robes, the cut, and the pattern, but unaccustomed to uniforms. The cooperation of the air crew was another problem entirely, as discovery would mean cancellation of the airline's landing privileges and an embargo on its fuel purchases.

I didn't think any crew would go for it, and a few questions to flight deck members told me how right I was. Ditto our own Air Force planes. Any request I made would go directly to the State Department.

Plan the second. This sounded farfetched on first glance, but after on-the-ground study, it seemed practical. Build a crate. Posing as someone else, register the contents of the crate as being fragile if exposed to high altitudes in an unpressurized cargo area. Call it a pet or medical equipment. Go down to the airline and fill out the forms to ship the crate somewhere. Holland seemed likely. Schiphol Airport is a vast complex, and the crate would be unnoticed. Once set, I'd nail myself inside the box, have it delivered to the cargo area, and wait. I'd be loaded on the next available flight, and away I'd go. One hitch. KLM was using only one aircraft model, a DC-8, that had a pressurized cargo hold. It left four days every week.

Miss that baby, and they'd stuff me into an unpressurized cargo area with no heat. At forty thousand feet, it's thirty below zero with no air to breathe. It would be a race to see if I turned blue from lack of oxygen before I froze stiff. 'Nuff said.

I might, however, be able to add a small margin of safety. What if I could find someone who would agree to fly out on the same plane? I'd have to go on one of the flights which carried passengers, because the pure cargo haulers didn't come with pressurized holds. Once on board, if I found myself in the wrong containment area, I might be able to signal. Then my accomplice would tell the flight crew, who would probably come down in altitude and land somewhere. I'd end up getting caught, but that's better than dead. My friend on board would be able to find out if the pressurization and heating systems were functioning properly, by asking after his pet. Again, if there were any negative answers, he could tell the truth and I'd end up in jail, which is still better, though not by much, than being suffocated and popsickled.

I knew just the guy who might help me. His name was Dennis, he came from Oklahoma, and he looked like a cowboy. But tougher. An oil-field hand, construction worker, and world traveler, he was only twenty-nine. He had enough experience and savvy for a man of sixty.

If I could put it all together just right, I might be able to pull it off. It was worth a try.

Judas Priest, I hawked that air base. After shaking the shadow they had on me each morning. I went out there daily. I met everyone from the head of baggage transit to the man who smoked the cigar butts from the urinals. I saw how they worked, where the cargo was held, how it was loaded, what sizes of packaging and crating were allowed, and a thousand other details. Then I made up my mind. Of all the ways, this was the safest. There was a lot to do, but it would be doing something. Win or lose, I was ready.

I'm not sure I've been clear, so before I go on, I'd like to make a point. I'd been in jail, by this juncture four times. The jails were not nice. I'd been told by people I trusted that Abdallah Fazza had no intention of letting me go. Our own, or, more to the point, my own consulate, even though they had a daily watch over my case, told me there was nothing they could do. I'd spent money, hundreds of thousands of dollars, and my own sweat, to work out a compromise. To no avail. The deal, although it could be a sweet one, was obviously doomed. I wanted to go home, badly. All this added up to sufficient motivation to take a chance. I was being held, against my will, and the authorities either sided with my captors, didn't give a damn, or were powerless to help.

Allah helps him who helps himself. I decided, on April 7, right or wrong, to do it Allah's way.

12 I Decide to Have Allah Help Me

April 1978

Smiling, I pushed the silver-capped U.S.-restaurant-type pour-for-yourself sugar dispenser across the top of the small yellow Formica table. The man opposite me, a British Airways second flight officer in full blue uniform with three gold stripes on his sleeves, picked it up and dumped an ounce into his plastic cup of tea, stirring the sweet gloop without looking down.

"Of the fields I know, Schiphol in Amsterdam is the one. Good approach control, good runway control, and even though there's a hell of a lot of traffic, the place is so big that when we make a cargo-only run, we're often the only plane parked in an entire area."

I nodded, making a note. My own uniform, of personal design and manufacture, was a deeper blue than his, and although the gold stripes on my cuff weren't as wide, there were four of them. I'd sewn them on myself.

"Do the KLM aircraft get any different treatment? From customs?"

"Not that I can tell. They seem to treat everyone the same. One thing about the Dutch. They're consistent." He tossed down the rest of his tea and stood up. "Thanks for the brew. Gotta go up to Weather and get the latest."

I stood, too, leaving a half finished cup on the table. Extending my hand, I finished our little talk. "Enjoyed it. Hope to see you again sometime. Where I can buy you a decent drink."

"Couldn't handle it anyway," he said, going out the door marked "Flight Personnel Lounge, Air Crew Only." As soon as he was gone, I policed the bright-yellow table, threw away our two used cups, and waited. I had time to buttonhole another couple of fliers before moving on out to the cargo area for three hours of watching routine movements.

It had been more than a week since I'd found out how impossible an escape across the border by land would be without involving myself with a group of smugglers or political militants. Those were two entanglements I had no intention of trying, having had ample opportunity to see the insides of some of Saudi Arabia's less depressing jails. If I got caught breaking the immigration laws, that would be one type of crime. Not nice, but no one would bother beating the bottoms of my feet on the off chance it might refresh my memory and open my mouth to tell the names of other "foreign" conspirators. In a conversation, which had been heated, Suliman had hinted that the penalty for my trying to escape would be the severance of my right foot. I put it out of my mind as another example of his misinformation. Nobody would ever believe I was using a cross-country route for a personal getaway. I'd probably be shot as an Israeli commando. I don't look like your average Arab.

The air route was best. It had some built-in probabilities of discomfort, but nothing compared to the weeks of a sea voyage. As soon as I made up my mind, I'd started gathering information.

The Dhahran Air Base is a disorderly mixture of military-civilian. It's hard to tell where one supervision starts and the other leaves off. This caused a lack of consistency in the style of management and allowed me, if I was willing to risk a little, the opportunity of access to any part of the field, by the simple expedient of posing as a respresentative of whichever side, military or civilian, was not in control of the area to be visited.

The first thing I did was to sew a uniform. I went about buying various and sundry materials such as cloth, braid, brass buttons, and an emblem or two. Then by doctoring up a blue suit I had in my luggage, I was able to make an acceptable appearance. It wasn't much like the uniform of any particular nation, but enough like so many as to pass muster. I had to keep dodging my shadow, but in the crowded soukh he was easily lost.

The hat gave me a problem, but on the second day of visiting the air base, I found a nice one that fit. Seven and three eighths, new and shiny, with scrambled eggs on the visor. I wore it out the door. It added a nice touch to my costume.

I also needed a private ·base of operations. Once again I imposed on Mohammed Al Qarim for the use of an apartment he maintained on the top floor of the building where he had his offices. He was quite sympathetic to my problems and, while powerless to do anything to clear them up, he did what he could do to help me personally.

That apartment gave me the room I needed to work. The uniform was only one project. Losing my tail each day also took time. But I had to, if I didn't want my movements reported.

Next, I talked to Dennis. I wasn't surprised when he agreed to help but I was overwhelmed by the enthusiasm he had for operation. He would do whatever he could to assist me. Even to running the risk of being jailed as my accomplice if I were caught.

I began haunting the airfield. I went daily, for a week, wearing my uniform, which I'd press every night, and carrying a clipboard to note things down. I gave so many conflicting stories about why I was there and what my duty assignment was I couldn't ever keep them all straight. I didn't try. By concentrating on seeing only a few people more than once, it didn't matter.

The amount of confusion at the field worked in my favor. No one remembered what I had said, only that they'd seen me and I was okay. I learned the names of some top security brass and would occasionally check with a gate guard to see if one of those officers had passed through. It gave me presence. A second useful ploy was to get one official staff member to introduce me to another. Because the first man seemed to know who I was, the second, third, and so on would accept me, too. Why not? I appeared to be a part of the foreign employee structure. The ever present sunglasses also helped preserve my anonymity.

To make things easier, I carried a supply of ball-point pens and trinkets for security guards and cargo handlers. They were always glad to see me around after that, and for the price of the present I could come and go almost anywhere, as I pleased.

I did a serious study of cargo routes, customs inspections, flight items, equipment flown, ground procedures, loading and unloading techniques, and the airports in France and Holland where it was most likely I would be shipped.

In a single week of daily contact, I had the operations of the

Dhahran field down to a schedule. It was time to make my connection.

I went through the process at the consulate of being sure my passport was up to date. The new one they'd issued me would get me back into the United States if I could ever make it out of the Middle East. That done, I sat down one evening and started drawing. The project was to construct a box large enough to contain me, but small enough to be eligible for shipment aboard a DC-8.

KLM had an ideal flight. Its cargo hold number two was pressurized and heated. It was my goal to be inside a crate loaded into that area, then, in the air, come out. When the plane started down for its landing, I would go back inside the box, be unloaded, and when the opportunity presented itself slip out and slip away. I'd worry about how to get back to the United States from that point. My replacement passport was good enough to take me from Europe to the States, so crossing over the final border would be easy.

That was my plan. I started in good spirits and three days later, with Dennis's help, the basic box was complete. I'd arranged to get it accepted as cargo in the pressurized area, and I had a deadline for having the crate on the ramp ready for transit. On April 18, I was scheduled to go.

There was an awful lot still to be done, but I felt better. I had a target date and I was acting to get myself out of what had become an even more taxing situation. My only question hinged on the four Saudi partners. If I could stay out of their way for another few days, and not end up in jail again, I could do it. We'd been in communication frequently, and I was certain they knew where I was living. If I could have, I'd have moved once more. With building the box and getting the supplies I'd need on the flight, it was impossible for me to relocate to a hotel. I had to stay where I was, take my chances, and do everything I could to stall until the eighteenth. Then, I hoped they'd miss me, because if the plans went right, I'd be long gone.

To add to their confusion, I started placing telephone calls to Suliman's and Saba's homes during periods when I was sure they'd be out. I counted on their Arabic nature. My calls showed them I was around and needed something, hence they would put off seeing me or asking what I wanted. It worked. I gained the time to put my operation into action.

13 The Escape

April 1978

I came wide-awake at sunrise. It was early to start the final countdown, but I was too edgy and excited for sleep. There were only a couple of things that could go wrong, so I decided to start checking on one of them.

My own special little shadow was still following me. Everywhere I went, he went, too, but a little behind and off to one side. He wasn't overly good at his work, because his presence was as obvious as a spinster schoolteacher at an L.A. swinger's club. That's an off analogy, but I hadn't gotten myself laid for over three months, and although I'd not reached the point where some of the Arab gang was starting to look good, my mind seemed to center on sex more than usual. It might be a bit early for my personal spy, whom I had named Silent Sam, but I went up to the roof for a look.

It was a typical Saudi morning. Dull, empty tan haze high in the air covering much of the blue sky, and a sun like a nuclear explosion. The unique, drab air color was caused by high-altitude sand particles swept up by storms from the desert floor. The atomic sun was courtesy of geography. It was already a normal 85 degrees, getting hotter literally by the minute.

No Silent Sam. No one else, either. No cars, no honkers, no vendors, no walkers, no talkers, no hookers. No police jeeps. They'd been bugging me frequently in the last day or so. Shaking my head over my lesser problem and even thinking of hookers, I went back inside the small suite of rooms.

I made a hot glass of instant tea, some toast, and watered a spoonful of instant orange juice. I drank sparingly, as I had eaten sparingly the previous two days. Tea was a diuretic, and soon I'd be in the box with limited sanitary facilities.

The only john I'd planned for use in my little crate was a plastic trash bag packed with Pampers to absorb waste liquids. Heavier problems would have to wait. I didn't expect to be in the box for more than a few hours.

The other gear I'd selected was inside, positioned along the walls in the right places so I could get it. On my trial runs in the box, I'd found a place for everything. My hope was everything would stay in place.

For the tenth time, I ran through it. Two foam-rubber cushions. I knew I'd need those. A heavy blanket. Even pressurized and heated, the hold temperature could fall near freezing. Between the cushions to insulate me from the floor, the still-warm air my body heat would create in the crate, igloo-like, and the blanket, I should be able to make it. A transistor radio with an earplug. Entertainment on every McDonald and Company cruise. Two sets of underwear. Can't be too fastidious. One briefcase with papers dealing with my problems here and other business or personal matters. Everywhere with a briefcase. Mark of status. A second briefcase, bigger than the first. If one is right, how can two be too many? This one was a tool kit, with hammer, short crowbar, pliers, small saw, screwdrivers, candles, a red-burning road flare, cigarette lighter, can of fluid, assorted nails, screws, and hooks. Other equipment included a large towel, a business suit, a mattress cover for additional body insulation, one roll of masking tape, some very strong, 150-pound test, Goldblatt (a fine brand) construction string, two quarts of bottled water, two plastic bags, and the previously mentioned eight (count 'em, eight) Pampers. I also had a bottle of chili pepper. Partially because it reminded me of Texas, partially because it might come in handy to stifle the smelling capacity of any guard dogs nosing around in Holland. Judas Priest, with me and the junk I'd gathered, all packed together into sixteen cubic feet, we were going to be a merry mess.

The box itself didn't look too bad from the outside. There were neat little labels, stenciled directions, and it had "Handle with Care—Household Effects" stickers all over in three languages.

I'd just finished my third peek about for any signs of Silent Sam or other minions of the law and was on my second glass of juice when I heard footstomps up the stairwell. I was sure it was Dennis because he was the only one I knew who always arrived like a steamroller.

His voice boomed through the still-closed door to the apartment and he was speaking as he came into the room, in a volume he considered sufficient for an intimate conversation but was more suited to addressing a company of troops on a parade field. "Well, now, podner, I've had a once-around looking for those slimy mothers, but I ain't seen none."

As I mentioned earlier, he was from Oklahoma. He'd won a baseball scholarship to the state college, which enabled him to study engineering. He looked like a first baseman. Tall, about six one, and no more than 180 pounds of bone and muscle. Thick shock of red hair always down over his forehead. Ever since he'd started to help me with my plan, his style had gotten more and more like a Saturday matinee Western movie hero.

"Cut out the shit, Dennis. Have some coffee and eat the rest of that damn bacon I swindled out of the Aramco compound." I was a little nervous about my next few hours and even though I knew the job couldn't be done alone, I hated to subject a friend to the threat of being strung up in front of the mosque for a few lashes and a defooting.

"Shit it is, son, and shit it'll be if we bump into the fuckin' Arab cops." He pronounced Arab as A-rab, which was better than his usual "sand nigger." He moved over the small, foul-smelling butane gas range where the waterpot was sitting.

Dennis was cool but disturbed. He seemed to be talking less about the event than he wanted to, and I felt it came from a genuine concern for my well-being.

"Have you got the truck?" I spoke to his back, because, cup of coffee in his huge hand, he'd moved over to the radio, fiddling with the dial trying to locate a station. We always made a thing out of bitching over the other's choice of music.

Whenever we met to talk about my plan, Dennis turned on the radio, based on the theory it would negate the efficiency of any bugs or microphones the Saudis had planted in the room. Often, at his request, we looked but never found any, which didn't surprise me. Unless they had a Western technician, they could never have made a remote pickup work. Even though he agreed, Dennis always worried about the possibility, and not without cause, because attempts to bug every first-class hotel room had been reported too often to ignore.

Finally, satisfied, he hummed along a little with the Vivaldi horn concerto he'd picked up on Radio Aramco. It was odd to hear his humming, slightly ahead of the music, because it showed he was familiar with the piece. Classical music was the last thing I would have thought this giant, rough, loud man would have enjoyed, but as I'd noted before, he was a well of contradictions.

"Of course I've got the truck. How do you think I got here? By camel? When I left last night I tol' you I'd be back with it, so here I am."

There was a short period of silence between us with the music filling the room. I reflected on what was coming next, then decided I'd better give him a last chance to back out.

"I've been thinking, Dennis. If this thing blows up, your ass is gonna be in the same crack as mine as far as the Saudi's are concerned. It could make a lot of trouble for you."

"You just figure that out?" He looked at me, smiling. "Fuck the slimy Saudi bastards. But you better have second thoughts. Your ass is really in a crack."

That was just what I needed. Half the reason, unconsciously or not, I'd offered to release him from his promise to help was because I wanted him to have a shot at talking me out of the plan. When he said the words, though, giving me the opportunity to start a conversation in which I could allow him to gradually talk me out of it, I couldn't take it. For some reason, my mind became set. I knew it was dangerous, and I was certain the accommodations I'd arranged were going to make this one of the most grueling, uncomfortable trips of my lifetime, but I'd come to a state of mind in which I would rather have been dead than stay where I was another day.

"Let's go up on the roof. One last look around for old Silent Sam or any of his chums," I replied, heading for the door. "Then let's get out to the airport. I need to be early so as not to miss my flight." A little joke. But I wasn't feeling very funny.

The two of us had a hell of a hard time with that box. I'd been smarter, but barely, than the man who built a sailboat in his basement only to find it was too large to get up the stairs.

I was going to have to spend several hours in the damn crate, so I'd made it as wide as I could. It cleared the door by only a half inch, but that wasn't the problem. The stairwell outside was folded back on itself once each floor, and getting it over the low balcony, lined up for the second half of the descent was some job.

The only wood I could locate was three-quarter-inch plywood, and so with just the minimal gear I was carrying tucked inside, the whole assembly weighed over a hundred pounds. No burden for the two of us, but it started me worrying about how Dennis would move it when I added my body and took away my pair of hands. I'd lost a lot of weight, down to 140 pounds, but still, including the crate, he'd need help to unload.

Ah, well, that was for later. For now, we were making enough racket to raise the dead, banging the stairs and walls as we worked our way down.

I'd hoped to get clear of the building without anyone seeing us, because that would be cleaner when my captors came by later, as they were sure to do, asking questions.

No such luck. We were almost outside when the Pakistani who acted as building porter, handyman, and off-hours manager came to the foot of the stairway and looked up at us. He slept and lived in a tiny, recessed alcove in the lobby.

"Ah, it is you, Mr. John." His usual smile was unusually amorous.

"Right, Mohammed."

He spent a long time studying the crate, and I maneuvered the end to hide Dennis's face from view. I'm positive the man had seen Dennis come and go several times, but I wanted to keep him unrecognized if I could, and not having him directly associated with the crate inside the building seemed a good idea.

"The box looks heavy."

"It is. And almost too large for the stairway. But we'll make it, now." I tried to appear casually cheerful.

He nodded, losing interest. "Well, Mr. John, please try not to damage the walls." With that, he went back inside his small suite of rooms.

He closed the curtain and Dennis and I started down again. The Paki had been friendly during the time I stayed in the building and had even invited me into his abode for tea. I had declined after seeing him in a mutual masturbation session with one of his buddies during a weekend. They whacked off in the lobby, right in front of me, hoping, I suppose, I'd join them. I didn't want to get him into trouble, so was glad he'd taken no more interest.

Out on the street, our work got easier. We had room for both of us to take a good hold, and made the short distance to the blue GMC pickup quickly. Dennis had lived in Saudi long enough to know how to park. He picked a place as close to where he wanted to be as he could find, then stopped. So he was blocking traffic. What the hell? That was their problem. I was pleased to see he'd been discreet this morning, and had actually put the vehicle alongside the curb, so cars could pass in the street, even though that meant our carrying the heavy crate another ten feet. Better than a traffic jam and half the city watching us.

He let the tailgate down with a bang after resting his end of the crate on the curb. The noise was startlingly loud, a metallic clanging, followed by a duller, still-ringing sound as we slid the crate into the bed. He slammed the tailgate, slipped in the retaining latches, and we climbed into the cab. I sat there as he started the engine, heaving a sigh of relief and a gasp of anticipation, combined. What had sounded so simple even an hour before now began to seem like a frightening, half-cocked plan of action. I was on my way, and as the engine roared to life, I felt, for the first time, a powerful sense of freedom.

As we drove through town, I went over the papers Dennis would need to check in the cargo when we got there. We'd made the arrangements days before after a full-scale walk-through, then followed-up daily, to be certain of the accuracy of all the documents. It also helped me pass time during those final, tense hours. The only problem was Dennis's passport. He hadn't been able to get all his clearances, so instead of having someone with the passengers above, who could maybe pull me out of a tight spot if I got shoved into the wrong cargo area, I'd be riding alone.

Once free of the narrow streets of the built up area, I ran through my last-minute checklist. As far as I could tell, everything which could be done had been. There was water in the bottles inside the crate, and I was already building my mental strength for the hour or two wait I calculated it would take from the time I was consigned as cargo until loaded onto the aircraft.

I wasn't very talkative. Dennis turned on the radio, and sat back, humming as he drove along. He didn't look at me or speak, sensing I'd rather be with my own thoughts at this moment. Frankly, I'd have enjoyed a little light conversation, but there wasn't much to say.

Completely clear of the buildings, he waited until we gained a straight stretch of narrow road with no other cars before pulling over onto the sand shoulder. Dennis had been watching his mirrors to spot any followers, but we were clear.

I climbed down, and started walking to the back of the vehicle. There was an odd lack of sound. No insects, no other cars, not even a far-off drone of machinery. Just me, the idling engine, and miles and miles of wasteland silence. The narrow blacktop had already turned oily from the sun, and heat shimmered up. I wished I could have built air conditioning inside my case, then laughed at the thought. Dennis looked at me oddly, but it wasn't worth elaborating.

He banged open the tailgate again, and I climbed up. It only took me a second to swing open the lid, and I stood, in the back of the truck, staring down into the crate. After a minute, I inventoried my supplies, made sure they were in their right places, and stepped inside. I started to sit down, but Dennis stopped me.

"John, you sure you wanna do this?"

I nodded. "I'm sure, Dennis."

"You certain you don't want to sleep on it? Think about it some more? It's damn dangerous, it seems to me."

I sat down and arranged my weight by sliding my butt forward. "Hell, yes, I'd like to think about it some more. But if I do, I probably won't go through with it. So let's get going, you dumb Okie." That phrase always got a comment out of Dennis, but this time he was silent.

I lay back, and nodding, he closed the lid, which I pushed up again, quickly enough to startle him.

"Dennis?"

"Yeah?"

"Thanks."

He nodded. "I'll see you on the other side, John." With that, he slammed down the top, and I could hear him snap the hasps home and click one, then the other padlock closed.

Like it or not, I was on my way. All by my lonesome. At that moment, in the darkness of the closed box, I didn't like it.

14 The Ordeal

April 1978

It was hot. Judas H. Priest, it was hot. Hotter than I thought it would be, and I've lived in hot places most of my adult life. It was dark, too, a sort of dim twilight, except where small searchlights of sun seeped through a partially open crack in a broken seam along the top of the crate.

Didn't smell very good, either. I hadn't thought of that, the fact my own body odor might be strong enough to alert a sentry dog or a passing guard. I hoped not too much of it was leaking out into the clear, still, sun-scorched, brilliant outside.

My not having planned for the odor problem started me on another round of mental gymnastics. What else, more critical perhaps, hadn't I considered? The rope, for sure. When the box was unloaded from the truck, the two Pakistani porters dropped their end. Jarred the living hell out of me. Worse, it knocked off the lid, and Dennis had to act damn fast or I would have been caught before starting. He slammed the top back on and wrapped a piece of orange nylon rope around the box to hold it in place while he hammered the screws back in. It was quick thinking. God only knows who or where he grabbed the rope from.

Judas, did it make things harder for me. Once they got the damn box onto the level concrete, it teeter-tottered on the half-inch thickness that ran underneath. When I moved too much, the weight change would rock the box back and forth like a stupid seesaw. The noise, at least from inside, as one edge of the crate then the other slammed into the concrete, was enough to wake the dead. I had some freedom of movement, but I had to be careful. The guards had been over looking for the source of the banging once already. And at times there were workers and porters all around me. I found if I timed my shifting to takeoffs or landings, the roar of the jet engines would cover my sound. Unless someone was right on top of me.

I was drenched in sweat. At the rate I was perspiring, I'd need a quart of water every few hours to prevent dehydration. A half dozen quarts was exactly what I didn't have. I had one. I'd packed two bottles of purified water, but one of the plastic containers had split during the jouncing when the Pakistanis had dropped their end of the huge crate.

Damned Saudis wouldn't turn a hand to help. They never worked at anything unless there was profit in it. And then only if there was no way to swindle it or get someone else to do the work part. The water in the cracked bottle had leaked out onto the plywood bottom of the packing crate, soaking the thick blanket I'd brought along to protect me from the high-altitude cold. Hell of a note.

I was going to be loaded aboard a DC-8 in a pressurized but only semi-insulated cargo space, shot up to forty thousand feet where the temperature was below freezing, kept there for six or seven hours, then lowered back to earth. I knew from my experience in the Army's Arctic survival training that any moisture, even small droplets, had to be avoided. A wet blanket would be no help in keeping warm.

I was sweating so much I had small puddles forming under my elbows where the drops ran down onto the floor of the box. There was enough moisture in my crate to frostbite a regiment. Still, the thought of a cooler place seemed almost welcome.

How hot was it? I wondered. For the fiftieth time, I moved my eye up next to one of the small holes I'd drilled to attach the rope handles. I had to lift my head and, without rocking, scrunch myself over to peek out. The light was blinding. I could see maybe 3 or 4 degrees in any of two directions. One, slanted down, out about three feet from the edge of the box. The pockmarked concrete of the staging area was a dull, dry tan, with light flecks of translucent mica where the sun's rays reflected, making sparkling pinpoints. The other view was up, through the busted lid. At what angle from my cozy cage I couldn't tell. But up. The sky was obscured from the high-altitude leftovers of last week's sandstorm.

How hot was it? I looked at my watch. Three-thirty P.M. The dial was still a light luminescent green, but it took my eyes a second to become accustomed to the dark of the interior again after the brightness outside. At three-thirty in downtown Dhahran, it would be about 110 degrees. On the loading ramp out here at the airport, where the energy of the sun was stored as heat deep in the concrete and yellow hardpan, it would be a little more. Like in the desert. Say 112, 113. Inside my box, who knows? More, for sure. Like, say, 130. Or maybe not that much. One twenty. Surely another 10 to 15 degrees, from the sun's direct shining onto the sides and top, plus my own body heat inside the cramped interior. Anyway, hot.

Judas Priest, hot. The only time I could remember being any hotter was back in '51 when I went through training school at Fort Bliss, Oklahoma, in the middle of the summer. They would turn us out in full class A uniforms, including ties, for a parade, and keep us standing in formation in the blazing sun for two or three hours at a crack. I'd had other people around me then, and no fear of getting caught. Or the sick-stomach feeling from going too long with too much adrenaline pumping into my gut.

I was miserable. In the four hours I'd been sitting there, I'd sweated my image onto the side and floor. I was sore already, and even the foam pillows couldn't keep my ass switching from numbness to a painful throbbing as I shifted my weight, trying to take pressure from one spot and place it in another, without banging out a staccato tattoo as the box rocked on the fulcrum of its rope. I was only partially successful.

The radio with the earplug I'd so carefully packed to give me something to take my mind off the rigors of confinement lay discarded in my briefcase. I'd tried twice, and both times all I got was a headful of sharp static. Must have been an antenna problem, because it had worked fine back in the apartment.

It wasn't enough I was wet. There was nothing in the dim darkness around me to dry off on. The worthless water bottle had seen to that.

Water. My mind went back to it again. I was trying to steel myself. With only a quart left, I had to ration, so I allowed one drink every forty-five minutes. That was at first. The hands on the watch dial crawled so slowly I honestly thought the damn thing was broken. Then, to cheer myself up, I switched to a swallow every half hour. It was still an eternity, but every time the minute hand hit six or twelve, it was a victory. And I felt superior and satisfied because I was getting a drink before it reached fifteen or forty-five. I was cheating fate.

To pass the time more quickly, I tried to focus my mind on a way to lock the lid down tighter so no one would peek in.

It was still inside the box. No air was moving, and I had to lie quietly, or a guard would finally get curious over why a packing crate marked "Household Effects" was banging itself to pieces. They'd come once, but written the sounds off to the rats.

I was afraid of getting caught. So damn afraid I even tried to fart silently, although that wasn't too much of a problem after the first hour or so. My constant stillness settled the gas in my fear-taut gut.

The tiniest puff of fresh air crept in through a broken joint which I used as my lookout. Had you felt it on your hand, you might have mistaken it for a breath of wind from a candle flame. Hot and sooty. To me, it seemed almost like a shot from an open refrigerator in an unair-conditioned apartment in the middle of a Texas August.

Back when Pat and I were first married, our honeymoon cottage was a little two-room blockhouse with a flat roof stuck way the hell and gone out from the center of Oklahoma City. It would get so hot I'd hose down the roof. I don't know if spraying it with water did any good, but it sure had an effect on the neighbors. When they saw me do it, they were certain the guy who had just moved in from New York was a nut case. I did it anyway, day after day, because it was better to do something than sit and swelter.

Later that same summer, we went uptown. We were able to buy a ten-inch oscillating electric fan. I still believe that fan saved Pat from miscarrying our first child.

Sure would like to have that fan right now. I'd hang it up on one side of my box, turn it on, and let it blow. I don't know what I'd do, though, if it made too much noise. I'd have to turn it off, because I had to escape. I couldn't do that if I got caught by the noise from the fan. It would be hard to have the fan here, with me, stuck up on one wall of my little room, and not use it.

My mind was wandering.

I looked at my watch. It was time for a drink. Time for another example of how dumb I was.

When I'd designed the box, I figured on enough length for my six-foot frame and sufficient depth to allow me to sit up, shoulders against one end, in reasonable comfort. But I forgot that to take a drink out of a large bottle I'd have to tip it up. What I'd left out was the tipping room so I could take a tipple.

My head was coming loose. To focus my brain, I went back to the repair work I'd started thinking about earlier. I was afraid the top might get knocked off or someone with thievery in mind might peer inside.

Slowly, laboriously, moving only when my sound would be covered, I got out my small selection of tools and hardware. One at a time, I started twisting two rows of screw eyes into the broken wood of the lid and the upper edge of the box side. It was hard work, doing it without moving my body. I used a screwdriver as a lever, passing the blade through the open end of the small, shiny, cadmium-plated hooks. After I'd set the twin rows, I'd lace the top and side back into contact with the construction twine. Then I'd tie it off, and hope it would hold.

Judas Priest. It was hot. The work I was doing didn't help, either.

I wondered how Dennis was making out. At least he was in a cool place. Better off than I was.

My watch said time for a drink. I couldn't see the dial or read the numbers until I wiped the sweat from my eyes and eyebrows.

The water was hot. A drink. Judas, who'd have thought I'd call a swallow of flat-tasting hot water, flavored like its plastic jug, a drink. What I needed was a beer. Or a scotch and soda. Or a glass of my iced instant tea.

Fat chance. The Saudi interpretation of the Koran said, "Don't drink." That came from Mohammed. The story behind his decision is probably apocryphal, but it's still funny. It seems a member of Mohammed's retinue got into his cups. In his drunken state, he told Mohammed where to get off the caravan. Then, adding to the insult, he barfed all over his lord and general. Who, thenceforth, frowned on indulgence in all forms of alcohol, especially before prayer time. The Saudis expanded this to total abstention. The average man on the street inside the Kingdom had better not get caught taking a drink. There is a special religious police who look for such violations. A dangerous group. Mohammed himself first created their sect to watch his encampments. They're bad news to anyone caught breaking the "law." No hesitation using traditional punishments set down by Mohammed and the Koran. Which are on the "eye for an eye" level of Hammurabi.

My vice was tea. Instant. Made in a tall, thick glass. No sugar or mint. Just instant tea.

There I went again.

My mind was drifting. And I was glad. It was hell inside the box, lying quietly. Any respite where my brain wandered and pulled my attention away from my plight was welcome. In fact, it might be necessary.

The heat had now caused sweat to stick my wet pants up into the crack of my ass. Even without moving, the cloth had chafed what felt like a half-dollar-sized hole in my skin near my backbone. I rolled onto one cheek slowly, so as not to rock the boat, bent my knees, and tried to cradle my head against my arm. Wherever my skin touched, there was instant sweat. Another trickle of liquid ran down my right shoulder, across my back, bound for the puddle on the floor. A reservoir, formed in the hollow made by my collarbone and my neck, was also released, and flowed away, adding to the pool.

From the outside, if the damn crate leaked, it would look like someone was trying to smuggle out ice cubes. Or bacon, and the grease was running. There might even be a spreading, dark wet spot on the tan concrete. The humidity would keep it from evaporating.

In the interior of Saudi Arabia, away from the coast, water evaporated as fast as it came. Someone ought to be able to use the arid dryness in a new refining or petrochemical process. No one had. All the techniques were designed by the Germans or Americans, built by the Americans, and finally, because they could get them cheaply and didn't have to trust them, operated by the English. The Japs were coming in a little here and there, but for technology as well as follow-through, to be sure what was built worked, the good old U.S. of A. still held sway.

Some sway. Off the track again. I looked at the glowing green numbers on my watch. Twenty minutes had passed. Also, my deadline for a drink had come and gone. It was time, I was pleased. I'd contrived to put the nagging problem of my thirst out of my now wayward mind, and not think of it for over ten minutes.

I expect my surging adrenaline helped, but I'm very one-track when it comes to situations like this. Once, in Alaska, I got good and lost, with only three candy bars in my pocket. I decided to save them for an emergency. On the third day of walking, when I finally found my way to a rescue cabin, I still had them. I was so hungry I gulped down a whole can of concentrated scrambled eggs with ham, a rather unpopular military ration. When I chased it with a glass of water the stomach cramps were so severe I ended up helplessly rolling on the floor in agony. If I'd nibbled on the candy bars instead of saving them I'd have been better off.

I decided to drink my fill. The problem was how to get a drink out of a plastic quart bottle twelve inches high when, in a semireclining position, the top of my head came to within a half inch of the lid of the crate. Earlier I had tilted the bottle up for my first swig, until it bumped the roof of my little cage, and the level of water was still below my mouth. Since liquid doesn't flow uphill, I'd had to slip into a fetal position and squnch down, to allow the edge of the plastic jug to angle up enough to let some water out into the side of my parched mouth.

Speaking of parched, my lips were cracking. Between putting in eyelet screws, I'd chewed off a tiny corner of a scaly piece of skin, and created a new sore spot. When I smiled and stretched my lips, it hurt, so I smiled and stretched them often, to see if it would still hurt, and when it did, I knew I'd found a new source of agony. Funny how little things mean a lot when you're alone and limited in your senses and movements for a few hours.

The drink of water was a minor exercise in contortionist skills. First, I'd get to the right time on the watch. Then I'd wait, not knowing how long, for the covering sound of a jet engine winding up. After squeezing down, angling around, and keeping my mouth up so I could suck at the one-inch spout of the "City of Mecca Sweetwater" jug, I got my drink. Maybe I hadn't planned as badly as I had thought. In this position it was impossible to drink too much at one time. The cramps in my legs and lower gut caused me to jerk straight, in a convulsive attempt to relieve them, and I did it without spilling the water. But I sucked some down my windpipe in an involuntary effort to breathe, so I went into a fit of coughing and gagging.

Ever try to cough and gag quietly? It's not easy. Nor advisable. My fear of being detected was great enough to keep me quiet. Teary-eyed, I changed positions again, as I felt another cramp coming on. To hell with the banging noise. I was able to coincide my movement with the sound of a passing jeep. Cramps were a sign of low potassium or calcium, both an indication of low water level or electrolytes in the body.

Judas Priest, no wonder. I guess they were low. Seven and a half hours in a sauna would lower anybody's electrolyte level. I found a comfortable place. Comfortable, that is, as long as I could ignore the raw spot on my tailbone.

What the hell was I doing here? Inside a two-by-four crate of my own manufacture, slapped down on a concrete apron at an air base in the middle of the Saudi desert, in bright sunshine, too scared to fart and afraid my strangled coughs would be heard from the outside by a passing guard. I was in such bad straits the little breath of hot air from the lookout crack felt refreshing. What was I doing here? And would I ever get out?

Another thought struck me. There were several F-5 military jets parked out there. In the general paranoia of the region, if I were discovered would they believe I was a stowaway or a spy-commando, sent to James Bond the place? Wonderful feeling I got from that line of reason.

I tried to rest for the fiftieth time, settling back as best I could. Closing my eyes was easy. Keeping them shut was another matter entirely because I wanted to stay alert in case someone came looking for me. Worse, if I tossed in my sleep, the banging box was bound to attract unwelcome attention.

What was I doing here? What had I done? Or better yet, who had I done? The whole damn mess was almost beyond my understanding.

The Ordeal II

April 1978

I must have dozed, then awakened, then dozed again, and repeated the cycle over and over, in a seemingly unending, semiconscious sequence. I recall coming out of the fog once when two guards approached. I was floating in my sweaty haze, lost in the dark gloom of my crate, when a noise snapped me to attention. I turned my head to look out the peephole, and when I did, my weight shifted and the rope rocker caused one end to bam against the concrete. The clatter had become common to me, but what brought me fully awake was the metallic snick of an automatic rifle bolt being slammed back and sliding home. Someone was out there holding a cocked sub-machine gun with a live round in the spout.

I didn't breathe. Straining my ears to listen, I could only hear the splat of a drop of sweat falling off my forehead onto my chest. My eye was glued to the peek hole, but there was nothing within my limited range of view. I opened my mouth and breathed as silently as I could, slowly exhaling. Still no sound except the roaring of my own breath in my ears.

"Ana taaban! Ashouf?"

The voice, which came not two feet from my head, scared me so badly I had to make a serious effort not to shake. The suddenness of it had broken into my concentration and it took all my control to keep from jerking my head around in response. I had a hard time making out the words.

"Taaban shway maarf mashouf!"

The second voice was a little farther away, but not much.

Scrunch. That's the nearest facsimile of the sound. It was like the noise of dirt falling onto the top of my casket. Big clods of soft wet earth. Out my peephole I could see a moving olive drab.

Confused, I could make no sense of it. Then I understood. Two royal guards. The first had asked the second if he could see anything. The other man had said no. One of the two, my guard, was standing right over the crate I was in, and what I could see was his uniform. The noise was from his resting his foot on top of my carton, while he looked things over.

I thought I'd been sweating before. Now, the addition of a strong dose of nervous tension made the water pop out of my skin like toothpaste from a squashed tube. If that guy shifted his weight wrong and rocked my box, he might recognize the racket. I lay as quiet and still as I could, afraid to blink my eyes, which burned from the perspiration flowing into them from my forehead.

"A deahu deene da, Mohammed."

A pause while my guard finished his look-see. His friend was urging him to come on, but he seemed loath to move off.

"Ela taffadal elataffadal." Come on, come on. The other was being more insistent.

"Lah! Lah! Ogan shway." Come on, like hell. "Ana binisma hunek." I'm sure I heard a noise over here.

"Ana, asmah henna." A rat, nothing more. Rats are everywhere.

Go on, go on, go on, go on. I was screaming at him with all the force of my mind. Go on, go along with your friend. Of all the times you might pick to become superguard and be responsible, this is the worst, and why in the hell are you doing it anyway, because any other time you wouldn't have given a damn, so go on. The strain of sixteen hours in the hot box was beginning to tell on my mental process.

Scrape. The disturbance startled me again, but I kept still. Out my peephole I could see the Arab moving, and through the thick wood I could hear footsteps. He was going away.

I let out a long, silent sigh. Thirty minutes later, with time passing as slowly as cold honey flows from a small-neck jar, I recall thinking how one more incident would stop my heart. Yet I craved it. Anything to give me the feeling I was alive in a real universe, anything which would bring me to my senses and make me a part of the world out there, just inches from my nose. The wood of the crate separated me from everyone and everything as completely as if I were locked in an underground dungeon.

I dozed and dreamed I was in a spaceship, circling the earth, cut off from the cool blue and white and green surface. When I came to, I had another worry. It was completely dark outside and there hadn't been, as far as I could recall the noise of a jet engine for several hours. Which might mean something or nothing.

Another idiosyncrasy of the Saudis: it has to do with holidays. There is no warning to Westerners, so holidays seemingly just happen. Actually, the Saudi weekend starts Thursday noon and ends Friday night. If that's not confusing enough, add fifty-three holidays to those weekends and you get 157 days off a year, or over five months out of every twelve devoted to down time. None of this counts the other, special days, vacation time, or sick leave. It's as though a day is selected at random and news of the celebration is spread by wildfire word of mouth. Men tell other men, who tell others, and then at dawn the next day, everyone takes off, no one shows up on the job, and Saudi Arabia slides to a gigantic halt, lock, stock, and Aramco, which has fought these labor breaks for fifty years without winning.

Some Westerners, however, work right through the Saudi holidays. All fifty-three of them. They also do a straight seven days a week, since it hurries up their rotation out of the country. There is little noticeable effect on individual efficiency, and the practice holds down the insanity level.

It came to me, lying in my little box, still sweating from the residual heat of the day, staring out into the darkness through my tiny peek hole, that I might, just might, be the victim of Unscheduled Holidayitis. If so, there was nothing I could do about it. Asleep, half sleep, and dreams, confused half awakenings, frozen with fright as I collected my faculties to see what had disturbed me, then relaxing, and drifting off again, until I had to pull myself out of the cycle because it seemed it would never end.

I looked at my Rolex dejectedly. The dull luster of the precious metal was hidden by the blackness inside my box. I'd selected a gold watch with a heavy band because I figured if I ever needed a quick bribe and was away from a source of cash it might come in handy. I hadn't needed to use it. Yet.

Sitting in the dark, I watched the minute hand touch, then edge exactly into the center of the tic above the small five-pointed crown marking the twelve position. The little hand read three, and since the date had changed, I'd been in my stifling hot, still, Stygian cage for exactly twenty hours. I'd lost so much weight my watch was loose on my wrist.

Still. If I sat still for another minute, I was going to scream. But the minute passed and I hadn't screamed, and before I knew I was into a third minute and still hadn't, and I couldn't wait much longer to move, but I didn't dare move until an aircraft passed overhead or the sound of a nearby jet could cover my own noise. The first engine blasts in hours were a relief. It wasn't a holiday.

I'd completed the six-hour task of fastening down the lid. The screw eyes and laced string did the job, neatly closing the gap at the top. I was in sorry shape. My ass, shoulders, and upper legs were raw from where I had forced them into the hot wood, and I was out of water. Judas Priest, it was hot. Hotter than I would have it, if I could have it. Sweat poured out of my skin like water from a lawn sprinkler.

I'd missed the last KLM flight, and my calculations, I'd had lots of time to make lots of calculations, indicated the air base would close soon for the Moslem weekend. I was in trouble. Once the facilities shut down, all the workmen would go home, leaving only the guards. I needed a crowd of people if I was going to leave my cage and get back to town without being detected.

I was also going swansee in the brain. Swansee? That isn't even a word, but it was what I was going in my head. My ears were ringing. It would be nice if someone would answer, but there was no one home.

Off into orbit again, this time controlled by the Saudi version of an IBM system. Saudi IBM is a local joke: *I* for in sha Allah or God willing; *B* for bukra, tomorrow/mañana; and *M* for mawfi, or all fouled up.

There. Judas Priest, there. A plane landing. In a second the noise grew louder and I moved around a lot, careful not to rock the crate too much so someone outside could see it, but it felt so good to move and relieve pressure from my right side.

After all the hours in the box, I still had no desire to take a leak. Must be some connection with all the sweating I was doing. The water went out the pores of my skin faster than through my kidneys. Or possibly there wasn't enough water left in me for a kidney trip. Just as well, though, because lying on my side in the cramped position I had to assume, there was no way I'd be able to go without peeing in my pants. And that would smell like day-old ammonia.

Ammonia reminded me of cleaning, and cleaning reminded me of Christmas, and that reminded me of the Christmas I spent in

Baghdad and the Christmas I'd just spent. Jailed and unjailed, and out on the streets in Al Khobar, a city of a thousand and one Arabian frights. My fellow violator of Islamic law and the cans of beer we shared together Christmas Day in my executive suite as he tried to cheer me up. I was the guy who was going to be home by Thanksgiving and our twenty-fifth wedding anniversary with gifts for all, and here it was Christmas, and there I was in the U.S. Firms Guest House which sounds grand, but was a shabby, four-story walk-up.

The U.S. Firms Guest House sure as hell was nicer than my present abode, and Judas H., it was getting hotter and now I'd been in here twenty-four hours and fifteen minutes.

If I could sleep, maybe I'd be better off. I closed my eyes and tried, but the trickle of sweat which kept running down my nose made it pretty hard. I wiped it away and forced myself to relax. I heard a noise. My adrenaline-soaked, overtaxed mind instantly conjured up the picture of large rats. A pack of them, moving in on my crate. The smell of the peanut candy bars I had along enraged the starving creatures and they would soon start gnawing through the sides to get in at me. I awoke shaking.

The outside sounds were normal. The rats had been another dream from the half-world which I was having more and more trouble telling from the real world.

It all became confused. Real, unreal, time, no time. Thoughts, sounds, smells, needs, all flowed together into a specially disoriented place occupied by me and me alone. When I looked again at my watch, and fuzzily realized I'd been in the crate on that runway for twenty-seven hours, I knew it was over.

My choices were two. I could stay where I was and die. Don't think I didn't give that one some earnest consideration. Or, I could try to maneuver past the guards, and if I made it, find myself where I'd left off in my fight with Abdallah Fazza, Suliman, and the rest. I decided I preferred that to staying another minute in the hell on earth I'd created for myself.

I lay still, calculating the days. Since there hadn't been an unscheduled holiday, it had to be something else. I'd been dropped off as cargo on Wednesday. It was now later in the day on Thursday. I'd missed the first plane; or, more likely, it hadn't come. Change of schedules, a mechanical failure, something, frequently made the cargo schedules irregular.

It hadn't come today, yet, either. Same reason, or something else. Did the Saudis miss me, and guess my plan? Paranoia crept through my mind after twenty-seven hours in a small box in the hot sun. I dismissed the thought. I didn't want to think about someone hacking off my foot while my four partners watched.

Tomorrow was Friday. A weekend day in Saudi, where Thursday afternoon and Friday correspond to our Saturday and Sunday. Judas Priest, it was a clear case of in sha Allah, the will of God. I'd packed myself up, they'd canceled two flights, and now I was going to have to stay in my home away from home for at least forty-eight more hours, while the Saudis made their version of weekend whoopie.

That thought finished me. Not the whoopie part, but the idea of forty-eight more hours like the wonderful twenty-seven I'd just passed. Funny how time does fly when you're having a great time. I was coming out of my box. I had to get out, get away, and get word to Dennis.

The "how" was already worked out. I had my fake uniform and I was going to use it. I couldn't dress fully inside the confines of the crate, but all I had to do was get to my feet, slip on the jacket, and clamp down my hat. Both were right there, handy by my side in the bag. The suit would be wrinkled, especially the trousers, but many members of the Arabic military are less than spiffy in their dress.

Then what? I would be on my feet, uniform jacket on, top back on my box, ready to go. Go where? I pondered the question. There is no doubt dehydration and the long imprisonment in the small dark crate had a stupefying effect on my brain. It was hard to concentrate. Harder still to think creatively or direct my thoughts forward.

Finally, disgusted with the effort, I said to hell with it. It took me ten whole minutes to undo the screws holding the hinges. I was intent on getting out. I undid the release bolts from the inside, rooted through my bag until I located the uniform jacket, and started to push off the lid, so I'd be able to sit up.

Something stopped me. What, I don't know, because I was not thinking well at all. I used the peephole and watched as a guard's boots walked by. Had I popped up the instant I'd started to, I'd have been caught outright.

I leaned back to catch my breath. That had been far too close. There was no way, I realized, I'd be able to tell when a guard or someone else was passing by. No way. The range of vision of my peek hole was too limited. I'd have to chance it. I lay there, listening. I might be able to hear footsteps.

After two more minutes I decided no one was walking by, I couldn't hear them if they were, or they were sneaking. It didn't make much difference, because I had to act.

I loosed the inside catches, which were none too secure, and pushed up on the lid. It moved a quarter of an inch, maximum, and I felt a sharp strain through my shoulder blades as it stopped. The damn thing was stuck.

I was trapped inside the box. What was I going to do? My eyes were wide, staring at the wood ten inches from my nose. I could see the grain clearly from the narrow gap which now ran around the joint between the side of the box and the lid. I moved and the whole crate rocked and banged. I moved and it banged again.

I was in a state of total terror. The noise I was making, plus a lid loose enough for any casual passerby to see, would surely bring someone. What in the hell was I going to do? I clenched my fists until the muscles in my forearms went sore, which calmed me a little. Using the tips of my fingers, I straightened the lid and pulled it back snug, into place.

Waiting for my breathing to slow back to normal, I thought about the problem. I was locked in. One of the hinges I'd designed had stuck, or one of the screws Dennis had hammered into the lid when it fell open was in a critical place. Maybe if I tried to lift at each end simultaneously, near my head with my hands, at the lower end with my feet. It might work. I lay still, gathering my energy, then, in spite of myself started to laugh.

It was the rope. The damn rope I'd teeter-tottered back and forth on for twenty-seven hours. It went around the box and held the top closed. I was choking back my laughter, relief flooding through my brain, when I heard the voice.

It's impossible to talk about something being frozen after being exposed to the Saudi heat for twenty-seven hours in a closed carton, but I resembled it. The relief I'd just experienced was instantaneously replaced by anxiety.

They'd heard or seen me. Would they try to get me to step out or blast through the sides with their machine guns? My gut tensed, anticipating the bullets.

Nothing came. The voices, chatting casually, now that the

thumping of my heart in my ears was low enough to let me hear, moved closer. They were talking about a falcon, a popular sport bird in the Kingdom. Apparently, one of the pair had an uncle who owned a champion. They slowed near me, and stopped altogether. There was a long silence, then the sound of a man pissing on the concrete. A guard had taken shelter behind the crates and was relieving his bladder. The other, waiting, began to hum an off-key, oddly rhythmed song, I recognized as one of the popular desert campfire Arabic ballads, a not too nifty ditty Abdallah had taught me in our happier days. It was about a Bedouin boy riding across the Empty Quarter on his camel. More nasal wailing than top-forty pop. Hard song even for the best of singers, although I admit I'm not skilled in music. My voice would throw the Mormon Tabernacle Choir off key.

I lay still, waiting for them to go away. Long silence. Longer silence.

Kathump. There was a crash, right next to my head. A loud bump, followed by a soft slithering. Same thing repeated. Thump, bang, slither. Confused, I silently waited and hoped for an answer. In the next second, I almost screamed. The crate tipped one way, without my moving, and the edge banged the apron. There was a voice, pleased. In a second, I heard the other voice, this one down near my feet. I was rocked back the other way. Giggles of delight. Like two kids the Saudi guards had seated themselves, one on each end of my crate, machine guns resting next to them, and were rocking the box backward and forward, laughing like two children. It wasn't a rough ride for me, because the fulcrum made by the rope was only a half inch high, but it was enough to give them playtime satisfaction.

Tired of their game, the two jumped to their feet. I couldn't see their faces, but I knew under their mandatory manly black mustaches and beards they were smiling gleefully, two mouths filled with irregular white teeth.

I heard them walk off slowly. Thanks be to Islam and Allah. One fact of Saudi life is that the punishment for theft does seem to curtail the practice. Anywhere else, one of those sentries, seeing a box lid held on only by a length of rope, would have slipped a hand inside to see what might be taken. Not in Saudi Arabia.

Waiting again. I was determined this time to get the hell out of there. One thing about old McDonald. It may take a little while, but he sure as hell knows when enough is enough. Twenty-seven hours was enough.

The guard incident was favorable, because unless there was another patrol, an unlikely occurrence based on pre-escape watching, the two were on their way to the end of the cargo-containment area, a half mile farther down the air base apron. Their backs would be toward me for several minutes.

It was time to leave my happy little home away from home. I fished around in the utility briefcase until I located my X-acto knife, which I'd used to start the screw holes earlier. I slipped in a new, fresh blade and thanked the Lord I had a father who'd taught me to keep my tools in good shape. It was sharp, as in razor. Enough to do the job quickly.

I twisted around until my left forearm was in line with my shoulders and pushed up on the lid. It immediately moved up a half inch, allowing the knife to slide out. I ran it down the seam until it stopped, and began to saw rapidly. Ten cuts and the lid popped free. I eased it up carefully.

In spite of my best intentions to jump right out, the sight of that dirty orange-blue-gray sky overwhelmed me. The brightness forced my eyes closed. The fresh air was overpoweringly sweet, and I just lay there, lid half off my box, staring for God only knows how long. Too long, that's for sure. Anyone who spotted me now would know what was going on.

I sat up, or tried to. The hours on my back, even changing position when I could, had deformed my bones and their attached muscles. Talk about hurt. Talk about weak. It was all I could do to get high enough in the crate to swing one arm over the edge. I pulled myself up to a sitting position. So much for the swiftness part of my act. If it hadn't been for the days I'd spent in the desert doing physical work, I'd never have made it. I was in top shape, and it still took me almost a minute to escape from my coffin and another minute to stretch. I remembered the uniform jacket. Reaching for it, I bent over too quickly, and the blood roared in my ears. I ignored it, digging in my things. Jacket. Here. I slipped it on, exhumed the hat, and straightened myself like an old man. Not too great, but I'd wear it with authority, I thought. One more dive into the crate for my briefcase full of papers. My mind seemed estranged from its body, almost as if I were watching myself from a high perch.

I put my case down and lifted the lid back into place,

wincing at the slam noise when it dropped. I untied Dennis's knot in the rope to have enough slack to join my cut ends together. I'd have to trust to no one's dropping the box again, as it seemed to me it would hold if it wasn't subjected to too much strain.

I straightened and stretched again. Jesus, it was good to be back on my feet. I was so elated in being free from my coffin I didn't mind the fact that I'd muffed my escape.

My immediate goal was to get the hell off the airstrip. I'd left most of my belongings back at the apartment, never thinking I'd see them again. As a part of my plan, I wanted the place to continue to have that lived-in look. I hoped it would keep the curious from becoming concerned over my whereabouts.

I looked around for the first time. Two Saudis, dressed in robes so they couldn't have been guards, stood talking not fifty yards away. They must have seen me, but were engrossed in their chitchat, and I ignored them. The windows of the Royal guards' barracks were all open and facing me, but apparently, no one had been watching.

Picking up my bag, I started through the cargo-holding area, marveling at the maze of crates and boxes piled there. Several pathways had been marked in faded red paint to indicate groupings of freight for a given airline. Interested, I moved back through the head-high row, realizing I only had a partial view. The avenues of access made irregular aisles, which intersected other aisles, like a gigantic maze, with walls of boxes, in some places only a couple of feet high and in others over my head.

Markings were made on the outside of the crates with chalk, and every section defined by the red lines was filled with crates with the same Arabic designations. I couldn't tell if I'd been waiting in the right place, except that each carton was addressed through a KLM route, which made me believe I'd at least been in the proper pew. For all the good it did me.

I walked through the bright sunshine, stepping into dense shadow when the stacks of cartons made the pathway more a corridor. If I had my bearings, I would come out near the cargo entrance gate, which meant if I didn't see any guards before I got there, I would shortly thereafter.

I was right. No one was patrolling my way, but there was one guard with an automatic rifle, watching the action at the big steel-mesh gate. Not that there was much action to watch. It looked like a slow day.

I sauntered out to the edge of freight section then stepped

into clean sight, and started counting the boxes stacked in front of me, while I tried to spot their routing.

It's a good thing I couldn't see myself, because I had a day's growth of stubble beard, my wrinkled one-off uniform jacket, and trousers that looked as if I'd slept in them, which of course I had. Looking like a skid-row derelict on an early Sunday morning in Baltimore, I was walking around the edge of a cargo area trying to appear as if I were checking crates.

I was pointing to them with one finger, shaking my head, and wishing I had my clipboard, because it was a pass to anyplace, when the guard called out to me.

"Min fadlack wahid dagigi hunek!" You there. Exclamation. Tone of a Saudi to one who is obviously not a superior. A little snotty, but polite enough to pass. Unhurried, I turned.

"Me? You are calling me in such a tone!" My Arabic had the advantage of being high-class now that I'd worked on it. I also spoke more slowly than was customary, to get the pronunciation right. It gave everything I said, so I was told, a more dignified and foreign sound. I forced my somewhat tired, bloodshot eyes to open with indignation, straightened my aching back, threw my shoulders out to put as good a line on my uniform as could be had, and stormed up to the gate in a walk, combining a parade adjutant's strut and a drum major's prance. The hat bill was down over my eyes so I had to hold my chin up to see, West Point style. I needed to appear military. I didn't want him to take too close a look at the I.D. pass buttoned to my left breast pocket. I'd made it from a luggage tag and my Texas driver's license.

"Good afternoon. Allah is good. Praise to Allah. May his blessings be upon your family." He responded appropriately. We went on for a minute more. Weather, family, God is good. The sight of an infidel speaking Arabic fascinated the man.

"Are you the guard at this station? How long have you been on duty? What was the name of the man who had this post before you?" All this in precise, carefully structured sentences which I hoped would show I was somewhere between angry and indignant, with someone's ass in the balance.

The guard, hit by the unexpected, slouched his way to a semblance of attention, not sure what was right or expected of him. He pegged me as one of the high echelon U.S. training advisers. I watched his action with the weapon. It was favorable.

Arabs are forever cocking their damn sub-machine guns. It's a macho sound to them, and it shows they mean business. It also causes a lot of accidents, because a blowing block weapon is hard to uncock. It always tosses out the chambered round, and if the cocker isn't careful, the receiver slams home and scoops up another. No Arab likes to be around a sub-machine gun that has the hammer relaxed but still has a live one in the ready hole, because they bump and drop the damn weapons so much. My guard didn't cock his. He didn't even swing it down from the strap on his shoulder.

By this time I was two feet away from him, and I leaned my face even closer, invading his personal space. Arabs find this threatening and sometimes react in a hostile manner. It is also a sign of relative station between two men, with the invader being higher in status than the invadee. In this case, it kept his eyeballs on me, not on my homemade pass.

I hadn't stopped talking since starting my tirade.

"I am ordered to come out here in the heat of the day to check a cargo, and I do, and what do I find? Twenty-seven crates, not twenty-nine as there should be. And why? Because the stupid Pakistanis who don't have the common good sense to stack them in the spaces where they belong. Or maybe they do, and two boxes have been lost. Through this gate. I've been going through those cargo squares, and I still can't find them. Climbing up and down for hours, trying to see the cursed shipping labels, which the Pakistani sons of camel dung have placed facing each other and in every other direction. They must have no supervision at all when they stack those boxes. It's like letting a bunch of monkeys work."

There was a lot more, delivered in the same tone, and as I said it, I forced the guard to turn his back on the cargo section and face the outside of the base, where I wanted to be, and suddenly, I found him between me and the fenced-in area where I'd been, and nothing but freedom behind me. I broke off the conversation, turned suddenly, took a short step away, still talking. Before the man could call out to stop me, I spun back, and was again nose to nose with him. "The name, man, the name of the guard before you. The boxes were missing when you came. If not missing, misplaced. The guard before you could have seen something."

He muttered that he didn't know the name of the guard he'd relieved, which was probably true. Then again, it might not have been, because the two could have come from the same tribe. Either way, it confused him. I turned away once again, and talking over my shoulder, said, "Well, if you don't know, Base Security will, and that's where I'm going, right now. You wait here. I'll be back."

I stormed away, still in full military stride, leaving the guard watching, puzzled, and more than a little worried.

It sounds like a zany thing to have tried, but considering the Arab psyche, it wasn't. The mixture of command and confusion, of accusation and confidence exchanged, of work and avoiding work all fit to make a logical frame of reference. The guard had a puzzle to unravel and little time to do it. He could see I wasn't Saudi, but I spoke Arabic and felt immensely superior to Pakistanis. I was most likely an adviser from a military mission. Tribal loyalty was not a question, as I was clearly not a native. Also I might not be too important, since I'd been sent on an errand of checking cargo. Unless the cargo was important, then I might be, too. If it sounds confusing on paper, imagine what it must have been like to the poor guy standing there. Especially in the Mideastern framework of his trying not to become involved in any action where he wasn't fully aware of what effect the outcome might have on his future.

I marched along the blacktop road to the first place I could step out of the guard's view, and did. I was drained of energy and leaned against one of the buildings. I didn't feel as confident as I'd hoped I sounded. Nothing like it. I was stiff, sore, frightened, and still somewhat disoriented from the long hours of confinement in the packing crate. I was also still on the air base, but in a better position now to make my way over to the main gate past the outer core of guards. From there, I wasn't sure what I'd do.

My uniform was far too wrinkled to risk going inside the main building where I could catch a cab. Besides, I was too rattled to be able to fend off any tough questions from men who might recognize me. I just went on, in the sun, through the main gate and out onto the edge of the highway.

My concern over the two workers who had been standing near the crate when I'd popped out grew with every passing minute. Had they investigated and turned in an alarm? I had no way to know.

It took me an hour of nervous walking before a car slowed. The driver, who spoke a little English, asked if I'd like a ride. Would I like a ride? I melted into the seat, dying of thirst. The drive into town seemed to last forever. I got dropped at a cab stand on the outskirts, and in a minute was on my way again.

I took off my uniform jacket. It was too hot anyway. I always figured in case someone was watching, it would be better to be spotted in my skivvy shirt than in the uniform. The one he probably wouldn't bother to report, the other he would mention.

Holding to my usual security precautions, I had the cab drop me a block from the apartment, so I could check before going inside. I spotted a makeshift refreshment stand a young Saudi boy had set up on the corner. He had a small washbasin, a few chunks of quickly melting ice, and four cans of Pepsi-Cola, priced at three riyals each. It was worth it to watch his wide-eyed amazement as I knocked back the first two. I drank all four, and only Allah knows how I kept them down.

The first thing I did after getting the door locked and putting down my briefcase was strip out of my smelly clothes. I headed into the bathroom, where I established the longest sustained leak for the *Guinness Book of World Records*, then had a sponge bath. No shower or tub naturally. Only then was I ready to tackle the phone system to call Dennis. In twenty minutes, when I finally got a connection, he answered the first ring. "Goddamn," he said, "are you OK? What happened?" I wasn't in the mood to exchange stories, just relieved I'd caught him. We spoke briefly and agreed to meet the following morning to regroup.

Eight hours later, in the dark, I awoke. It had been a rough nap. Fitful snatches of sleep interrupted by anxiety dreams over noises. Had they found me out? Were they coming for me? Lying quietly on my foam pad, staring at the ceiling, I felt for a second like I was back in my box. Then I recognized the room. It was a good feeling. I thought about the time I'd spent on the airstrip, but it was a blurred memory, all run together and stuck at the edges with tension, fear, and restless turmoil. An aching muscle tightness lingered, but the only sharp recollection was the sheer physical discomfort. The blisters and raw spots still smarted, but as far as I could tell none were infected.

My part of the plan had worked. The box had been placed in the right slot, I'd stayed much longer than I had ever anticipated I might need to, and had been able to walk away undetected when I had to get out. That portion was sound. I couldn't control the aircraft schedules, but the chances of their running erratically twice in the same seven- or ten-day period were low. That's when I asked myself the killer question. Low enough to try it again? If I was going to, it would have to be soon. Soonest. The crate was still there. If I took a day to rest up, could talk Dennis into going out with me to secure the lid after I slipped inside, then in all likelihood I'd be loaded onto one of the planes.

I relaxed a long time, thinking about it. It was the only way, but the scars from the last thirty hours were fresh, and those made from my captivity and the jailing seemed pallid because of the patina of time. I called upon a mental resource I rarely used, re-creating as nearly as I could my anger and frustration brought on by the kangaroo court hearings, the unjust way Fazza and Company had been able to jail me without the necessity of posting their share of the bond or doing as required by their own customs, and the fateful words more than one person had spoken to me: "You'll never go home."

Bullshit. I was going home. I turned over and went back to sleep. I would need all the rest I could get because it was back in the box as soon as I had everything set.

Not going home, bullshit, I thought as I drifted off. We'll just see who's not going home.

16 Try, Try Again

Dennis came the next morning at four-thirty. When he saw me, I could tell by his face how I looked.

"Shit, John." He put out his hand. "I was damn glad to hear from you. You know what the hell happened?" He went on without stopping.

"What the hell happened was the plane did a no-show. Cargo overload and a flight canceled because of a sandstorm. What happened to you? Let me get some coffee." He started away, then stopped. "I tried to get back to you, but when they crossed off the flight, they closed the field. I couldn't go out to the cargo area to tip you off." He went to the kitchen.

I heard him puttering around. He came back carrying a cup, and stepped over to the radio, twisting the dial to find a station. To my surprise, he settled on one of the Arabic musicales. "You know, John, some of their stuff is getting through to me."

I nodded, thinking, Judas, Dennis needs to go home more than I do.

"Sort of like Smetana. Must be some Oriental influence in all that Slavic stuff."

I nodded again, and pulled up two old rusty, wobbly metal folding chairs. "Dennis, I wonder if you'd do me another favor?"

"Anything but like the last time. I sweated blood when those Pakis dropped the goddamned box and the lid popped off. Again, when I couldn't alert you to the canceled flight."

"Yeah. Thanks for trying." I smiled. "That rope was some idea. Where did it come from?" I saw from his face how bad he was

227

feeling about my stay in the crate, so I wanted to change the subject. I was lucky enough to have him risk his neck. If I'd been caught, it would have been his ass too.

"I had it in the back of the truck. Thought I might need it for something."

"It saved the day. It also gave me hell."

He looked up curiously. "How's that?"

I told him and it took fifteen minutes. When I got to the end, where I bluffed the guard, he was laughing so hard he could hardly hold his coffee.

"Jesus, John, that took nerve. You can come and go as you please."

"If my heart'll stand it. Which it won't. Got to ask you again. You still game to help me?"

"Just tell me what flight."

I told him. "I wanna go back into the cargo area. I'm guessing the backlogged shipments have been pulled off the flight line to a priority loading zone. While you wait outside, I'll go locate it. I'll pose as an officer and you as a pissed-off cargo recipient. When I get to the crate, and the coast is clear, I'm gonna clamber inside, and lock down the lid. No rope this time. I don't want another rocking-horse ride."

He stared at me incredulously, then gave a low whistle. "You sure as hell don't learn fast, do you, podner?"

"There was nothing wrong with the plan."

"Nothin' except the damned airplanes come in and out of here when they want and not on any schedule you might have figured out."

"They're more reliable than that."

"But supposin' they're not. You really willin' to spend another day of your life in the case?"

I thought for a minute. My mind was already made up, but the hell his words recalled stopped me for a second. "Won't be as bad this time. Won't be as long."

"Maybe, then again, maybe not. You willin' if it is?"

"You goddamn betcha. It's a better'n stayin' here until I'm too old to do anything."

"Shit, John. I know you're hooked on the forever and ever part, but nothin' lasts that long. Something'll happen sooner or later if you just sit still."

I'd been through all that reasoning, and I agreed. Something would happen. Sooner or later. At the Saudis' discretion. And I was damn sure tired of waiting on their terms. The next act, and the next, if I had anything to do with it, were going to be mine.

"There's no other way I can tell you, Dennis. When you got to go, you got to go, and I gotta go. So I'm gone."

That was the kind of declaration he understood perfectly, and he nodded approval. "Know how you mean it, ol' buddy. What do I do outside while you look for the crate?"

"Cool it. If I get caught, get the word out. Find where they've jailed me and do what you can to get me out. Fast. Okay?"

"Okay. When do we make our play?"

"Tomorrow. I've got a couple of things to check out today, got to buy some more bottles of water, and then I'll be ready. Can you be here at one-thirty?"

"Hell, yes. Need anything else?"

"Only your best wishes. I'll clean up my uniform and be ready for action."

He swallowed the rest of the lukewarm black instant Folger's, and put the cup down on the rough formica table.

"Then I gotta run. Be back tomorrow about one-thirty, ready to drive you out. I'll bring some extra nuts and bolts."

"I don't think I'll be able to secure it shut from the inside."

"Then we got to fix it so you can." He smiled.

Before I could say thanks, he was up, and in a fluid movement rare in such a large man, gone.

I spent most of that day making contact with Suliman and his pals to keep them from getting suspicious. We discussed cement and other construction matters. It worked. I was set to try again. I didn't want another twenty-plus hours in the coffin, but if that was what it took, I was ready. I was going home, and that was one thing for damn sure.

True to his word, I heard Dennis's truck early the next afternoon. I had been up before dawn, and like the last time made trips back and forth onto the roof to look around for Silent Sam and Company. No one in sight, but I knew I was still under surveillance.

It's hard to describe the positive slant of my attitude. The horror of the thirty hours I'd spent on the airstrip hadn't faded. I'd replaced it with resolve. I was getting out. If it took as much from me this time, so be it. I was even willing to try again after that if something else went wrong.

I didn't stay in the apartment long enough to get Dennis a cup of coffee. He had started up the stairs when I met him, coming down. I was dressed in a white shirt, the uniform trousers, which looked ordinary worn without the jacket and shiny shoes. Hard to keep shoes shiny with the constantly blowing dust, but impressive if it could be managed. Getting the uniform cleaned had been a chore.

Laundry, that is washing, had always been done in the home, by servant women. But the need to handle the demand of newly arrived workers, religious pilgrims, and foreigners bent on doing business had broadened the spectrum. Almost every hotel had its own service, which was good and quick, but not cheap.

My uniform had cost me eight bucks and had taken a full day to do. Even so, I looked great. In the time available, I'd added gold braid and shined the bill of my cap. Very spit-and-polish. Like an English general. I packed hat and coat into a garbage bag so no one would see me wearing it out of the house. It was hard getting into the uniform jacket while perching in the front seat of the hot bouncing truck, but I made it.

I rode out to the airport sitting next to Dennis. Passing through the gate, I snapped a salute to the guard, who returned it smartly. I leaned over to Dennis. "Goddamn. Hate to leave now, just when I'm getting these troops into shape." My sense of humor often was wasted on him. He gave me a puzzled look.

We drove up to the entrance of the cargo compound and Dennis screeched to a halt at the guard post. I held my breath, but as far as I could tell, the man on duty wasn't the same as when I'd walked out. Same mustache, same beard, and same machine gun, but different face. I thought. I was so tired and tense that day, I really wasn't able to remember.

As we stopped, I rolled down my window. The guard ambled over, weapon slung on his shoulder. His red beret and khaki uniform marked him as a privileged Royal guard regular.

We exchanged the mandatory comments and praise-to-Allah greeting. Then I could get to the point. "Where is the space for the KLM flight to Schiphol?" In Arabic, Schiphol, the name of the airport outside Amsterdam, sounded quite foreign.

His reaction to my use of Arabic was normal. Dull shock followed by an enthusiasm to ask me an endless series of questions, stockpiled over the years for just such an occastion. It took a long time before I came back to my business.

"I'm here to inspect the next cargo loading for the plane for Amsterdam. There is a discrepancy."

There were so many discrepancies I knew he'd not be surprised to hear about another. He wasn't, but his elite training brought him to attention.

"No cars."

"No cars where?"

"Inside. It is still a holiday. No vehicles are allowed inside today. If you want to go in, you'll have to walk." He was civil, and the ploy had worked. Now there was no question of our getting in, only the way.

"Okay." I pointed ahead for Dennis. "Park over there." I was still speaking Arabic, and looked at the guard for approval. He nodded, and Dennis backed the truck, then drove forward a few yards to stop along the side of the road. We both climbed out and I put on my hat.

Dennis leaned against the hood, looking at the Saudi guard. We'd talked it over on the drive out. I would go in alone, to look around. When I found the box, I'd come back to get his help with the top. If I got caught, he would get word to Terence. It would cost big bucks to bail me out, but I was secure in my belief those two would take my IOU and spring me.

Marching in style, I passed the observant guard and was back inside the cargo compound. I started my search for the delayed-priority boxes.

It's funny, but if you don't know a place very well, and you walk from here to there, when you go back, and walk from there to here, it looks completely strange. That's what happened to me. I had been through the cargo area several times. Coming at it from this direction, though, I might just as well have never even seen the layout before. When I'd gone through, even in practice, I'd been looking for people, making notes on movements, that sort of thing. Only a portion of my mind had been occupied by the geography.

It took me a half hour, and two or three false starts, but I finally located the staging site for the held-over loads.

I searched every crate. There was no sign of mine. Thinking I might have made a mistake, I retraced my steps from where I thought the box had rested on the apron back to within rock-throwing distance of the main gate. I was in the right loading zone. No doubt. But no box. No doubt of that fact either.

Since it was Friday afternoon, the equivalent of our Sunday, only a few work crews were on duty. I had the area almost to myself. The missing box worried me. What if I had overlooked it? Face it, after my time spent in the packing crate, when I left the air base I was less than my usual sharp self. I could be wrong.

Standing in the bright sun, the temperature already over 90 and the humidity not too far behind, I tried to picture exactly where the box had been placed. Nothing was there now. Fifty yards away an Air Force F-5E with its engine pin wheeling impatiently awaited clearance. Looking down, I spotted some skid marks where wood had been ground into the rough surface. A faint dayglow orange line, about two and a half feet back from the wood scrapes, showed bright orange against the gray concrete.

Dayglow line. That came through to me. This was the spot after all. The rope Dennis had tied around the crate and upon which I'd teeter-tottered back and forth for hours, had left a faint yet defined impression in the rough concrete. The outside fibers had been scraped away, and they, along with the dye, had remained on the gray apron after the box had been taken elsewhere.

I didn't want to look overly interested since I was being watched by a pair of clerks who were having a cup of coffee while sitting inside an air-conditioned cargo office. There might also be a stake-out if the guards had found the crate and figured what it was for. It would be better if I drifted around.

As I turned away, the pilot of the F-5E opened the throttle enough to start his taxi roll and I was engulfed in a cloud of hot, shimmering, kerosene-smelling air.

The box was gone. The question was, where? If the security patrol came along and for some reason got suspicious, they might have impounded it. Or, again, they could have opened it. If they did, I was in trouble right now for even being inside the cargo compound. They'd figure whoever built it would come back for a free ride out of the country. They'd be watching.

The F-5E engine ran up into a loud scream, and I waited, patiently, for the racket to die down enough to allow me to think again. Inside the crate, I'd known the noise was horrendous, but it was nothing to the decibels out in the open air. Deafening. So deafening I didn't hear the big forklift as it rumbled up alongside the crate I was standing next to, slipped in its two front teeth and started to hoist it jerkily.

When the crate moved, I jumped three feet into the air and almost wet my pants. I'd been standing there, expecting God knows what to happen, and suddenly the box I'd been using for shade came up two feet off the ground. For an instant, I felt the Saudi security had surrounded me.

The plane roared off, clearing onto the runway, the freight-train noise dwindling rapidly, being replaced by the well-muffled rumble of the forklift. As soon as I heard the small engine, I knew what had happened, and peered around the side of the rising box to see who the operator was.

By his oily, dirty turban, I could tell he was a Paki. I stalked down the row of boxes, looking to see if the operator had cohorts and an ambush set up.

I found neither. It was a lone Pakistani running the forklift, probably trying to clean up some of the detained cargo from the previous week.

Usually, Pakis could be trusted. They disliked the Saudis, who had superior attitudes toward them. Quietly, I walked out until I was close enough to touch the driver on his arm. When I did, he jerked so hard he almost fell out of the seat. His face was a mask of alarmed fear, and he threw up both his hands, as if to ward me off.

"Allah, be merciful," he squealed, in Arabic with a thick accent.

"Allah is merciful and kind," I replied, using my best high-class tone. The sound of my voice relaxed him. Pakistanis are superstitious. They have a wide folklore assortment of demons and things that go bump in the dark of night. His surprise and shock at seeing someone meant one of two things: he was being watched, and that meant security was onto the box, and was watching the area; or he was up to something illegal and believed I'd caught him at it.

Putting my foot up onto the floor of the driver's area of the forklift, I swung aboard next to the sweating little man. The machine, which had been Saudi Air Force dark green at one time, but was now a scratched and battered gray, idled slowly, its engine making a pop-pop sound in the oppressive air. The smell of burned jet fuel from the afterburner takeoffs the hotshot military pilots were making at the other end of the field, was intensified by the heat.

From my vantage point, a couple of feet off the ground, I

looked carefully around, but could see only worn red lines painted onto the concrete and more or less random rows of crates and boxes. Most were not too carefully stacked, as they spilled out into the spaces left open to be used as aisles. Nowhere were the cargo packages piled so high a man could stand behind them in any comfort. As far as I could tell, we were alone. There were no watchers.

I faced the Paki, who had calmed himself a little. Eyeing him, I figured he'd been up to something or was about to be up to no good when I'd surprised him. He looked guilty.

"Oh, sir, you scared me." He had a strong English accent, but pronounced "sir" more like an Indian.

I stood quietly, watching. His eyes kept darting to my uniform, which marked me as some official. That, I decided, was most likely what had startled him so badly. If I had been wearing normal civilian clothes, his reaction would have been to nod and drive away.

"How long have you been on duty?" I got the tone of my voice tough, to match the appearance I felt I was making. It would be easier to get more out of the man if he remained unsure of himself.

"Since last night, sir."

"I am here looking for a lost piece of cargo. Not to spy on your activities. You understand?"

He nodded.

In those few sentences, we'd spoken English, Arabic, and a touch of French. Funny, when you want to, and you've been around a little in the Middle East, you can communicate. Guess it depends on how great your desire is for information.

"Did you see a crate for KLM out on the apron over there?" I pointed around the corner.

"There are many crates, sir. We brought many back through customs. The sandstorms have canceled several flights."

"Drive around so I can show you."

He engaged the gear, and the trolley jerked forward. Swinging the wheel sharply, he negotiated the corner, and jammed on the brakes, a look of panic on his face again. Dennis, towering above the level of the crates, had stepped out of the shadows. Having grown restless, the big man had come after me, to see if I needed help.

"Easy," I told him, "he's with me. We're looking for a unit of lost cargo."

I had to wait until the fear subsided.

"Have you seen it? A big crate. With a bright red-orange rope around the middle." At that moment, I was glad I'd put the rope back into place before leaving. If I hadn't, there would have been nothing special about the box to make it describable to anyone. It was hard enough as it was, working through three languages.

There was a long silence as the Pakistani sized things up. I was positive he was hiding something, which is what frightened him, but what it was, I couldn't say. And didn't care. He seemed to realize that, finally, and decided to cooperate.

"Yes, sir, I saw it. I, in fact, loaded it myself."

"Loaded it? Onto what?"

"The KLM special that flew in, to make up for some of the late cargo due to the sandstorm the other day. A big backlog had built up."

I didn't know whether to believe him or not, but he'd at least said something I could verify. I climbed down off the forklift and, with Dennis, started back to the car. As we passed the gate, I threw the guard a smart salute, which he acknowledged.

"Did you find your missing cargo?"

"I think so. Thank you."

"Thank not me, but Allah, for it is as he wills it."

Twenty minutes later, we were on our way back to town and the apartment. It was getting to be a habit of mine, leaving the apartment, saying good-bye to everything, then dragging back later, hunting for the refuge.

The one stop we'd made, at the freight offices in the terminal, allowed me to confirm the Pakistani's story. There'd been an additional KLM flight in, and the major portion of the cargo backlog had been taken. Which meant it was most unlikely the authorities had my box. It also meant I was back to square one. Or square zero. I still had the plan, my mind was made up to escape, and inadvertently, I'd run a test on shipping a box. Now I knew I could manage that end. The problem was, my box was gone, and there was nothing else to do but start construction on a new one or try one of my other discarded plans. I mulled over the matter and opted for the crate. I didn't look forward to another session cooped up inside, but I did believe now, after my previous try, I could handle the project better. Spirits lower than a snake's belly in Death Valley, I started designing the new container.

My Mark II model was a vast improvement. I constructed it a

lot lighter, provided a better peek hole, and built in a special removable-end trapdoor device, so Dennis and I could carry the empty box out into the cargo area, confirm where we put it, and then I could slip inside. I'd thought of doing that the first time, but felt the guard would be too alert. Now I knew better. Once we had the papers processed and the box in the right place, it would be easy. All we had to do was time the shift change, go in while one man was watching the gate, just before his relief arrived, and wait. Dennis could exit alone, and the new man at the control point would never know two of us had gone in earlier. Being able to get into the box after I was sure it was in the right loading area, and not have the risk of being dropped again, was a much better concept. I added a series of ventilation holes, covered by a confusion of nailheads, and three skids, so the bottom would rest a couple of inches off the hot concrete and increase air circulation. Discouragement diminished as my plans expanded.

Four days later, my second crate was a reality. I don't know what my ex-Saudi partners thought about the reports they received concerning the volume of lumber I was buying, but surely they were puzzled. Maybe they thought I'd gone into the room-remodeling business. At any rate, although Silent Sam lurked about occasionally and I saw Suliman once, they did nothing to harass me, aside from the customary intimidating telephone calls and a not too veiled threat to have me back in the hoosegow. Because I suspected Sam searched my apartment, I used the demands of the court for obtaining the materials for the second crate, by letting it be known I was going to ship some "tools" to Fazza. I even made up a thin plywood cover, stenciled, "Tool Box, Heritage Building Systems." Once away from town, we'd pull that off to reveal the real address.

During the time I constructed the box, I went back to the air base, to get the proper papers filled out and to determine that no changes had been made in schedules. Having been through the routine before, it went quickly. Several people still recognized me, and we had some interesting conversations while I tried to guarantee the crate would be packed in a pressurized and heated cargo hold. With their assurances ringing in my ears, I signed the last document and had everything set to make the third try.

Everything, that is, except my own mind. I wish I could honestly say I was heroic about it, but to tell the truth, I dreaded the thought of having to spend another twenty-five to thirty hours inside

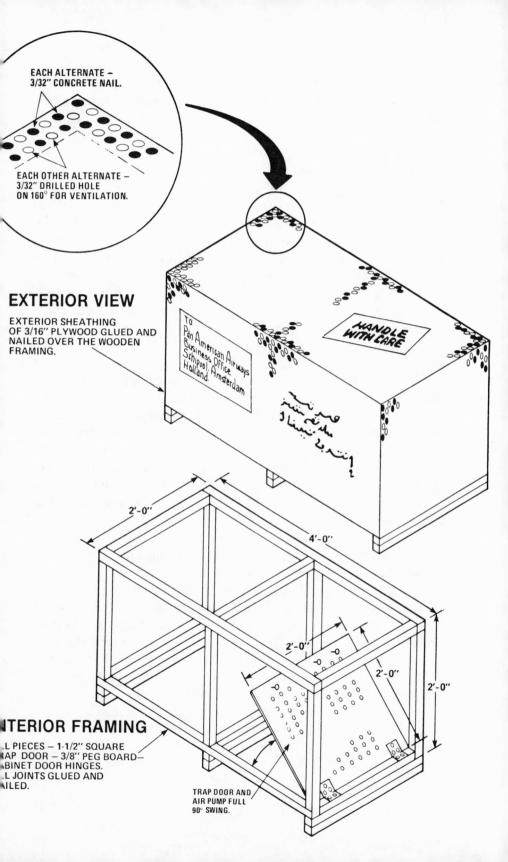

EACH ALTERNATE –
3/32" CONCRETE NAIL.

EACH OTHER ALTERNATE –
3/32" DRILLED HOLE
ON 160° FOR VENTILATION.

EXTERIOR VIEW

EXTERIOR SHEATHING
OF 3/16" PLYWOOD GLUED AND
NAILED OVER THE WOODEN
FRAMING.

TO:
Pan American Airways
Business Office
Schipool. Amsterdam
Holland.

HANDLE
WITH CARE

2'-0"

4'-0"

2'-0"

2'-0"

2'-0"

NTERIOR FRAMING

L PIECES – 1-1/2" SQUARE
RAP DOOR – 3/8" PEG BOARD–
BINET DOOR HINGES.
L JOINTS GLUED AND
AILED.

TRAP DOOR AND
AIR PUMP FULL
90° SWING.

that damn coffin. Make that dread and despair. I really didn't want to do it, but there was no choice. I kept telling myself how silly I was. Three days after the incident, my bones still ached and I had raw places all over my body.

Physical comfort, in the new Mark II, however, was improved. A little, but any helped.

I passed the shipping information along to Dennis, and with his newly approved documents, he was able to get a passenger ticket on the same flight. It took me another day to buy the gear I might need: tools, string, three bottles of sweet water, none of them cracked; some tape to patch one if it did bust a seam. My earlier design of a portable john, Pampers inside a plastic bag, was still workable, so I made one of those, too. At last, I was ready. Dennis, who'd come over a couple of nights to help with the construction, arranged for the truck again.

I put in a few last minute touches and tired, went to bed early.

It was like déjà vu. Moving the big box down the stairs, the building manager looking on, the truck waiting, the ride out to the airport. We left earlier in the day to take advantage of a guard shift, and when we stopped off the road, we loaded up two fifty-pound sacks of cement as ballast.

Getting the crate inside the cargo compound was easy. Like the last time, we drove to the gate, unloaded it from the bed, and a team of Pakis carried it in. Unlike the last time, I was walking along behind them, enjoying the feeling.

The porters located the proper storage area after a few false tries, and set the box down. I passed out cigarette lighters and oranges for a tip, and the two went away, talking.

It took half an hour to get all the documents right. A Saudi national had taken charge of the KLM cargo routing and I tried to impress him with the necessity of placing the crate into a heated, pressurized hold. He did his best to ignore me. During the final forms session I remember thinking about the "Household Effects" I'd declared the contents to be. Struck me as funny, but in reality, I was indeed Pat's favorite household appliance.

With the paperwork done, we got out of there.

Dennis dropped me off at the apartment, but came back later bearing a special surprise.

"Knew you wouldn't be getting a drink on the flight," he said, "so I brought you some as a farewell present." What he had was a jar of 180-proof moonshine called "sadeki." It tasted like old garbage smelled, but was stronger than blazes. I figured on having one drink to relax, but before I knew it, I'd gotten so relaxed I went to sleep right there on the floor.

The next morning, we ate at four-thirty, then made the drive again. We were passed through the gate with no problems and not even stopped at the cargo area checkpoint. It was 5:45 A.M. when the pickup rattled to a halt next to the crate.

I climbed out and looked carefully around. A few people moving around. A normal workday. It was another Saudi morning. Hot already, blue spots in the sky where the orange haze was breaking up, bright sun, humid. I was wasting time.

Dennis had stopped the truck to screen us from anyone passing, so we had some cover. We worked so smoothly together it was as if we'd practiced the action before. The trapdoor came open, we wrestled out the sacks of cement, and as I slipped inside, he shoved the bags into the cab on the passenger's side.

Dennis stretched. "I sure as hell am glad it's you, not me, going in there."

"I wish I could say the same."

The lid came down; it got dark. Working quickly, I fastened the inside catches to secure it.

Dennis knocked twice on the outside of the crate. Then, he must have bent over when he spoke, because his voice was close and surprisingly clear.

"Good luck, John."

I heard his footsteps as he walked away over the hot, rough concrete, then the noise of the pickup truck's starter. The engine sound died away in the distance, replaced by the far off chatter of guards and laborers. My only thought at that second was to hope he got away safely.

17 If at First You Don't Succeed

Judas Priest. I may have called my new box the Mark II, but it was still torture. Although the improvements helped, it was like saying to a man who has to lie on a bed of nails that you've cut off most of the sharpest points. He's in for an uncomfortable experience. Even so, it was a relief not to be rocking back and forth.

Uncomfortable is too mild a word. After two hours, it was almost intolerable, bordering on unbearable. The trapdoor was a curse as well as a blessing. I designed it to open and close quickly. Fanning it in and out, I cooled the inside, exchanging the air with a pumping action. As I learned when a large rat bumped into it while skittering by, it would also allow company to enter. Bad thought. That would have caused a commotion for sure. Alone, I was making too much noise even though the crate was rock-solid, resting on the skids I'd attached for bottom ventilation. It would have been wild with a four-legged visitor.

I was hot. Hard to believe I'd forgotten how hot it had been. The smell of newly sawn wood, a resinous, lingering aroma, mingled with the human scent given off by my sweat-soaked body. It brought back recollections of last time. Lying in the dark, tense with anticipation, drenched, the air permeated with that odor, I remembered exactly how hot it had been. And how hot it was now.

How hot it was. That line started me on a series of "it was so hots," like, "It was so hot I saw a dog chasing a cat and they were

240

both walking," or "It was so hot people were putting cans of beer in the campfires to cool them off." I must have thought of twenty crummy jokes, and some were funny to me at the time. I should have written them down, but it was hard to do in the dark. Besides, I was too cramped to move. They may have only been funny to my wandering mind, too. That's how I passed the time. Bad jokes and my mind meandering up and down the used, long-unopened file drawers of a memory corridor.

I reached a semi-delirious point sooner than before, because some thoughts were so vivid they were like dreams in color.

The improved peek holes bettered my connection with the outside world. More by accident than by exact planning, I'd placed one handy to my eye, so I could look out without turning my head. The vivid white shaft of light it allowed in was a cheery spot in the otherwise gloomy dark.

After four hours, my mind had drifted badly, withdrawing from the rigors of close confinement. I let it. Anything was better than sitting there, dripping sweat, stomach knotting at every noise. The greatest difference in this time and the last, though was the absence of the rope. I could move without rocking. It gave me more freedom of action. Only a small amount, but go back to the guy on the bed of nails. Every little bit is appreciated.

I was lost in space, thoughts rambling, my eye pressed against the peephole, seeing nothing, when slowly a change of light through the aperture brought me back to consciousness. It took seconds, and I mentally wrestled with what had happened. The bright sunlight had been replaced by an orangish moving glow. I refocused my vision closer, then jerked back so fast and hard I raised a huge bump where my head struck the corner. What I'd been looking at was the rear end of a scorpion, probing into the hole, his little poison tip lancing about on segmented tail. The wood of the box was a half inch thick at that point and the barb could easily have penetrated. If it had, I would have gotten it right in the eyeball. I don't know what damage a scorpion sting in the eye could have wrought and don't want to, but I'm reasonably confident it would have ended my trip this time around.

I watched the flicking tail, wondering what to do. The hole was big enough for the entire creature to slip in, and I can assure you, if it did, I was getting out, detected or undetected. People die from the fiery sting of those little gray monsters. Even if they don't, they go through some horrific aftereffects. I'd been stung once, and it was like a cattle-prod electric shock straight to the nervous system.

My first reaction was to use the plug I had handy for closing the hole, which would cut off his tail. I thought better of it when I realized I'd have the poisonous barb inside with me. Instead, I used the stopper to force the little bastard out, then I shut the hole and waited. While I sat, anticipating the creature would now go away, it dawned on me he might settle down on the plug, so when I pulled it out, I'd bring him in. That's a good indication of the charming frame of mind I'd attained.

After five minutes, I worked the plug loose, checked it before putting it in my lap, and tried to spot the bug. He was gone. But I didn't relax, because I could see, moving toward me, two guards. All I could spot was the bottom edges of their khaki pants and their rough jump boots.

By listening closely, I could hear them as they walked, feet slapping and scraping across the concrete. They weren't talking, and the machine guns they carried made metallic noises banging against their hips.

They were coming right at me, which meant they had to have stepped out of the main aisle, as the box had been placed well back out of view.

All kinds of ideas ran through my mind as the legs approached. Security had found the other crate, staked out the area, and was waiting for me to try again. Or someone had seen something, so they were coming to investigate. I thought of several other options, equally awful.

I was trapped. There was nothing I could do but wait. So I did, as quietly as possible. The men approached, still not speaking. I could see only khaki now, they were so close. Then they were past me and must have turned a corner, because I couldn't hear their footsteps any longer.

It had been all in my mind. They were just the regular guards, making irregular rounds. I was in a superstress sweat for nothing.

Over the next hour, my state of worry made little improvement. The oppression of the heat, the fear of detection, and my jangled nerves all ganged up on me.

When I'd climbed into the box, I figured on a four-to-five-hour wait. I reckoned an hour to move the cargo on board, and, just to be safe, gave myself an additional four to five hours for a margin of error. The luminous hands on my watch showed five minutes to one and I was getting progressively more concerned that something else had gone wrong. At one on the dot, after stewing in my own juice for the fiftieth time, I heard one of the most welcome conglomerations of sound I've ever experienced.

The muted roar of at least two forklifts, accompanied by the whine of their gears and the voices of several men, drifted down one of the passageways. I anticipated anything as the noise came closer. Finally, through the peephole, I could see the crew leader, a dark Pakistani with a paper-laden clipboard. Accompanied by his second in command, he came right into the square where I was lying and started examining shipping labels, checking numbers against the documents on the clipboard. I held my breath while one called out the eight digits to the other. I'd placed the shipping tag just a little above my view port, so it shouldn't have been any surprise when I looked out to see the assistant cargo manager's nose. It almost scared me shitless. His face was pressed so close to the peephole I could see pores in his pimply skin. As far as I could tell, there was no way he could miss my eye. He straightened, called something out about two more, and moved on to the next crate. I breathed again, and as soon as I controlled my shaking hands, plugged up the peephole.

Time passed. The men were still milling around. They didn't seem to be in any hurry. Then a new rumble, which I recognized as a Mercedes diesel truck arriving, got everyone busy. I heard boxes being picked up and dropped with casual abandon, the rasp of the forklift prongs on the concrete as they were slid under a box, the gunning of the engine as a lift was made, then the harsh scrape as the bin was slipped into the back of the truck.

There was no way to count how many times that happened before I was moved. My crate was rocked back by two men and the lift picked me up in one stomach-twisting movement. As I felt myself being hoisted, there was a turning motion when the forklift rotated and charged forward toward the truck. My box and I rocked sharply, bounced on the prongs as the driver sped us over the apron, then teetered on the verge of falling off as he quickly dumped us onto the open bed. Two other men shifted me. In a minute, there was a loud bang, and I realized another crate had been placed on top of mine. I was glad I'd made my carton as strong as I had.

The loading went on for a half hour. Then the men took a break. The next session lasted fifteen minutes, composed mostly of tying boxes down for the drive to the other part of the air base.

There was a roar, I was tossed back in my crate, and the truck started to move. Slowly at first, then, judging from the jouncing I was getting, faster. How that driver could make such a rough trip across the smooth concrete of the apron is more than I can imagine. I was pitched every which way, picking up splinters, banging my head and an elbow, then the small of my back and a knee. Wonderful way to travel, inside a box on a flatbed truck driven by a destruction-derby freak. I finally got the hang of it, and by bracing both knees and my hands in the corners, I kept myself from getting any worse scrapes.

We stopped for a few moments. Over the noise of the engine, I could hear conversation. It must have been routine, so I supposed it was the gate to the cargo compound and the driver had to check out.

We were on our way again, but this time over a service road. I only thought it was rough before. Now, when the truck would slam a wheel into a chuckhole, it would jar me violently. Because of my spread out bracing position, I couldn't look at my watch, so I don't have any idea how long we drove. It seemed like a year, but it's not more than five minutes from the storage and holding area to the plane-loading ramps.

We screeched to a rough halt, the sound of the engine died, and I recognized the voice of the man I'd seen earlier with the clipboard. He was talking with someone about placing the load and apparently had the various weights written down on his shipping forms, because they were discussing how to distribute the cargo. I couldn't follow much, but one sentence stood out loud and clear. They had too much weight. The makeup flight hadn't been able to take everything, so now there was a backlog. And I, judging from the short time ago the papers on my present crate had been filed, was in an iffy position. All I could do was wait, sitting in my dark little home away from home, dripping sweat.

Normally, I'm not a worrier. But at this point, I had good reason to be concerned. If they didn't take me on this trip, it would be forty-eight more hours. One thing I knew. I couldn't last another twenty-four hours in the crate, no matter how much I might want to.

If I didn't get loaded in, I'd have to stay put until they took the overage cargo back to the holding area, then try to make my getaway. Dennis would love that. He'd have to wangle another flight, if he could figure out I wasn't aboard with him, and come out with me a fourth time.

The next thirty minutes of waiting verged on intolerable. Every second seemed to drag by, one at a time, each as long as a normal minute. I kept telling myself it was okay, I was going to make it, they were going to load me. In the back of my mind, I didn't believe it. I expected to be left behind.

There were footsteps and voices all around me as the men skidded boxes to the edge of the truck bed, then tilted them up so the forklift could get its twin beaks underneath. Very little talking, but a lot of grunting.

Time stretched on endlessly. Without warning, I felt my box pushed forward. I sat anxiously. They could be moving me over to get at some more deserving, earlier arriving cargo blocked behind me.

No, they continued to push me, bumpity bump, across the grating metal of the truck bed, until I wanted to scream. What I needed now was for someone to shove me clean off the damn thing. We stopped, and I felt my box being tilted back slowly. The men allowed it to slam down. As I tried to swallow a grunt, I heard the forklift engine rev, felt the jerk from the start of the boost, and got that semisick vertigo once again as I was swung and raised at the same time. Bounce, bounce some more, then, with an added roar, I was tilted back so that gravity stuffed me down into the lower end of the crate. I could picture what was happening from my days spent observing base operations. The lift had been run up to its full capacity so my box was on the same level as the main loading door of the DC-8. I was fifteen or more feet in the air, none too steadily balanced on the lifting fork. I didn't like it, but considering the alternative, it wasn't too bad. I could still be on the truck, with more hours of waiting in store for me.

The voices this time were different, more hollow, because they were speaking inside the airplane. Hands latched on and I was half skidded, half carried across the space. The edge of my trapdoor caught on a projection and jerked open about ten inches. As I slammed it shut, I could see dark-skinned hands on the crate.

pulling it away from the piece of hardware we'd snagged. All I needed was for someone to stand me on one end. With my luck, it would be head first. Tie-down noises and voices receded. The peek hole was no good. I tried it, but the light was too dim. The final sounds had been new to me. The impact of the box on light alloy rang differently from steel. For the first time I appreciated the frailty of an airplane.

No great deductive powers were needed to figure out I was on board a plane. Was it the right one? In the proper hold? With heat and pressurization? If not, come takeoff, I was going to be in a hell of a fix.

More waiting. Breaking the monotony, the cargo hatch was slammed shut and latched. Like it or not, for better or worse, I was included in the flight manifest.

I only thought I'd been uptight during the loading process. Now I knew what nervous was. It was still hot, too. I'd hoped once I was out of the direct sunlight, I would be able to cool off a little. Insulation or no, the sun beating down on that big shiny aluminum body was enough to make its inside like an oven. It was 2 degrees warmer than a pizza cooker on Saturday night. That wasn't from my earlier series of reveries about the heat. My mind wasn't wandering now. Not a bit. It was sitting on the hard cold edge of reality, wondering if I'd finally managed, after all those years of trying, to do myself in.

Sinking feeling number one: If I were installed in the heated-insulated-oxygenated part of the plane, why was it so easy for me to hear the sound of the service truck and the noises from the refueling crew?

Deeper sinking feeling: Now I could hear the power generator vehicle as its speed started the first of the big jet engines.

Deepest sinking feeling: The engine caught, and the air suddenly smelled of burned kerosene. The fragrance lingered as the rest of the powerful engines chugged to life, one by one. If it was leaky enough to allow that strong a smell, it sure as hell wouldn't hold much heat or oxygen at fifty thousand feet.

Lurch, then light bounces. Too late to worry about it. Maybe I could build a small fire to keep my toes warm, if my candles or flares would burn at that altitude.

The long taxi out to the edge of the field and the active runway took five minutes. I could imagine the flight officers going through their checklists, talking on the radio, and settling in for their long haul. With the door closed, Dennis would be well into his first bourbon. I've never had takeoff jitters when riding as a passenger. As cargo it was different. The experience made me quite sympathetic toward people who get nervous. I also worried about the possibility of a last-minute search. Anxiety ran through my mind like a bird dog through a cotton field.

We came to a ponderous stop, then started again, as the aircraft began to turn into a lineup for the runway. Full power came on, and the slow, ever-quickening acceleration built, pushing me back into the bottom of my box; a few bounces, a sudden smoothness, an organlike note from the hydraulic system, and the thump-whump of the landing gear retracting. The outer gear-fairing doors slammed shut with a distinctly different sound. One long turn out of the runway pattern onto course, and with engines still at full, because of the hot humid air, we climbed. It was a hell of a lot louder where I was riding than on top with the paying passengers.

I was out of Saudi Arabia. Whether or not I'd make it to wherever it was I was headed was another matter. My plan had worked. I was free.

Filled with triumph, I spent the next couple of minutes undoing the internal fasteners so I could pop my trapdoor and climb out. I knew better than to move about very much because even on automatic pilot my weight might affect the trim enough to cause a crew member to be sent down to see if anything had broken loose. I figured if I got out of my crate, had a stretch, and looked around, it would be okay, as long as I stayed on top of my box or close by.

The trapdoor was undone and open. I slithered out like a cobra, between the end of the crate and the curved wall of the fuselage. We were in an ear-popping climb, fast, up to the altitude where jet engines use fuel more economically. We must have passed ten thousand feet by the time I stood up. That's the point where people start to need oxygen; not as badly as they do at fifty or seventy, but it starts at ten. I took short, shallow breaths, imagining it was already a little harder to breathe.

Judas Priest, it was dark. Not a sign of light. The brightest glare came from the luminous dial on my wristwatch.

I half reentered the crate, bumping my head again in the same spot where I'd banged it during the loading process, and fumbled for the small key-chain flashlight my son had sent me for

Christmas. It took another minute to find it while I kept swallowing to unstop my ears. Then I was back out, sitting upright on top of my box. No imagination this time, it was colder. My sweat-drenched clothes were chilly but were drying fast, draining body heat in the low humidity of high altitude.

I turned on the light and made a quick sweep. Not much to see: boxes and bags scattered, tied down; walls hung with sheets of quilted, gray-green padding, and scarred, gouged paint showing the yellow primer everywhere the quilting stopped. The floor was covered by tracklike shiny runners a half inch high.

Second look around, the light making a pitiful puddle of brilliance wherever it focused. A sign: beat-up red stencil, scratched so badly it was almost unreadable. There was a picture. I squinted at it for a long moment. It was a silhouette of a boxer dog on the bulkhead. No lettering. It was a shabby illustration, but it looked better than any Picasso I've ever seen. It meant I wasn't going to freeze or suffocate.

18 Tastes Like Freedom

April 1978

I may have been on the final leg of my plan, but the trip sure as hell wasn't over. Seven hours in a dark cargo hold at forty thousand feet doesn't sound too bad on paper, and physically, it wasn't. I wrapped up in my mattress cover, settled down like Dracula in my box, clicked off the flashlight, and tried to relax. It was a little chilly; down to the upper fifties or low sixties, but after the months of unrelenting heat, it felt pretty good to snuggle up under a cover. Breathing was fine. There was a weak smell of hydraulic fluid and hot oil in the air, but these are normal odors around aircraft. They didn't creep into my mind enough to interrupt my train of thought. I wish they had, though, because that was the hard part.

I thought about Dennis, riding above me. Soft seat, movie probably on, hot and cold running stewardesses. Per our plan, I was sure he'd made the necessary inquiries about his special cargo. He'd be on his second drink by now.

I hoped I was going to land at Schiphol. That's what my manifest said. But cargo transit isn't like a passenger ticket. I could be off-loaded at a special stop to make room for higher-priority goods. Not likely, but possible. I hoped for one of the largest airports in the world.

Built after World War II on the site of a previous facility, it became, in the sixties, a major international arrival-departure point. Schiphol was, and still is, a key air cargo center for much of Western Europe. Especially for matériel bound south for Saudi, which meant the Dutch had added reason for keeping their ties with the Kingdom in good order. It would be bad for me if I got caught.

249

I don't know if it was the altitude, the unending darkness of the cargo hold, or my cumulative experiences over the past few days, but something forced me from my normal positive outlook into a pessimistic view. This in turn brought man's most futile activity, worry.

First, I worried about getting away from the aircraft. If I was going to be picked up on the ground at Schiphol, it had to be away from the DC-8 that brought me in. There could be no connection with me and Saudi Arabia or they'd send me back. I don't know now why I was so certain they would send me back, but in the chilly dark, I was sure of it. There was also the chance Silent Sam had missed me and set off an alarm, which would mean a cargo search when we landed.

If I could possibly be lucky enough to get free of the plane before detection, the next point would be to move over into the passenger terminal, where I could blend in with the crowd. A lot of people would be wearing wrinkled clothes.

I only had a vague idea where these two parts of the field were from a brochure diagram I'd studied one afternoon in the air-base office in Dhahran. I'd been confident of my ability to find my way around. Now my confidence was gone. I knew my detection was imminent.

If I did make it to where the people were, I was safe. My passport showed I was an American. I could board any plane going to the States or to a country which didn't require a visa. Canada, say.

To break my mental flow, I climbed in and out of my crate for practice. Then, still wrapped up, I shook out my suit to dry the perspiration I'd picked up on the ground. It was better outside the box. After three hours of aimless anxiety and fretting over conditions I couldn't control, the low harmonic droning noise coming through the skin of the aircraft from the engines and air friction combined with the oil smell to drop me off into a trance.

The change of engine pitch and a sharp nose-down attitude jolted me. The pilot was able to conserve fuel by staying at altitude longer, then making an abrupt approach down to the more trafficked levels of air space. He did a hell of a job. I suppose it was his NATO training added to a couple of thousand hours in a Saber jet. Or, it might have felt steeper because I wasn't strapped into a seat and had never had the experience before. Either way, he flipped that sucker around, pulling g's, and we got down to controlled air space so fast it caught me off guard. I'd planned to close myself in after taking a final stretch on the long descent approach, which I felt I'd be able to detect by the increasing cabin pressure. I barely had time to change from my sweaty, rumpled, fake uniform to my now dried but wrinkled business suit. I pulled everything inside, closed up shop, and went to work locking my trapdoor down so I could be carried off the plane without being dumped out.

The hot rocks up front kept the throttles on most of the way. We screeched in with a no-bounce landing and taxied at a speed that would have qualified any Indianapolis racer. That pilot was good, in a hurry to make a date, or both, because we were stopped and ground crews were opening hatches almost before I'd had time to latch mine closed.

The first voices came to me. Through my peek hole I got a blinding eyeful of white light as someone popped the door open and one of the small searchlights used for night unloading was stuck inside. I was struck by the language. It was the first time in months I'd heard working people speak anything but a Paki dialect or Arabic. This was more guttural. Sharper. Germanic. Western. It sounded good even though I couldn't understand a word.

The men were as briskly efficient as the Pakistanis who had loaded things onto the plane at the other end were lackadaisical. Working in teams, they shifted the boxes onto the low floor rails, then pushed them to the door. A loader would accept a full complement, then trundle off rapidly, its place being taken by another so quickly the men inside didn't have to interrupt their constant shoving crates out the hatch.

They started moving my box, and I shut down the observation holes so no one would accidentally catch sight of me. Adrenaline was scouring my system, keying me into action. All the doubt and nagging worry of a few hours before had vanished with my nap.

I was out the door and into another of those moving-downward-while-turning spiral motions which gave me vertigo. The loading machine was lowering the cargo container as it turned and sped away into the floodlit night.

We must have gone a long way, because it took over ten minutes before there was a gentle thunk, coupled to a slight jar, and I could hear the machine chug away quietly across the smooth concrete. My ride had been jouncy, but in no way as rough as the one in Saudi.

I lay still and listened. Motors, well muffled, sounded distant. The rattle and squeak from a chain of baggage cars being pulled by a tractor blended with the slashing roar of a jet on takeoff run to come drifting across the emptiness of the field. No voices or footsteps. I unstopped the peephole and used my limited view to check my surroundings. No one in sight.

I lay still and listened. This was the danger point. I had to open my hatch, get out, and get away from the box quickly.

I undid the latches and unfastened the trapdoor. With few movements and working as fast as I could, I opened up, wiggled and slithered my way out, reached in, grabbed my briefcase with all my papers, and shut the hatch back so the crate would look normal. No sense calling attention to it, and possibly myself, any more than I could help. A short step down, off the trolley, and I was landed.

I shook out my suit jacket, slipped it on, picked up my case, and started marching smartly away, trying my best to look like a lost businessman.

Ten feet down a narrow aisle between crates stacked as high as my head, I was at a crossing. Which way? I went straight without breaking pace. Out of the corner of my eye, I spotted a man in a bulky coverall, wearing a yellow nylon jacket. His bent over back turned, so he didn't spot me. I kept on, trying to look arrogant and walk softly at the same time.

Another intersection. Right this time. There were overhead sodium vapor lamps lighting the area with an orange cast. Where the crates were stacked high, the shadows were dark, black velvet. I was moving through a world with no blends. Everything was a contrast. Light to dark, rough to smooth, enormous volumes of frightening sound to silence. Endless avenues through an infinity of crates. It was confusing enough that I began to fret about walking around in a circle, like people who are lost in the woods are said to do.

I needn't have worried. The continuous aisles kept me going in a straight line or at a 90-degree angle from my original track.

I went for the longest time, passing group after group of busy, moving workers. They were all too engrossed in their jobs to even look up, although since most of them were around the idling engines of the loading machines, it wasn't possible for them to hear my footsteps.

I turned left. More aisles, more orange light. A burned smell of kerosene wafted over from the run-up area at the start of an active runway.

Still no end to the cargo storage. More people. No one noticed me. I began to feel like I might be stuck wandering through the relentless sameness of the box-edge aisles for the rest of my life. There had to be a beginning and an end to the boundless storage area. Surely, I thought, when the first truck had driven up with the first crate of cargo, they'd stacked it someplace. That was the start. And the last crate unloaded had to have been put somewhere else. That was the other end. Trouble was, I'd been walking for five minutes and I seemed no closer to either.

Footsteps ahead. Different sound. Harder. Quicker. A man came under one of the orange lights. There was just enough water in the air not to be foggy, but there was still a halo. Uniform. Uh oh.

"Whysixxgggidavagen?"

I know that doesn't make sense, but neither did what he said to me. The same guttural language I'd been hearing.

"I'm sorry. I don't understand."

"Ah, English."

"No, American."

"Ah, American."

He walked right up to me. Boots, spiffy green uniform with a cross belt the old Army used to call a "Sam Brown."

"What are you doing in this area?"

He looked me slowly up and down. I was conscious of the state of my wrinkled suit. Messy. It looked like a used rag to me. I hoped it didn't look as bad to him.

"Checking on some of our stuff." It wasn't much of an answer, but it might lead me somewhere.

"Ah. Your 'stuff.'"

"No. Our stuff. We've been on this deal for two days now. Not even a chance to go to bed or change. Got to get the stuff to Saudi."

I could have bit my tongue when I said "Saudi," because I wanted no association with that place. But it was a magic word.

"Of course. Did you find your 'stuff'?"

"Not mine, ours. Yes. I did. And now I've got to go report." I walked by him smartly, looking like I knew where I was headed.

I expected a challenge at each step, but he just stood there, watching me. I could tell he was standing, because there were no sounds from his footsteps. I made a turn at the next intersection, then leaned against a huge crate, breathing deeply and listening carefully. Nothing. He'd gone on his way. I went mine, too.

After ten minutes of wandering, I got my bearings. The cargo had been placed in a warehouse so huge it had its own internal, free-standing light sources, on poles. The floor was concrete, exactly like the ramp. Because of the shadows, I hadn't realized I was inside until I finally passed a monstrous door, which, unlike several others, was partially open. I walked through it into an overcast night. I was standing on the edge of an enormous flight apron. There must have been forty 747s and DC-8s and some other type of aircraft I couldn't identify parked in rows. A few had their engines going, but most were silent. I recognized markings for KLM, Air France, Pan American; and the colors, red, green, blue, were vivid in the sharper, whiter lights surrounding the area.

It was nine-thirty in Saudi, but here the sun hadn't completely set and the planes had a pinkish glow. I looked around to get my bearings. My guess was the passenger terminal was across a taxiway from me, behind a twelve-foot woven-wire fence topped with six strands of barbed wire. To my right, the barrier stretched as far down the flight line as I could see. To my left, though, was what might be a gate. It was a hell of a long walk. I toyed with the idea of trying to climb over, but the prickly wire on top stopped me. I'd had enough of getting stuck by steel barbs when we used the concertina wire in the Army. Besides, if I were spotted, I'd have to find a way of talking myself out of trouble. Resigned, I started to my left.

Reminding myself of the necessity to appear businesslike, I picked up the pace and did my best to look resolute.

From three hundred yards away, I could see I'd been right. It was a gate. I knew, because I saw two uniformed security guards come through it and start toward me. I didn't know much about Dutch airports, but I was sure it was over for me. A lone man wandering around a Western airfield would be the subject of a quick arrest for questioning. European security made our U.S. version look like Romper Room antics.

Mind racing, I reached into my pants pocket and removed the one document I hoped might help. The bill of lading for my own box, consigned to the Pan American Airlines business office in the passenger terminal here at this field. When the two officers were about fifty yards away, I waved the flimsy paper in the air and shouted at them.

"You, there! At last! Finally someone who can help. Where is this box of cargo?"

They looked at me as if I were deranged, but I continued on, frowning.

"I've walked all over this damn place, and no one can tell me."

As they closed to within a couple of feet, I gushed words out, holding on to the initiative I'd gained.

"Now look here." I showed them the waybill. It was my only valid paper with the name Schiphol on it.

I must have caught them by complete surprise, a crazy American, on their field where he had no right to be giving them hell because he didn't know where to go to find his shipment.

Both pointed together to the huge cargo building behind me. One spoke English of a sort, far superior to my non-existent Dutch, so I had the language barrier to help me. After several minutes of conversation, conducted with gestures, arm waves, raised voices, and third-grade grammar, the two watchmen had patched together my story. Through more sign language and simple phrases, I agreed going to the Pan American office would be the best solution. The guards, one on each side, escorted me to the gate, walked me through, and opened a door into a long narrow tunnel which ran inside the passenger building. I thanked them, and, shaking their heads over the insanity of Americans, they went back to their rounds.

As soon as we were separated, I stripped off my suit coat and tie, put on my sunglasses to give myself a different appearance, and started down the brightly lit, tan hallway.

Opening one of the double doors at the top of a crew stairway led me to a crowd of passengers milling around the terminal building. I was tired, cold, relieved, and happy. I'd made it. Even if I was picked up now, I had my passport. I was at least quasi legal. No one would notice me in the midst of several hundred other disgruntled, worn out passengers unless my feet actually were a few inches off the ground. I was safe.

I went directly to the KLM counter to page Dennis. He was scanning faces. With a big grin, he rushed over as soon as he saw me.

"Goddamn, John, you did it. I was sure some worried when I didn't hear anything from you."

"You were worried, you dumb Okie. What do you think *I* was? I thought about you, sitting up there patting the stewardesses' butts, sipping on bourbon."

He smiled from ear to ear and all he could say, over and over, was, "Well, goddamn, John."

He opened one of the two flight bags he was carrying and gave me a slightly squashed cowboy hat and a pair of Western boots. I slipped into the men's room. When I came out a couple of minutes later, I guarantee no one would have recognized me as the man who'd just been stopped by the guards.

I used the time to straighten my clothes, tuck in my shirt, and make myself more presentable. The attention people paid to the hat unfocused their notice of my rumpled appearance. I was beginning to get the first edge of a high.

Dennis and I walked over to a small booth to get a bite to eat and a drink. That Heineken's beer was tart, lightly bitter, foamy. Tasted like freedom.

19 Epilogue

I looked out the small window as the Air Canada 747 went into a gentle bank. Below, growing larger by the second, was a sea of endless green; pines and oaks spotted with silvery-barked hackberries. An occasional road or powerline easement ran through, making an open scar in the dense foliage. Scattered ponds with muddy brown water flickered brightly in the late-afternoon sun. Far off, on the horizon, the towering skyline of downtown Houston jutted out of the flat prairie.

I was anxious to be home. Only a few more minutes, I kept telling myself. Just a few more, and after all I've been through, surely I can wait a few more minutes. Maybe it was because of all I'd been through that I was having such trouble.

I'd come back via Montreal. It was the easiest route and the flight-departure time gave me a short break. I checked into a hotel, showered, shaved, and got my clothes as neat as possible. It was a welcome layover.

No jet fighter landing this time; slow, sedate, ponderous. A jolt coinciding with a squeal as the outer surface of a couple dozen rubber tires got ground into vapor fineness was followed by the roar of the retro thrust and a smell of jet fuel in the cabin. The belt pulled at my waist as I was pushed forward from deceleration. Then the worst wait, during the long, long taxi period as the plane was guided into its dock.

"Passengers will please remain seated until the aircraft has arrived at the terminal and has come to a complete stop," the mechanical voice snapped over the intercom. I lost the rest as I joined many of the homeward bound people in ignoring the request, standing to get my few possessions from the overhead locker where I'd stuffed them after boarding.

I kept myself braced because there is always a jolt at the end of the rolling when the ship comes to a final halt. The second I felt it, I started down the aisle for the forward exit. I waited, grinning at the stewardess as she looked out the window, watching for the signal to open the door. Finally, nodding her head, she threw the latch, and it swung out. I stepped through, half ran up the slope of the boarding tunnel, and burst into the open space of the terminal. Pat spotted me, and she, along with the kids, started running across the rug covered floor, arms out. I grabbed her, gave her a hug and a kiss, tried to hug her and all the kids at the same time, and then realized we were blocking the aircraft exit aisle and had already held up ten or fifteen people.

We moved out of the way as a group and I stood looking at Pat and my family, blinking back tears and feeling little cold lines where they ran down my face and dried in the chill from the air conditioner.

20 Final Comments

A lot has happened since my return from the Kingdom.

At first, there was a flurry of interest by the news media and I spent some weeks doing television shows and being interviewed for articles. This led to a few more weeks of appearing as a guest speaker before many groups, and to writing several statements about the Middle East situation.

During this same time, I was also trying to reorient myself to the sweetness of American life and to piece together the remnants of my shattered business. Pat and the kids closed in around me, providing the support I so badly needed, and after a few months, my life settled back to normal.

When I finally got a true look at my financial situation, I was aghast, because in addition to being broke, I also owed money to numerous people and firms. But I was back home, healthy, and the challenge of starting over was exciting. In a year, my new company, dealing in commercial real estate and investment construction, began to show signs of prospering and a few months later, after banking my first deal, I could tell the light at the end of the tunnel wasn't the headlamp of an oncoming freight train.

On a sad note, Dennis, my friend who helped me escape, was killed in June 1980. He died in a car wreck not far from Houston, trying to avoid a head-on collision into a previous accident. He swerved off the road and crashed. I flew to Tulsa riding shotgun over his body. It was damned odd, not to mention sad, flying up there, with him in the cargo hold this time, and me in the seat above. I miss that rough Okie and owe him more than I ever could repay.

Naturally, I hear from friends in Saudi Arabia occasionally. There was some hell raised when the partners discovered I'd gotten away, but not much they could do about it except harass me, which they tried. Threatening phone calls were made to me and my family.

259

I am convinced, however, that if an Arab calls you on the telephone with a dire threat, you really don't have much to concern yourself about. Somehow, the mere act of making the call and placing you on notice of his hatred will allow him to consider any violent acts he'd been contemplating accomplished.

Now that I've got my life pretty well back into shape, the biggest worry I have concerns the Arab world, their oil, and our dependence upon them for supply. It's not just the money, although they have caused a major shift in world financial power.

What troubles me is the Arab attitude toward the West and especially America. A combination of fear, mistrust, insulted honor, and at the same time disrespect does not make for good partnerships or strong alliances. Yet to a large extent, these are the blocks we are building upon. Unless the leaders of our government take time to understand the Arab and his elaborate culture, we're going to be in for a hard time.

They always say, "Close on a bright note," and even though I'm not too sure who "they" might be, it sounds like a good idea, so here goes.

I still have friends throughout the Moslem world: Saudis as well as Iranians, Pakistanis, Iraqis, and some people in between. They are all basically moral, although each has a different sense of justice and fair play. But none that I know relishes war. Or wants one fought in his backyard. Life is hard enough for them without one more of the four horsemen riding roughshod and unhindered through their towns and villages.

Since that's one point where we can all come to agreement, maybe that's the common ground on which we can act together to prevent the conflict building between East and West.